FOOTBALL GROUNDS OF LONDON

FOOTBALL GROUNDS OF LONDON

**Alex White
& Bob Lilliman**

TEMPUS

First published 2005

Tempus Publishing Ltd
The Mill, Brimscombe Port
Stroud, Gloucestershire GL5 2QG
www.tempus-publishing.com

British Library Cataloguing in Publication Data.
A catalogue record for this book is available from the British Library.

ISBN 0 7524 3182 X

Typesetting and origination by Tempus Publishing.
Printed and bound in Great Britain

Introduction

My interest in London football grounds goes back someway. During the late 1980s, I wrote an article for the *Footballer* magazine called 'The Lost Grounds of London'. From this my interest grew and I visited many of these grounds. Bob Lilliman, who has supplied most of the photographs for this book from his personal archive, has visited every ground in the London area and many throughout the British Isles. His comments replace my own when I have not visited a particular ground. He has been taking photographs of grounds since the early 1970s and seems to have been one of the few people doing this at this time. He therefore has a unique collection of photographs of football grounds throughout the country, as well as the London area.

I decided to include all grounds within the M25, but had originally intended to only cover those within the Greater London boundaries when I started the book. This means Egham are not featured in the book, but the likes of Dartford, Crockenhill and Farleigh Rovers are. I was fortunate to visit many of these gems before they were bulldozed. The saddest loses have been Dulwich Hamlet's Champion Hill ground, Ilford's Lynn Road ground, Southall's Western Road ground, as well as Tooting & Mitcham United's ground at Sandy Lane and Wimbledon's Plough Lane arena. Many Millwall supporters also miss the old Den, which was always an intimidating venue for away fans, including a Fulham supporter like myself. When I was a teenager, I regularly attended matches at Fulham, Chelsea and Wimbledon, my local clubs. I was also fortunate to watch Queens Park Rangers play at the White City. This was a huge ground that had little atmosphere when the crowds were small, which is the main reason Rangers decided to return to Loftus Road. I have watched Fulham play at Loftus Road for the last two seasons but, as I write this, they have returned to a newly refurbished Craven Cottage.

When Fulham played their last game at the Cottage in July 2002, I thought that it would be the last at the venue. Fortunately, I have been proved wrong and over £8 million has been spent to bring the ground up to the required standard. Many grounds, especially League grounds, have changed out of all recognition during the last fifteen years or so. These changes have been mainly brought about following the advice of various government reports after ground disasters in the 1980s. The terrible fire at Valley Parade, the Heysel Disaster and the appalling incident at Hillsborough – when over ninety people were crushed to death – means that grounds have changed forever. More and more grounds are becoming all-seater and many supporters miss being able to stand at a football match.

Many non-League grounds have also changed a great deal and some clubs have built new grounds, including Kingstonian, Tooting & Mitcham United and Dulwich Hamlet. Hopefully, Wealdstone are about to play on their new venue. East London has been hit the most when it comes to grounds disappearing. Grounds at Walthamstow Avenue,

Ilford, Rainham Town, Thames and Leytonstone have been swallowed up by redevelopment and have now disappeared under new housing estates. Charlton Athletic looked as though they would never return to The Valley but fan power helped them return to their historical home. Since then the ground has been almost completely rebuilt into a modern stadium.

This book contains information on all League and non-League grounds inside the M25. To be included in the book, a club must have senior status with their local FA. This means that clubs playing as low down as the Spartan South Midland League, the Kent League, the Combined Counties League and the Essex Senior League have been included. I hope you enjoy the book!

ALEX WHITE

I had no interest in football for my first fourteen years due to attending the rugger-playing Bedford Modern School. In December 1965 I saw Bedford Town beat Brighton 2-1 in an FA Cup second round replay. My watching activities involved 'Eagles' home games, the odd away game, matches on holiday, then gradually other local teams. From 1969 to 1972 my football education continued with frequent visits to Filbert Street and other League and non-League clubs within fifty miles of Leicester. I also took a degree in Classics at Leicester University. Working for Bedfordshire Libraries, then taking a librarianship qualification at Ealing Tech, opened up the grounds of London and the Home Counties. Being employed by Surrey libraries from 1974 to 1979 enabled me to delve into the Isthmian, Athenian, Sussex, Hellenic and Hampshire Leagues. From December 1979 I have worked for Wandsworth Libraries and continued with my football-watching obsession, clocking up my 2,000th new ground at Thoresby Colliery Welfare in August 2003. Meeting up with Alex White, through us both playing for Putney Manresa FC on Sundays, destined me to become a part-time Fulham supporter.

My interest in photography started in the summer of 1966 with a Kodak Brownie 127, which first accompanied me to football to the Abbey Stadium, Cambridge, on 5 April 1969, evidenced by two fuzzy black-and-white photos. Black-and-white was replaced by colour photos, then colour slides, and later back to colour photos. In 1971 I bought a Zenith E camera, and suddenly taking ground photos developed from a casual interest into a consuming passion. Football trips and holidays all over Britain enabled me to photograph grounds. As a result I have at least 8,000 slides and too many photos to count. These have been used in the Yore *Gone But Not Forgotten* series, *Football Grounds of Staffordshire and Shropshire*, the *Football Grounds Fact Book* and regularly in *Groundtastic* magazine.

BOB LILLIMAN

Addlestone, March 1974. The stand built on to the front of the dressing room had eight rows of wooden benches. On the other side was covered accommodation on the halfway line.

ADDLESTONE & WEYBRIDGE TOWN
Ground: Liberty Lane, Addlestone, Weybridge, Surrey.

It was a sad day when Addlestone & Weybridge Town went to the wall in April 1985. Addlestone FC were formed as long ago as 1885. They moved grounds in 1900 from the Crockford Park Road ground to a new one at North Lodge. Twelve months later they were on the move again to a field opposite the Black Horse Inn in New Haw Road and their headquarters were at the close-by Duke's Head Hotel. They folded briefly in 1906 but were quickly re-formed by some of the former members of the club. Around 1919 they moved to Green Lane and entered the Surrey Intermediate League. Addlestone joined the Surrey Senior League in 1924 and also moved to a better ground at Alexander Road. That season they entered the FA Cup for the first time, but lost at near-rivals Egham. With the club in financial difficulties they dropped out of senior football in 1930 to rejoin the Surrey Intermediate League and they moved to Victory Park.

After the Second World War the club played at the Co-op Field. They joined the Parthenon League in 1954 and they purchased the freehold of Liberty Lane, which was a former orchard. After three seasons they moved to the Surrey County Premier League. Addlestone joined the Spartan League in 1964 and the Athenian League Division Two in 1971. They finished as runners-up in 1974/75 and after finishing third in both 1975/76 and 1976/77 they turned professional and became members of the Southern League Division One (South) in 1977. They changed their name to

Addlestone & Weybridge Town in 1980 and won promotion to the Premier Division in 1982. Unfortunately they were immediately relegated, finishing in bottom place in 1982/83 with only 5 wins in 38 matches, in which they scored just 24 goals. The club's last season in the Southern League came in 1984/85 when they finished eighth. They were beset with financial problems and sold their ground for redevelopment and folded. The last match at Liberty Lane was played on 27 April 1985 – almost 100 years after the club was formed.

The Weybridge Town part of the club (renamed in 1989) was probably originally BAe Weybridge who played in the Combined Counties League during the early 1980s. This club had been formed in 1909 and had previously played in the Metropolitan and Surrey Senior Leagues and their ground was at Kings Head Lane, Byfleet. They were Combined Counties League Champions in 1986, 1988 & 1989. They also won the League Cup in 1989 when they beat Farnham Town 5-1 at Woking.

Addlestone first entered the FA Cup in 1965/66 but lost 9-0 at Woking in the first qualifying round. Later that season they recorded their record attendance at Liberty Lane when 2,027 saw another encounter with local rivals Woking. In the FA Cup they reached the third qualifying round in 1975/76 and 1979/80. They lost 4-2 at Tooting & Mitcham in 1975 and lost 3-1 at Welling United in 1979 after beating Sutton United in an earlier round. However, their best run came in 1980/81 when they reached the first round proper for their first and only time. Here they met Brentford but their ground was not used for the tie, which was moved to Griffin Park. They drew the first encounter 2-2 but lost the replay, also at Brentford, 2-0. Their best efforts in the FA Trophy came in 1979/80 when they beat Tonbridge, Bognor Regis Town and Bromley before losing at home to Dartford 1-2. They also had two excellent runs in the FA Vase. They reached the quarter-final in 1974/75 before losing at eventual winners Epsom & Ewell 2-0 and the following season they reached the quarter-final again before losing 3-0 at Stamford after beating Banstead Athletic, Leggett's Old Boys, Dartford Amateurs, Tunbridge Wells and Abingdon Town.

BOB'S FIRST TIME: This came on 6 December 1975 when Addlestone met Dartford Amateurs in a FA Vase tie at Liberty Lane. After a goal-less first half, Addlestone won 2-1 in front of an attendance of 174. They eventually reached the sixth round of the competition before succumbing 3-0 at Stamford. An alleyway from Liberty Lane gave access to the social club, with the ground on the left. The ground was quite basic at this time. The stand, with eight rows of benches, was built on to the front of the dressing rooms and was close to a corner flag on the side of the pitch. On the opposite side there was a low covered area by the halfway line. There were three floodlights on each side of the pitch.

Arsenal, May 1983. This view of the east stand shows the sparse crowd attracted by England's game against Czechoslovakia in the European Youth Championships.

ARSENAL
Ground: Arsenal Stadium, Avenill Road, Highbury, London N5.

Woolwich Arsenal was a struggling club by the time they left Plumstead to move to North London in 1913. Although their ground was close to Plumstead station, supporters still found it increasingly difficult to get there due to the poor service and distance from the city centre. There were plenty of other clubs in London by 1913 and Woolwich Arsenal was increasingly losing supporters to these sides (for the early history see Woolwich Arsenal). The decision to move the club to North London was made by Henry Norris, a wealthy estate agent and property developer and a former director of Fulham FC. He helped with finding and buying the new ground at Highbury and, but for his intervention, Arsenal could have easily gone to the wall. Other football clubs in that area of London objected to Arsenal's move, as did Islington Borough Council and local residents but, before the days of planning applications and various other regulations, it was not too difficult for the club to get around these.

The new ground was situated on playing fields belonging to the St John's College of Divinity and cost Arsenal £20,000 for a twenty-one-year lease on the land, which was negotiated with the owners, the Ecclesiastical Commissioners. At the start the club was not allowed to play home matches on holy days. The club quickly changed its name from Woolwich Arsenal to plain Arsenal upon their move.

This was yet another stadium designed by Archibald Leitch. It had a main stand on the east side and three large banks of open terracing. The two-tier stand, which housed 9,000, had an unusual multi-span roof in which the individual letters of the word 'Arsenal' were painted on each gable front. When the ground opened for the first match against Leicester City in September 1913, it was some way from being completed because of building delays. However, the new ground had easy access due to the close proximity of Gillespie Road underground station. Highbury staged its first international match in May 1920 and was regularly used for these until England moved to Wembley for all their games. In the mid-1920s, Arsenal FC purchased the ground outright for £64,000. This security of tenure meant that Arsenal could redevelop the ground to a higher standard. This began in 1931 with larger and better banking at the North End and the following summer work began on a new west stand. This was designed by architect Claude Waterlow Ferrier and broke new ground in stadium design. It was a double-decker stand and cost £50,000 to build. When first built it had seats for 4,000 and terracing for another 17,000. It was opened in December 1932 and soon afterwards the Arsenal manager Herbert Chapman persuaded London Transport to change the name of Gillespie Road underground station to 'Arsenal'. A 12ft-diameter clock was erected on top of the North Bank but in 1935, when this end was covered, the clock was moved to the opposite end of the ground and henceforth this was known as the Clock End. They continued to improve the Arsenal Stadium and in 1936 work began on a new east stand on Avenell Road. It was identical to the west stand but, in addition, it housed all the offices, players' and executive facilities and a new main entrance from the road was also built. The east stand had 4,000 seats each in the top and lower tier and a narrow paddock in front of the stand. Opened in October 1936, it cost £130,000 to complete. The stadium changed little after this until the 1990s and both stands are now listed buildings.

Arsenal were forced to leave Highbury and play at White Hart Lane for a while during the Second World War when incendiary bombs destroyed the North Bank roof. Floodlights were placed on the stands' roofs in 1951 and these have been updated a number of times since. The North Bank roof was rebuilt, exactly the same as the previous one, in 1954. Arsenal installed an under-soil heating system in 1964, and this was upgraded six years later. Extra seating accommodation for 5,500 was put into the paddock in front of the west stand in 1969. Fifty-three executive boxes were built at the Clock End and completed by August 1989, but looked ugly and out of place at Highbury. The terracing was retained but the stand's cantilevered roof covered barely half the terrace, and the concrete stilts meant many restricted views for spectators. A smaller replica clock replaced the original one at the Clock End. At the rear, a sports centre and conference complex was built. The following year, another ugly addition was a three-storey block to house a stadium control room and a first-aid area, next to the east stand. That well-known expert on football grounds, Simon Inglis, described it as, 'akin to bolting a tool box onto the side of a Rolls Royce.' Arsenal also spent £3 million on the entrances, emergency routes, toilets, kiosks and press facility in the east stand.

The Taylor Report would bring big changes to the ground, as Highbury would have to become an all-seater stadium. Many people objected to the original plans for the North Bank and Clock End and this led to protracted objections to the plan. In the end, Islington Council gave Arsenal six weeks to come up with designs more in keeping with the existing stadium and its environs. In the new plan, the North Bank design was lower than the original one, less obtrusive to local residents and would not have wrap-around corners, but still managed to hold almost the same number of seats as the original plan. The North Bankers were still not happy but could not prevent the bulldozers moving in during the summer of 1992. After a season as a three-sided ground, the North Bank Stand was opened on 14 August 1993 and soon gained praise for the quality of its design and range of facilities on its concourse. The new seated areas in the Clock End and East and West paddocks were ready for use in November 1993 and the whole project cost a massive £22.5m. Highbury became the first ground in Britain to install giant video screens. The ground's capacity was now just over 38,000 but this was not deemed high enough if Arsenal were to remain a major force in British and European football.

The solution was to build a new stadium in the vicinity of Highbury called the Ashburton Grove Project. This was first mooted in 1999 and would be an all-seater 60,000 capacity stadium. After five years of negotiations, seeking planning consent and raising the money for the project, the go-ahead was finally given in February 2004.

ALEX'S FIRST TIME: This was for a North London derby between Arsenal and Tottenham Hotspur on 16 September 1967. Arsenal won easily 4-0, with goals from Jon Radford, Terry Neill, Colin Addison and George Graham before a massive crowd of 62,836. I had a great view from the paddock in the east stand despite the size of the attendance.

ASHFORD TOWN (MIDDLESEX)
Ground: Short Lane, Stanwell, Middlesex.

Ashford Town sometimes get confused with their rivals in Kent, who are also called Ashford Town. The club's rise has been rapid in recent years, not only up the leagues but also with great improvements to their Short Lane ground. Ashford Town Football Club was formed in 1964 and first competed in the Hounslow & District League. They rapidly advanced through the various divisions of that league and at one stage absorbed Staines Youth Club FC. The club were elected to the Surrey Intermediate League (Western) in 1967 and, after a season of consolidation, rapidly rose to the Premier Division and easily won the title in 1975/76. Ashford Town became founder members of the Surrey County Premier League in 1982 and they played their first match in the new league at Farleigh Rovers on 4 September 1982. The club acquired their own ground in August 1985, when a long lease was signed with Spelthorne Borough Council, enabling the club to move to its present home at Short Lane, Stanwell. Prior to this, Ashford played at Clockhouse Lane Recreation Ground. The

Ashford Town, July 2004. The stand holds about 150 people. There are two bits of cover on the opposite side.

new ground was basically a field with no facilities, but these were quickly developed and the first match took place there in February 1986. Their clubhouse, which is now thriving, was built in 1987 and Fulham were the visitors to mark its opening.

Ashford Town became members of the Combined Counties League after senior status was granted in May 1990. The ground continued to be developed and floodlights were erected in September 1995, while the pitch is railed off and partly walled, with standing covered accommodation for 100 people. A purpose-built 100-seater stand was built in 1998. Extra terracing has been erected behind the Short Lane goal and the ground has been fully enclosed to comply with the Isthmian League's ground regulations. During their ten-year membership of the Combined Counties, the club never finished below sixth place and won the League championship for four successive seasons before rising to the Rymans (Isthmian) League in 2000. With the ground up to the required standard they finished in third place in the Third Division and secured promotion at the first attempt. The club took its place in the newly regionalised Ryman set up for season 2002/03 in Division One (South). The record attendance for Short Lane is 750 for a pre-season friendly with neighbours Brentford on 29 July 1998.

ALEX'S FIRST TIME: This was for a match to open their new clubhouse on 29 July 1987 when a Fulham side, made up of reserve and juniors players, won 1-0 thanks to a goal from Chris Pike (who later found fame at Cardiff City and Hereford United). A crowd of 522 attended this game on a lovely summer evening.

Aveley, March 1973. The main stand offers an elevated view. The wooden tip-up seats accommodated about 400. Opposite is a covered shelter.

AVELEY
Ground: Mill Field, Mill Road, Aveley, Essex.

Aveley have had little success over the years but have gamely struggled on at their Mill Field ground. Founded in 1927, the Essex FA granted Aveley senior status in 1949 and they were elected to the London League Division Two. Prior to this, Aveley had played in the Thurrock Combination League. The following season they were elected into the top division and became Champions in 1951/52. Aveley purchased their present ground Mill Field and were soon nicknamed the Millers. The ground was opened in November 1953 when a select Grays XI provided the opposition for its commemorative match. Over the next three years impressive terracing around the ground was built and in 1957 the brick-built main stand with more than 300 seats materialised with changing rooms. Grays Athletic also sold them a small stand for £100 that was known as the Pepper Stand at Grays. After finishing as Champions again in 1954/55, Aveley were elected to the Delphian League in 1957/58 and they moved up to the Athenian League in 1963/64. The club's floodlights were installed and used for the first time in November 1967. The Millers had a successful season in 1970/71, in which they reached the first round proper of the FA Cup where they lost 1-0 at Yeovil Town. They were also FA Amateur Cup quarter-finalists, losing 2-0 to Slough at Mill Road, before a record attendance of 3,741, and were also Champions of the Athenian League.

Aveley were elected to the Isthmian League in 1973/74 and competed without success in Division One until relegated to Division Two (North) at the end of 1985/86. Aveley gained promotion back to Division One following a tremendous end-of-season run-in in 1989/90. Recent successes have seen Aveley as winners of the Essex Thameside Trophy in 1979/80, winners of the Hornchurch Charity Cup in 1982/83 and runners-up in 1983/84. Aveley reached the fourth qualifying round of the FA Cup in 1984/85 where they lost at home to Dagenham. The Millers won the East Anglian Cup in 1988/89, defeating Cambridge City in the final, and they also won the AC Delco Cup, beating St Albans City 3-0 in the final tie in 1990. The club had their best season in the FA Vase during 1994/95, when they reached the fourth round before losing 4-0 at Wivenhoe Town.

BOB'S FIRST TIME: This was for an Isthmian League Division One encounter between Aveley and Windsor & Eton played on 20 August 1983. The visitors won 2-0 before an attendance of 120. There was a substantial elevated stand behind ten steps of terracing that stretched the length of the pitch. Opposite was a long, low covered tin stand with six concrete steps, stretching along the middle third of the pitch.

BANSTEAD ATHLETIC
Ground: Merland Rise, Tadworth, Surrey.

Banstead share their Merland Rise ground with the homeless Epsom & Ewell. This was supposed to be a temporary arrangement but they have now been with them since 1991. Banstead Athletic were founded as Banstead Juniors in 1944, after the demise of two clubs, Banstead and Banstead Hospital, during the Second World War. Playing on a council-owned pitch on the Tattenham Way Recreation Ground, the club was renamed Banstead Athletic in 1946. They moved to their present ground at Merland Rise in April 1950 but it was very basic, with only a roped-off pitch and small cover at this time. There was also a small shared wooden building that was used as a clubhouse and dressing room. The club accepted the council's offer, in 1952, of a field close to this area for their sole use. Athletic entered the FA Cup for the first time in 1950/51 but lost 3-1 at Sutton United in the extra-preliminary round.

The ground remained undeveloped until 1966 when a lease on the land was obtained by the football club. The existing small cover was rebuilt and extended and is still in use today. Soon afterwards the ground was fenced in and a clubhouse was built and opened in August 1969. This was followed by another large hall for bigger functions, which was built behind the first clubhouse/function hall and opened in 1972. In an attempt to rise up the non-League system, new dressing rooms and floodlights were built in 1979. They rebuilt the stand and extended the bar in 1983, hard standing was built around the pitch in 1985 and a fence was built around the ground along with a new boardroom the following year. They were in dispute with their landlord in the early 1990s but they eventually gained another twenty-five-year lease and built a six-foot high solid metal fence and two areas of covered terracing along with a new toilet block in 1992.

Crowds at Merland Rise have always been on the small side but the club had two excellent runs in the FA Vase during the 1990s. They reached the quarter-final in

Banstead Athletic, September 1973. At the time, this bit of cover was the only shelter for spectators. This has now been replaced by a stand and there is cover opposite and behind one goal.

1992/93 where they lost 1-0 at Bridlington Town and in 1996/97 they went one better, losing at the semi-final stage to Whitby Town 1-0 at Merland Rise, in what was the biggest game in the club's history. They beat Bracknell Town, Truro City, Reading Town, Herne Bay and Northwood on the way to the semi-finals. The club entered the newly reorganised Isthmian League Division One (South) in 2002.

ALEX'S FIRST TIME: After watching Old Salesians play an FA Vase match we popped up to Merland Rise to see the second half of an Athenian League encounter with Chalfont St Peters on 13 November 1982. A bleak place on a cold November afternoon, about fifty spectators huddled under cover away from the biting wind as Banstead lost 4-3. I revisited the ground for a full match in February 1990.

BARKING & EAST HAM UNITED
Grounds: Mayesbrook Park, Lodge Avenue, Dagenham, Essex.

Barking Football Club has existed in various forms since 1880. Barking Rovers first used the town's name in their title, playing matches on the Vicarage Field (which was opened in 1884). Barking Rovers were accused of damaging the Vicarage Field cricket pitch in 1889 and were forced to move to Eastbury Field. Shortly afterwards they folded, but almost immediately a new club, Barking Woodville, was founded, and although successful, they too folded around 1900. Barking Institute, who were formed

Barking, September 1972. Vicarage Field was within a year of abandonment in favour of Mayesbrook Park. This fine venue with substantial terracing behind one goal lay unused for several years before becoming a shopping centre.

in 1899 as Barking Working Lads Institute, then occupied the Vicarage Field. Barking Institute's name changed to Barking in 1902.

Barking Institute initially joined the Leyton and District League, winning it at the first attempt, and progressed to the London and South Essex Leagues, playing in both for several seasons. In 1912 their application to join the Isthmian League was rejected but they were founder members of the Athenian League but resigned after only two matches and did not rejoin until 1923.

The club became known as Barking Town in 1919, and Vicarage Field was the scene of much success. Barking took great strides forward, and with a series of cup and league successes the way was paved for the club's greatest period in the mid-1920s when their splendid team reached the Amateur Cup final for the only time in their history in 1927 but lost to Leyton 3-1 at The Den. They reached the FA Cup first round proper for the first time in 1926/27, where they lost at Gillingham. Barking Town became Barking again in 1931 and they pulled off the Athenian League championship in 1934/35. A local firm called Sanders & Foster were commissioned to build a new grandstand in 1937 with dressing rooms underneath. On the opposite railway side, extensive new covered terracing was built to cope with the large crowds, which disappeared in the early 1960s with the coming of television. During the Second World War matches in the South Essex Combination were played at the Merry Fiddlers Ground, Dagenham as the Vicarage Field was converted to an anti-aircraft site. Barking was a newly elected member of the Isthmian League for 1952/53 and floodlights were installed at the Vicarage Field six years later.

Barking were required to leave the Vicarage Field by the local council and were provided with their present ground in Mayesbrook Park in 1973. The cost of the upkeep of Vicarage Field had become prohibitive after fire damage to the main stand.

The Vicarage Field was sold as the local council wished to build a new road that never came to fruition. The ground was eventually redeveloped as a shopping centre after lying unused for over fifteen years. Rail travellers could not miss seeing the faded letters of Barking Football Club on the back of the covered terrace, opposite the main stand.

Mayesbrook Park is not the most interesting ground in the London area and has a long low covered seated stand down one side; with the other three sides open standing. Behind the near goal is the clubhouse with a car park behind. Barking won the Isthmian League title in 1978/79 and in that year the club was awarded the title of FA Non-League Team of the Year. Barking reached the second round of the FA Cup in 1978/79 after beating Oxford United 1-0 at Mayesbrook Park in the first round and again in 1981/82 where they lost to Gillingham 3-1 after a 1-1 draw at the Priestfield Stadium.

After thirty-nine years at Premier Division level the club suffered the first relegation in its history in 1991. This was followed by a drop into Division Two in 1996 and the club was on the brink of extinction when new owners saved it. The new owners restored the club's finances and instituted an ongoing programme of ground improvements, including the building of a new stand in 2000, and the club were promoted back to Division One in 2000/01. The following season, the club changed its name to Barking & East Ham United in order to perpetuate the name of East Ham United, who had lost their Ferndale Sports Ground and amalgamated with Barking.

BOB'S FIRST TIME: In a match played on a Sunday morning at 11 a.m. at Mayesbrook Park, Barking beat Leyton 4-0 on 3 February 1974. This ensured that Barking won their section of the Premier Midweek Floodlit League. The only spectator facility at this time was a lorry trailer with six rows of seats with a canvas back and roof. Eventually, an elongated corrugated asbestos bus shelter replaced this.

BARKINGSIDE
Ground: Oakside, Station Road, Barkingside, Essex.

Barkingside's attempts to improve their ground almost lead to their demise in 2000. Since the arrival of Ford United their Oakside ground has taken on a new lease of life. Barkingside were formed in 1898 and played at Fulwell Cross Playing Fields from 1898 (opposite the State Cinema in Barkingside High Street), Clayhall Recreation Ground from 1921, Hainhult Playing Fields from 1930 and Barkingside Recreation Ground from 1933 before moving to their present ground at Oakside in 1957. Besides a clubhouse and a small stand there was little on the ground until recent years. The record home attendance for Barkingside came in 1957 in a London League encounter with the Arsenal 'A' team, watched by 957 spectators. Barkingside initially played in the Ilford & District League but disbanded in 1923 due to lack of support. They soon reformed, as Barkingside Boys Guild then became Barkingside Old Boys before becoming plain Barkingside during the 1930s. They competed in the Ilford Minor League from 1925-44. After the Second World War they appeared in the South Essex League and the

Barkingside, January 1978. This cover on the railway side of the ground was the only shelter at this date.

Walthamstow League before gaining senior status and moving up into the London League in 1950. They finished as runners-up at the end of their first season. A fire destroyed their clubhouse in the early 1970s and they were forced to play some matches at Woodford Avenue. Barkingside played in the London league in its various forms until 1975 when they joined the Spartan League. Their best performance in a cup competition came in 1987/88 when they reached the semi-final of the Essex Senior Trophy before losing 3-1 at Wivenhoe. Barkingside came closest to winning the Spartan League in 1990/91 when they finished as runners-up, a single point behind Champions Walthamstow Pennant. They also had their best season in the FA Vase, reaching the third round before losing 2-5 at Walthamstow Pennant.

Barkingside became founder members of the Spartan South Midlands League Premier Division (South) in 1997/98 and won the title that season. They won 30 of their 44 matches and finished with 96 points. The following season, they were League Champions again but left the league in 1999 due to financial difficulties. They resurfaced again in 2000/01, playing in the Essex Senior League. Ford United moved into the ground in the summer of 2001 due to lease problems on their Rush Green Road ground. They bought out the lease at Oakside and now Barkingside are tenants of their own ground. Barkingside had developed the ground a great deal during the late 1990s in an attempt to gain entry to the Isthmian League, but this nearly led to the club's demise. Improved social and spectator facilities were built in 1997, which included an extended clubhouse, a new turnstile block plus a new 200-seat stand at the car-park end. In November 2003, Ford United met Port Vale at Oakside in an FA Cup first-round replay and narrowly lost 2-1 before a crowd of just under 2,000.

ALEX'S FIRST TIME: This was a match between Barkingside and Ulysses in the Spartan League on 14 April 1987 that the home side won 2-1. The ground was very basic and run down at this time. The station was next to the ground but there is a long walk between the two as there was no direct access. Ulysses seemed to be a team of doctors connected to London University and three of their side turned up after the match had started.

Barnet, October 1975. Underhill seems not to have changed much over the years, apart from uncovered seats behind one goal. The covered side remains much the same today apart from new cladding.

BARNET
Ground: Underhill Stadium, Barnet Lane, Barnet, Herts.

Barnet was a Football League club from 1991 to 2001 but would struggle to return if they won the Conference League due to the poor facilities at Underhill. They were formed in 1888 and their first ground was at Queens Road where they played until 1901, at which time they moved to a ground in nearby Totteridge Lane. In 1906 they amalgamated with Barnet Alston Works, and as Barnet Alston FC won the London League Division One championship in 1906/07. They moved to their present ground at Underhill in 1907, with the first match being played on 7 September 1907 against Crystal Palace reserves. When the Athenian League was formed in 1912, Barnet Alston were among the nine founder members, and at the end of the first season they finished runners-up to Catford Southend. They would go on to win the Athenian League title on eight occasions between 1930-1966. Barnet dropped the name of Alston from their title in 1919. Their most successful period came just after the Second World War, when in the first three seasons the club won every amateur honour open to them. In season 1945/46 Barnet beat Bishop Auckland 3-2 in the FA Amateur Cup final. Two years later they again reached the final but lost to Leytonstone 1-0. Their third appearance in the final came in season 1958/59 when, with six teenagers in their side, they were beaten 3-2 by Crook Town before a Wembley crowd of 60,000. Barnet were at Wembley once again in 1971/72, this time as a professional club, but lost 3-0 to Stafford Rangers in the final of the FA Challenge Trophy.

Underhill had its record attendance during 1951/52 when 11,026 attended an FA Amateur Cup fourth round encounter with Wycombe Wanderers. Before a stand was built in 1926, the club headquarters were in the Red Lion pub, on Barnet Hill. But Underhill as we know it today was mainly developed during the 1960s. Floodlights were installed in 1962, while the current Main Stand and covers on the East and South terraces were built between 1964-66 at a total cost of £75,000.

After winning the Athenian League title yet again in 1965/66, the club decided to turn professional and joined the Southern League. They won the First Division title in their first season and stayed in the Premier Division until 1975 when they were relegated. They were champions of the First Division (South) in 1976/77 and three seasons later became founder members of the newly formed Alliance Premier League (later called the Conference). After finishing as runners-up of the Conference in 1987/88 and 1989/90, Barnet finally took the title in 1990/91 and entered the Football League for the first time. One million pounds were spent on upgrading the ground for League football and then complying with the demands of the Taylor Report. This was spent on barriers, turnstiles, first-aid areas and police facilities, and on the partial easing of the pitch's slope. In order to meet the League's 1,000-seat minimum, 237 seats were also bolted onto a terrace, although many of the seats offer views of only half the pitch. A new social club was also built to replace one destroyed by fire in January 1991. They had the lowest capacity in the League, only 3,219 in December 1993. Since then the south terrace tin roof has been taken down, followed by the clearance of the terrace itself, and it was replaced in 1995 by temporary uncovered seating. They had a season in Division Two in 1993/94 but were quickly relegated. There have been numerous proposals to relocate the club. In early 1995, there was also a plan for a new 500-seat south stand at Underhill, costing £875,000. This never materialised. In recent years, the club has sought to develop Copthill Stadium, a sports complex some three miles south of Underhill, into a 10,000 all-seater ground. Used primarily by two local athletics clubs and, until 1995, by the London Broncos Rugby League Club, the stadium has a 600-seat stand and three sides of low banking, but would need a great deal of money spent on it to bring it up to standard.

Barnet lost their League status in 2001 and went back to the Conference League. They have recently attempted to build a new ground on land to the south of Underhill but after obtaining planning permission this was taken away from them when a new council took over and changed the previous decision. With their present ground, Barnet would not be allowed back into the League unless they relocated or vastly improve the facilities at Underhill.

ALEX'S FIRST TIME: Being a Fulham supporter many of my visits to grounds have been to see my favourites as opposition. I visited Underhill for the first time on 8 August 1984 when Barnet beat a Fulham XI 5-3 before a crowd of 250. My first impression was of the sloping pitch, which made the terracing look lop-sided and was later amazed to hear that this ground had been considered good enough for League football, as Underhill seemed like a typical non-League ground.

Beckenham Town, May 1983. By 1983 this steel stand holding sixty-two spectators had replaced the previous structure of five rows of planks on wooden poles with no roof.

BECKENHAM TOWN

Ground: Eden Park Avenue, Beckenham, Kent.

Beckenham Town Football Club began life in 1971, metamorphosing out of Stanhope Rovers, a local junior club operating most successfully in the South-East London Amateur League. Rovers had started up in 1959 as the brainchild of teenage footballers. An earlier Beckenham Town incarnation, formed in 1878, had played its home games at Balmoral Avenue until 1939, then at Stanhope Grove from 1946 before becoming defunct in 1969. Stanhope Rovers changed their name to Beckenham Town in 1971 when they became the senior club in the town. In the midst of its final death rattle, Beckenham Town had signed its name and possessions over to neighbouring Bromley Football Club, who allowed the new club to assume the title of Beckenham Town (1971), while simultaneously claiming the red and white colours synonymous with Beckenham Town down the years. As Beckenham Town, the club continued to compete in the South-East London Amateur League with distinction, gaining intermediate status. Town achieved senior status in 1975 and made the leap to the London Spartan League for the start of the 1975/76 campaign, where they took their place in Senior Division One. On gaining promotion to the Premier Division in 1977/78, Beckenham went on to achieve a creditable sixth position in the top flight. In July 1980, Beckenham moved to their present ground at Eden Park Avenue, which they obtained from the London Borough of Bromley on a twenty-five-year lease and, with an eye to the future, they formed a limited company at the same time.

On 16 August 1980, Whyteleafe became the first team to meet Beckenham Town in a competitive fixture at their new headquarters in what was to be Town's penultimate season in the Spartan League. Since removing to the Kent League in 1982/83, major honours have so far eluded Beckenham, although they did reach the final of the Kent

League Cup in 1985. Eden Park Avenue has a railed-off pitch and a small 100-seater stand with clubhouse, and recently installed floodlights to make the ground sufficient for Kent League requirements. The record attendance at Eden Park Avenue is 720 for a FA Cup tie against Berkhamsted in 1994.

ALEX'S FIRST TIME: This was a Kent League match between Beckenham Town and Ramsgate on 31 March 1990, which Ramsgate won 1-0. There is very little cover on this ground so take your umbrella, but the clubhouse is quite roomy and welcoming.

BECKTON UNITED
Ground: Manor Way, East Ham, London E6.

Beckton United struggled for years without much success but gave up the ghost in 1995. This was despite the area undergoing some sort of revival due to the London Dockland Railway extension to Beckton. The club was formed as Ceevor FC in 1966 and played in local football until 1979 when they gained senior status with the Football Association. They changed their name to Beckton United during the 1970s and joined the London Spartan League for season 1979/80, finishing in tenth place at the end of their first season. They usually finished in mid-table during the 1980s and had their best run in the FA Vase during 1985/86 when they reached the third round. They beat Eastbourne Town 2-1 at the Saffrons, then beat Romsey Town (4-1) and Gorleston (2-1) at Manor Way before losing at home 3-0 to Stevenage Borough. Beckton struggled during 1989/90 and finished second from bottom of the London Spartan League. They struggled again in 1991/92 and gained only 20 points from 36 games and finished one off the bottom again. This included an 8-0 defeat at Hanwell Town. After two more seasons of struggle Beckton United were demoted to the First Division in 1994/95, as they did not have floodlights and finished tenth out of thirteen

Beckton United, October 1981. A plastic structure supported by metal poles offered shelter. By 1996 it had gone, to be replaced by a giant steel structure on the opposite side, the prime function of which was to stop golfers getting wet.

clubs. They did reach the final of the Division One Cup but lost 2-0 to Walthamstow Trojans. The club seems to have folded around 1995.

When their ground was visited in 1981, it consisted of a cricket pavilion in one corner, with a roped-off pitch. There was a tiny cover on the cricket side made from steel poles and plastic with an estimated capacity of only fifteen. By 1996, a huge steel construction had been built along the Manor Way side of the ground and was used as a golf driving range across the pitch. This area of the ground had been built over by 2004, although the football pitch remains in the shadow of the 'Beckton Alps', which is made up from clinker from the old gasworks.

BOB'S FIRST TIME: This was on 17 October 1981 when Fisher Athletic were the visitors to Manor Way in the London Spartan League. The visitors were unbeaten in the league at that time and the game ended in a rather brutal 0-0 draw before a crowd of sixty.

BEDFONT
Ground: The Orchard, Hatton Road, Bedfont, Middlesex.

The club was initially formed in 1900 as Bedfont Institute and in 1968 amalgamated with two local clubs, Bedfont Rangers (founded 1950) and Fairholme United (founded 1953). They played their home matches at Bedfont Recreation Ground until 1980. The club was joined by Interharvester in 1973 and in 1988 Bedfont Eagles joined to form the modern-day club. Bedfont moved into intermediate football in 1968 when they joined the Middlesex League, winning the Premier League in 1973/74 and the Premier Cup in 1970/71 and 1976/77. The Middlesex Intermediate Cup was added to the collection twice, in 1969/70 and 1976/77. The club moved into the Surrey County Premier League in 1983, winning that division in 1984/85 and 1986/87. The club located to their present

Bedfont, July 2004. The stand holding 105 people replaced a tiny bit of cover. There is also cover behind one goal.

23

ground, The Orchard, in 1980 and opened a clubhouse four years later. They put a rail around the pitch in 1986 and created a hard training area in 1989. In recent years, a new stand and clubhouse extension have been completed.

Senior status was gained in 1987 and promotion into the Combined Counties League quickly followed. Since joining, the club have twice been to League Cup finals and won the Challenge Vase in 1992/93, beating Sandhurst Town 2-1 at Woking. Their best finishes in the Combined Counties League have been in 1996/97 and 1999/2000, when they were third in the table. Bedfont do not have a great cup record. Their best in the FA Cup is the second qualifying round and they have twice reached the third qualifying round of the FA Vase. They lost 6-1 at Boston in 1993/94 and 1-0 at Porthleven in 1999/2000.

BOB'S FIRST TIME: This was for a Combined Counties League match played on August Bank Holiday 1987, – the first of three games that Bob saw that day. Bedfont were newly promoted as Champions of the Surrey Premier League and easily beat Westfield with five second-half goals before 58 spectators. The only spectator facilities were a low cover behind the dugouts and there were three training lights for midweek fitness sessions.

BOREHAM WOOD
Ground: Meadow Park, Broughinge Road, Boreham Wood, Hertfordshire.

Boreham Wood FC was founded in 1948 following the amalgamation of Boreham Wood Rovers and Royal Retournez. During the 1950s, the club progressed through the Mid-Herts League into the Parthenon League and then entered the Spartan League in 1957. The club played at Eldon Avenue from 1948 until 1963, when they moved to their present venue at Meadow Park. A stand was soon built at the ground, but this had a huge sloping roof that impeded the supporters' view of a game and a covered terrace was also constructed. The club finished runners-up to Hampton in 1965/66 and moved into the Athenian League Division Two, finishing ninth at the end of their first season. The club joined the Isthmian League Second Division in 1974.

Boreham Wood entered the FA Cup for the first time in 1970/71 and won their first tie at Leyton 4-2 in the first qualifying round. They reached the first round proper for the first time in 1973/74 when they met Southend United at Roots Hall, but lost 3-0. They reached the first round again in 1977/78 but, after a 0-0 draw at Meadow Park, they lost the replay against Swindon Town at the County Ground 2-0. They won the Second Division title in 1976/77 by 16 points and gained promotion to the First Division. Boreham Wood appointed Bob Makin as first-team manager in 1993 and he took the club to the First Division championship in 1994/95 by 22 points over Worthing.

Boreham Wood were still in contention for the championship until the last day of the 1995/96 season but finished behind Hayes and Enfield. The club won the

Boreham Wood, October 1975. Five rows of wooden benches under a wooden roof made up the main stand. Opposite was a covered terrace stretching the length of the pitch. Unusually for the time there were four corner floodlight pylons.

Isthmian League Cup the following season and also had an excellent run in the FA Cup. After beating Tring Town, Aylesbury United, Edgware Town and Thatcham Town in the qualifying rounds, Boreham Wood were drawn against Rushden & Diamonds in the first round. They pulled off a big surprise as they won the replay 3-2 at Rushden to enter the second round for the first time. Here they met local rivals Luton Town, but lost 3-2 at Broughinge Road. The following season they again reached the second round after beating Rushden & Diamonds and Hayes, before going out to Cheltenham Town. They drew 1-1 at Whaddon Road but lost the home replay 2-0. Since then, Boreham Wood have again reached the first round three times. They lost to Luton Town again in 1998/99, crashed 5-0 at home to Torquay United in 2002/03 and lost 4-0 at Blackpool in 2003/04. Surprisingly, the club does not have such a good record in the FA Trophy.

During the 1990s the club upgraded their Broughinge Road ground every season and the Football Conference grading was obtained in 1996. They were runners-up in the Premier Division in 1997/98 and celebrated their fiftieth anniversary by playing a full Arsenal first team on 10 July 1998. The match drew a record attendance of 2,832 and Arsenal's manager, Arsene Wenger, officially opened the club's new stand. The club were relegated from the Premier Division in 2000 but were quick to return the following season as they clinched the Division One championship with an 85-point haul. A new record attendance at Meadow Park was created on 13 July 2001 when Arsenal were again the visitors, and somehow 4,030 spectators fitted into the ground. Things didn't go well in 2002/03 and they were eventually relegated after finishing twenty-second. The Wood could only finish ninth the following season in the First Division (North).

ALEX'S FIRST TIME: This was for a match between Boreham Wood and Uxbridge in the Isthmian League Division One. This match was played on 5 February 1994, and the Wood won 1-0 before a crowd of 142. We attempted to sit in the main stand but the view of the match was so poor that we decided to stand behind the goal.

BRENTFORD
Ground: Griffin Park, Braemar Road, Brentford, Middlesex.

Brentford FC was formed at a public meeting on 10 October 1889. The club's first ground was called the Clifden House Ground and Edwin Underwood, who had been elected as the club president and owned the land, offered the use of his field at a nominal rent. Brentford were able to use the Griffin public house as a clubhouse and changing rooms, which is situated next to their present Griffin Park ground. The ground had a private entrance close to the Griffin pub and was fenced off so the club could take a gate. The first match took place on 23 November 1889 against Kew but the club had to move in 1892 when the land was to be developed for housing. Brentford moved to Benn's Field at Little Ealing but this was not very accessible and fans found it difficult to get to. The first match at this new venue was against a team called Clarence on 15 October 1892 and the players used the Plough Inn for dressing rooms. The field was large enough to contain two separate pitches but it was easy for fans to watch games without paying due to lack of fencing.

The club was on the move again, this time to a pitch in Windmill Lane, Brentford. This ground was known as Shotter's Field and the first match took place there on 22 December 1894 when the Bees played the 8th Hussars. The venue was completely lacking in facilities for spectators and initially not enclosed until large hoardings were erected in April 1896 to stop spectators from getting a free view. The ground was very expensive to rent and this eventually led to the club moving again. With Brentford steadily attracting more support, these noisy crowds were not welcomed in this quiet rural neighbourhood. Attendances were by now around the 3,000 mark and the club clearly needed a better ground that they could develop. They were due to move to a sports ground on the site of the Boston Park cricket pitch in York Road but this fell through and the club were homeless.

The club had to search around yet again for a suitable alternative venue, and eventually one was found. The new ground, known as Crossroads, was situated in South Ealing and was some way from Brentford but was close to District Line trains. Work was well underway in levelling the field by August 1898. Some facilities were provided when a corrugated iron pavilion, with dressing rooms, was completed by September, and a refreshment bar was also built, but the venue did not have any

Brentford, April 1978. The substantial covered end was demolished in the mid-1980s, to be replaced by a tiny stand with six rows of seats above ten steps of terracing, with housing behind it.

cover for spectators. The first match on 1 September 1898 attracted 2,000 fans but attendances dropped alarmingly as the season developed and they stayed at South Ealing for only two seasons. Their next move was to Boston Park Cricket Ground. The first game at the ground drew a 3,000 gate for the visit of Chesham Generals on 15 September 1900. This was a vast improvement over the Crossroads ground due to its proximity to Brentford, but the ground contained only two pavilions, and no real spectator facilities. A seated stand was built that held around 800 spectators, but the ground struggled to cope and 12,000 somehow squeezed into the venue for a match with local rivals Fulham in 1903. The leasing arrangement meant that football at the cricket ground was not possible after the start of April, which caused the club some fixture problems. Factories were eventually built on the site in the 1920s.

Brentford announced in May 1904 that they were to move to a former orchard owned by the Chiswick brewers Fullers. The first match was played at Griffin Park against Plymouth Argyle on 1 September 1904, before an attendance of 5,500, for this Western League fixture. Houses already surrounded the ground at this time and members of the public were allowed to cut down the orchard and keep the timber. The two stands were brought from Boston Park; one became the main stand on the Braemar Road side, the other, dubbed the 'Flower Pot Stand', was placed on the New Road banking. Griffin Park itself was named after the emblem of

Fullers brewery. Just before the first game, a borough surveyor deemed the main stand to be unsafe, forcing the players to change at the public baths in Clifden Road and four months later the stand roof collapsed. A new main stand was not erected until 1927, costing £5,000, and it was opened by the FA secretary, Frederick Wall.

The Bees were playing in the First Division by 1935 and they had made some improvements to the ground. This included a cover over the New Road terrace in 1931. Half the Brook Road End terrace was built in 1933 and the rest was completed two years later. At the same time, angled corners of seating were added to the Main Stand wings. The first floodlights were mounted on both side stands by 1954, but by this time Brentford were back down in the Third Division. These were replaced by new corner pylons in 1963. Brentford nearly went out of business in January 1967 when chairman Jack Dunnett announced an agreement for QPR to take over Griffin Park. This never took place and Dunnett moved on. There was a possibility that Brentford might relocate to Hillingdon Borough's Leas Stadium, and in 1974, a move to the site of the local market was also discussed but never happened. A fire destroyed the eastern half of the main stand in February 1983 and it cost £800,000 to restore the damage. The fire disaster at Valley Parade, Bradford in 1985 led to the ground's capacity being severely reduced from 37,000 to 9,500.

Brentford briefly solved their financial problems when they sold part of their site, a small car park behind the Brook Road terrace, to make room for two blocks of private flats. This also helped finance a narrow, basic double-decker Family Stand that took the place of the covered terracing that had now been demolished. As part of a £230,000 refurbishment in 1991, 850 seats were placed in the corners of the main stand and the Ealing Road terrace was also refurbished. The club wanted to put a roof over the Ealing Road terrace and convert it to seating but local residents objected and the plans were rejected by Hounslow Council.

Brentford's debts have been increasing and the club plans to clear these by relocating to another site and selling the valuable land for a housing development. Many plans have been mooted and the most recent one was made in early 2004 when a plan was made for a move to a new site close to Kew Bridge railway station.

ALEX'S FIRST TIME: I visited the ground on 1 April 1975 for a match between Brentford and Newport County in the Fourth Division. The game ended in a lifeless 0-0 draw before a crowd of 5,560. The Brook Road terrace was still in situ at this time and was a steep covered terrace that could accommodate many spectators and afforded a good view of the match.

BRIMSDOWN ROVERS/ENFIELD TOWN
Ground: Brimsdown Social & Sports Club, Goldsdown Road, Enfield, Middlesex.

Enfield Town now share Brimsdown's ground at Goldsdown Road and this has led to great improvements in the facilities at the ground. Brimsdown Rovers were formed as

Brimsdown Rovers, March 1983. Facilities were rudimentary: this wooden shelter was it.

Durham Rovers in 1947 by a group of Geordies who were working in the area who chose to play in the colours of Newcastle United, black and white stripes (still their colours today). They entered the Enfield Alliance, playing on local park pitches. They changed their name to Brimsdown Rovers in 1947 and played at the King George VI Playing Fields in Enfield. They finished as runners-up of the Alliance in 1947/48, moving up to the Premier Division. They joined the Northern Suburban League in 1950 and again won promotion to its Premier Division at the end of their first season in the league. They eventually won the title on six occasions. The club moved to their current home in 1956. This was offered to them by Enfield Council and was initially waste ground. The club quickly developed it into a sports complex and the football club became part of the Brimsdown Sports & Social Club.

Brimsdown Rovers joined the London Spartan League in 1976 and were promoted to the Senior Division in 1982. They were promoted to the Premier Section in 1983/84 where they finished third, after gaining senior status from the London FA. They reached the Spartan League Cup final in 1987 but lost 4-0 to League Champions Yeading at Hanwell Town's ground. The following year, Brimsdown lost in the final again, this time to Edgware Town. They were runners-up in the Spartan League to Northwood in 1991/92 and the following season they were Champions with 97 points from 42 games. That season, they lost again in the League Cup final against Hanwell Town in an exciting 4-3 encounter. Brimsdown reached the third qualifying round of the FA Cup and played Chesham United at their Goldsdown Road ground on 12 October 1991. A new record crowd of 412 saw a 2-2 draw but Chesham won the replay 2-1. They had pulled off a surprise by beating St Albans City in the previous round. Brimsdown Rovers became founder members of the Spartan South Midlands League in 1997/98 but were relegated to the Senior Division in 1999 with only 15 points from 44 games. Brimsdown had made some improvement at their ground. A new dressing-room complex was built in 1985 and the following year a floodlit training area was developed.

With the recent problems at Enfield FC, their supporters decided to break away and form their own team, Enfield Town. They ground-share with Brimsdown Rovers as the ground is in the London Borough of Enfield. Town joined the Essex Senior League and are attracting much better crowds than their mother club Enfield, who have been homeless since the sale of Southbury Road. Brimsdown have applied to the local council to try and improve facilities on the ground, which were very basic. A new 106-seat stand was built on the cricket side of the pitch and new covered accommodation erected for 100 fans. A new perimeter fence is to be erected to meet the minimum Isthmian League standards so that Enfield Town can move up to that level.

ALEX'S FIRST TIME: This was for a FA Vase first round encounter between Brimsdown Rovers and Leavesden Hospital on 18 October 1986. The match ended in a 1-0 victory for the home side before an official attendance of fifteen (I counted fifty present). The roped-off pitch was some way from the clubhouse and there was no cover in the ground.

BROMLEY

Ground: Hayes Lane, Bromley, Kent.

Bromley FC were formed in 1892 and initially played at the Queensmead Recreation Ground before moving the following year to the Glebe Road site, where they remained for seven years until it was required for housing. This ground had an entrance off Station Road and the footballers and cricketers of Bromley Town had a pavilion each, while the football pitch also had the benefit of a members' stand. They moved a few hundred yards to the vacant Plaistow Cricket Ground in 1900, which backed onto the previous ground and was, along with the cricket club, separated by a hawthorn hedge. This was home until 1904 when they lost the ground to housing development.

Following talks involving the various sports clubs and the Norman family, who were large landowners, they were all offered facilities on a long lease in Hayes Lane, just a hundred yards from the present ground. The official opening was on 3 September 1904 by the Mayor of Bromley. There was little on the ground but changing rooms were quickly built. This sports ground lasted until 1938 when a new road was planned across the site and new housing built to accompany it. The landowners again offered the clubs another site just 100 yards away, and although Bromley FC and the bowls club agreed, the tennis club folded and the cricket club went elsewhere. Their former ground was eventually only partially built on and the rest reverted to agriculture.

In 1934, the club officials began to discuss ways of building this new ground. Preliminary work was started and a campaign launched to raise funds. The areas set aside for terraces were thrown open for the dumping of hard core. Profits from winning the 1938 FA Amateur Cup were diverted into the building of the new ground. Over a quarter of mile of fencing was erected to enclose the ground, while around the pitch itself white picket fencing set in concrete was put in place. Instead of moving the stand from the old ground, a completely new one was erected. An elegant timber structure with an elevated seating tier and a pitch roof extended at the front to provide additional cover for those standing below. Stanley Rous officially opened the new Hayes Lane stadium on 3 September 1938, after which they lost 6-1 to Walthamstow Avenue. The club's superb timber main stand had around 2,000 seats, and the banked-up perimeter was sufficient to assemble a crowd of 10,789 to watch a match against a Nigerian XI on 24 September 1949. The club managed to find the finance to buy the Hayes Lane ground outright in 1941, despite the restrictions caused by the Second World War. After hostilities ended the supporters' club presented the club with an electric clock that was placed on top of the stand roof.

Another timely FA Amateur Cup win in 1949 provided the funding for further developments of the ground. The first FA Amateur Cup final to be played at Wembley drew a crowd of 90,000, and after tax Bromley were left with £3,000 to invest in the facilities at Hayes Lane. The banking and walkway around the pitch were concreted, while at the same time the north terrace and south open seating terrace were both given covers, bringing the total capacity up to 15,000 with 4,000 under cover. There were also 3,000 seating places available of which 2,000 were under cover. Bromley joined the Isthmian League in 1952, and in the years that followed further improvements saw the provision of glass screen ends for the main stand and the

Bromley, October 1973. The wood and tin structure on the left had gone by 1980. The wooden main stand held about 560 on seven rows of wood benches.

erection of floodlights in 1960. Bromley FC switched these on on 27 September 1960 when an Isthmian League XI played Japan's national side at Hayes Lane.

The loss of the main stand in 1992 was a calamitous blow: the fire depriving the ground of its major asset and focal point. The club was forced to ground-share at Dulwich and others while a replacement stand was built. A more modest 320-seater stand was erected with the black seats and white facings to fit in with the colour scheme of the surroundings. The most distinctive features of Hayes Lane are the two end terraces with open bench seating, some of which has lost its wooden planks in recent years, in the south stand. An identical cover stands at the rear of the north terrace with narrow crash barriers. The two roofs are made of corrugated iron and supported by white painted struts. The white picket fencing that used to surround the pitch has sadly now disappeared.

ALEX'S FIRST TIME: It was 15 August 1987, Bromley 1 Maidstone United 1 in a pre-season friendly. It was a great loss when the original stand burned down in 1992 but the ground remains one of my favourites as it has the feel of a proper football ground and a unique atmosphere of its own.

BROOK HOUSE
Ground: Farm Park, Kingshill Avenue, Hayes, Middlesex.

In a very short period Brook House have risen from being a Sunday morning side playing in the Hayes & District Sunday League to a club with senior status competing in the South Midlands League in recent years. After its formation in 1974 the club quickly moved up the various divisions of the Hayes & District League and won the Middlesex Junior Cup in 1980. The first proper structure to be built at Farm Park was called the 'Tea Hut' but a new clubhouse replaced it in 1984. The team won the Hayes & District Sunday League Division One in 1981 and Saturday football was introduced to Farm Park when they entered the South-West Middlesex League and they were soon founder members of the Middlesex County League.

Senior status arrived at Farm Park in 1989 as the club was elected to the Spartan Premier Division and on 9 February 1992, Brook House had a record gate when they entertained Chelsea FC at Farm Park to celebrate the official opening of the club's floodlights. Brook House played in the FA Cup for the first time on 1 September 1992 and a new 100-seater stand was built at the ground around this time. A new members' bar was opened on 19 December 1993 and new dressing rooms were built in 1998.

Brook House became champions of the Spartan South Midlands Premier Division in 1998 and were presented with the 100-year-old Dewar Challenge Trophy in the same year as the new dressing rooms were built. The club became a limited company the following year and both Watford FC and Crewe Alexandra visited Farm Park for pre-season friendlies that were part of the transfer deal when Brook House players were

Brook House, August 1989. This cover is now a toilet block. A 100-seat stand has been built behind the dugouts, plus two bits of cover on the opposite side.

sold to each of these clubs. That season, the team were runners-up in the South Midlands Spartan Premier Division and also won the Premier League Cup.

BOB'S FIRST TIME: Brook House played Wembley in a pre-season friendly on 1 August 1989, in a 1-1 draw at Farm Park. The ground was very basic at this time and the players had to make a long trek from the dressing rooms to the pitch. They were elected to the Spartan League top division at the end of 1988/89 despite only finishing fifth in Division One.

CARSHALTON ATHLETIC
Ground: War Memorial Ground, Colston Avenue, Carshalton, Surrey.

Carshalton Athletic have suffered many financial problems in recent years but have always bounced back with the help of new financial backers. Mill Lane Mission was formed in 1903 and joined the Croydon & District League. They changed their name to Carshalton Athletic four years later and in 1908 they amalgamated with Carshalton St Andrews FC (formed in 1897) from the Southern Suburban League. They played their matches on the Wrythe Recreation Ground until 1914. During the war the land was used for agricultural purposes and when football resumed, the rec. was not available, so a local market gardener lent the club a field half a mile away known as Culvers Park, and this was used until the urban district council announced they wished to build an estate on this land. Carshalton wrote to the UDC requesting the lease on five acres of land that were no longer needed for agriculture, and due to other development in the area the council gave them permission to fence in the ground and build a small club house and dressing rooms. The estimated cost of this work was £1,000, and the opening match was played on New Year's Day 1921 against Thornhill, but the ground was not completed until the start of 1922/23. The ground was named the War Memorial Ground in memory of those players and officials who were killed during the First World War.

Carshalton became founder members of the Surrey Senior League in 1922. However, after just one season they switched to Division One of the London League. Three seasons later, they gained promotion to the Premier Division. The Robins acquired the Jockey Club grandstand from Epsom Racecourse during the close season of 1926, which had become obsolete after a new stand replaced it. This was transported and rebuilt by club officials and supporters and was the main stand for the next forty-one years until a severe gale demolished it. Extensive concrete terracing was laid down along the recreation ground side in 1949, and this was extended around the top end soon afterwards. A crowd of 8,200 crammed into Colston Avenue for an FA Cup tie with local rivals Tooting & Mitcham United in October 1950. The opposite side was concreted in 1953, and in the next ten years was covered in sections to give the stepped appearance seen today. A new clubhouse was built in 1959, and eight years later floodlights were introduced. In more recent times a covered terrace with new turnstiles was completed with the removal of banking from one end. Carshalton

Carshalton Athletic, April 1976. Reputedly the former jockey stand at Epsom, this tiny structure provided the only seats. On the opposite side a covered terrace ran the length of the pitch.

remained in the London League until 1946 when they joined the Corinthian League. Carshalton gradually developed into a very strong side by the early 1950s and the Corinthian League championship was won in both 1953 and 1954. They reached the quarter-finals of the FA Amateur Cup for the first time in 1955 but Hounslow Town beat them 6-1 after a replay; they also got as far as the last eight in 1960 but were defeated by four goals to nil at Kingstonian in front of a crowd of 7,000. Carshalton transferred to the Athenian League in 1956 but found very limited success.

After the main stand was blown down in 1968, a temporary stand was used until the current structure was completed in the spring of 1972. This stand was on the small side. The Robins were one of seventeen clubs invited to become members of the newly extended Isthmian League in 1973. They eventually achieved promotion at the end of the 1976/77 campaign when they came second to Boreham Wood and they have remained in the Premier Division ever since 1977 except for the odd blip. They have also done well in the FA Cup in recent years, getting to the second round proper in 1982 and the first round proper in 1987 when they were beaten 1-4 at Torquay United and 2-3 at Welling United respectively.

ALEX'S FIRST TIME: This was on 14 October 1986 when Carshalton Athletic lost 3-1 to Dover Athletic in the FA Cup third qualifying round replay before an attendance of 453. The first match at the Crabble had ended in a 3-3 draw. A good atmosphere in a pleasant ground with plenty of cover to protect you from the elements, Colston Avenue is part of a recreation ground.

CHARLTON ATHLETIC
Ground: The Valley, Floyd Road, Charlton, London SE7.

Charlton Athletic lost The Valley then reclaimed it, developing it into an excellent modern stadium thanks to the fighting spirit of their fans. They were formed by a group of youngsters in 1905. Their first ground was waste ground called Siemens Meadow, close to what is now Eastmoor Street. This was an open space with no facilities. Their second ground was Woolwich Common, where they moved in 1907. This still exists and was very much like most park pitches that you would find today. The club competed in the Lewisham League at this time. A year later they moved again to Pound Park (now Coxmount Road). The pitch was surrounded by a hedge and was privately owned. At the club's AGM in May 1913, they decided to seek senior status and find another ground with better facilities. They took on a lease at the Angerstein Athletic Ground, Horn Lane that was close to the Blackwall Tunnel approaches. They shared the ground with Deptford Invicta, moving up in status to join the Southern Suburban League. This was an enclosed ground, but the only facilities were changing rooms for the players. The ground was taken over for a petrol dump during the First World War.

The club was a small amateur club until 1919 when they decided to move to The Valley. This was a derelict sand and chalk pit known locally as 'The Swamp'. Volunteers dug out a pitch and banking was built around it. For the inaugural match in September 1919 against Summerstown, there was no stand, fences or turnstiles, so a collecting box was passed around and the players had to change in a house in Ransom Road.

Charlton turned professional in 1920 and joined the Southern League. A year later, they were elected to the Football League despite The Valley still being a very basic ground, albeit one with huge potential. Charlton paid £3,000 for the site but had little money with which to develop it. The club went more and more into debt with their builders, Humphreys, whom they owed £21,000 for work carried out during 1921/22. To prevent bankruptcy they sold one of the best players, Alf Kingsley, to Fulham.

The most expensive addition to the ground was the new main stand. It had four spans above a single tier of 2,500 seats, and looked half completed, as it did not run down the whole of the west side of the pitch. The area of the ground that held most spectators was on the east side and was variously called the Mound, Cliff or East Bank. This bank was huge and reached up to Charlton Lane, but was initially only properly terraced at the bottom. This very basic stadium could not cope with large crowds and when Bolton Wanderers visited for an FA Cup match in March 1923, a crowd of 40,023 caused havoc as barriers gave way, sending dozens of fans tumbling onto the pitch. Fortunately, there were no serious injuries but Charlton faced a number of compensation claims.

The club was lucky to survive their next decision, which was to leave The Valley and move to The Mound at Catford, which was four miles away. The ground was used by Catford Southend and was situated in the present Mountsfield Park. Humphreys made a number of improvements to the new ground from May 1923. The Catford move proved to be disastrous and it is not clear why they did it. The Mound's construction was hurried, resulting in the death of a worker, and the pitch later subsided due to faulty workmanship. There was no seating at the ground, which forced Charlton to stage a FA Cup tie with Wolves back at The Valley and drew the season's highest gate of over 20,000. Charlton played at The Mound from December 1923 to May 1924 and the crowds dwindled alarmingly; only 1,000 saw the final match, before the club made the decision to return to The Valley. Catford Southend used the Mound for one further season, but they were wound up in January 1927.

Back at The Valley and £57,000 in debt, Charlton struggled on, still largely thanks to their builders Humphreys. Charlton found wealthy new owners in 1931 when the Gliksten brothers, Albert and Stanley, joined the board and they ended up investing over £100,000 in the club. The ground improvements were modest and started in 1934 when the north terrace was covered. They also spent £5,000 on concrete terracing on the upper levels of the East Bank and fences were erected behind the south end to stop onlookers watching games from the neighbouring allotments. Jimmy Seed became the manager of Charlton Athletic and the club rose from the Third to the First Division in successive seasons and they finished as runners-up in the First Division in 1936/37. A new attendance record was set in 1938 when 75,031 spectators paid to watch a FA Cup tie with Aston Villa.

During the Second World War, the north stand took a direct hit, and bombed-out Millwall shared with Charlton during 1943/44. Despite two Cup Final appearances in 1946 and 1947 and regular gates of 30,000 plus, ground improvements were limited, but 750 seats were placed in the main stand paddock in 1950. Floodlights were installed

Charlton Athletic, September 1985. The Valley as it looked five days after its 'last game'.

in September 1961 and the ground remained the same until the late 1970s. The Valley was only filled twice during this time, for rock concerts featuring The Who, in 1974 and 1976. Charlton were finally forced to do something about the ground in 1979 when The Valley became designated under the Safety of Sports Grounds Act. The Greater London Council cut its capacity to 20,000 due to subsistence on the terraces and weakened barriers, as well as a lack of suitable entrances and exits to handle the crowds. Three major developments took place, at a total cost of £450,000, between 1979-1981. They replaced the distinctive, but life-expired, Main Stand roof with a square, modern cover and erected a similar roof over the South Bank. The GLC cut the ground's capacity even further in 1980, to just 13,000. The biggest problem was the East Bank, but the directors did nothing to improve it, despite warnings. The south stand was officially renamed after Jimmy Seed in August 1981. Poor decisions by the previous owner meant that the club were now £1.5m in debt by March 1984 and went into receivership soon afterwards. The new owner John Fryer, was the managing director of the property company, Sunleys, and this company loaned the club £2 million to save it, just thirty-five minutes before a final Football League deadline to close it down. The Gliksten family still owned The Valley at this time.

The GLC ordered the closure of the East Bank in August 1985. This was just after the Bradford fire when all local authorities were anxiously reviewing their safety policies. Charlton could not complain as they had been warned since 1979 that repairs were needed, and none were done. One report on the ground stated that ninety per cent of the barriers tested had failed. The board challenged the GLC's ruling in the courts, but lost. Shortly afterwards, they declared that repairs to the East Bank would cost £2m due to a large sewer that ran at an awkward angle under the terrace and would make repair work very complicated, but this was later found to be a gross exaggeration. The club refused to carry out the repairs and used it as an excuse to leave The Valley and seek a ground share at Selhurst Park with Crystal Palace. Most fans thought this was the end of The Valley and the 'last' match was played there on Saturday 21 September 1985. A sad and disillusioned crowd of 8,858 saw their favourites beat Stoke 2-0.

Charlton Athletic were to stay at Selhurst Park for six years followed by a further season in exile at Upton Park. Gates were often poor even though the club were in the top division for most of this time. The Valley remained intact but it was vandalised and very overgrown. The supporters began to organise themselves in the fight to bring the club back to The Valley. Fryer stood down as chairman during the summer of 1987 and new directors helped finance the £350,000 purchase of the club's training ground at New Eltham and this enabled the club to have a base closer to The Valley. Soon afterwards, Gliksten sold The Valley to a housing company for £2.6m, ending his family's link with the club, and Roger Alwyn and Michael Norris bought the Charlton club from Sunleys in June 1988 for £3.25m. There was talk of a new ground at Angerstein Wharf but nothing came of it.

Things looked up when it was announced on 23 March 1989 that the club would be returning to The Valley. However, there were lots of problems to overcome before this could happen. The club organised a clean-up day when the fans turned up at The Valley to clear the weeds and undergrowth in April 1989. The old main stand was pulled down, when it could have been refurbished, and the floodlights were dismantled and sold off. However, the pitch was reseeded and plans were put to the local council in August 1989 for a 25,000 all-seater stadium plus a new housing project to be included at the site. The club hoped that these flats and houses would mostly cover the costs of rebuilding the stadium. Greenwich Council would not give planning permission to these plans. In the hope of changing this decision, the supporters formed themselves into the Valley Party and stood for election at the council elections. They polled 10.9 per cent of the vote and this forced the council to again go into negotiations with the club over the development of The Valley. A revised plan was entered but the ground capacity would initially only be 16,800 and the housing element was greatly reduced to only twelve houses. Therefore, the funding for the new ground would have to come from another source.

The plans were finally passed on 2 April 1991 and there were 1,500 fans waiting outside the town hall for the decision. They were euphoric but there were soon more delays with the building work. The west stand would initially be a temporary one and was rented on a season-by-season basis. It had a pitched roof supported on eight columns. The ground-sharing agreement had come to an end with Crystal Palace so the club played at Upton Park while the ground was being built. This work was halted when the club struggled to come up with the funds for the project. However, Charlton bought the freehold on the ground in August 1992 for £1.25m. New directors joined the board and they contributed finance to enable work to start again on the ground.

The Valley was finally ready and the first match took place on 5 December 1992 – but the new east stand was not ready so the crowd was only 8,337. The existing south and north stands were refurbished and used again but the east stand was not ready until the autumn of 1993 and held 5,787 seats, eight executive boxes and a fans' lounge. It was officially opened on 2 April 1994, five years after the first clear-up of the ground. The temporary west stand was removed during the summer of 1997 and a new one was started. This cost £750,000 to build, held over 8,000 seats and brought the ground's capacity up to 20,000. Next on the list was a new north stand which was partially ready for use by August 2001 and finished later that season. Charlton announced plans to raise the ground's capacity to 40,000 in November 2003. This would place an upper tier on the east stand and the Jimmy Seed (South) Stand would be redeveloped with a second tier and include infills on the south-east and south-west corners.

ALEX'S FIRST TIME: Fulham were in free fall from the First to the Third Division and this was not helped by a 5-3 defeat at The Valley on 30 November 1968 in the Second Division. A crowd of 17,217 fitted easily into such a vast arena. I stood on the East Bank and had an excellent view of the match. The only cover for spectators was the roofed north terrace and the strange-looking main stand.

CHELSEA
Ground: Stamford Bridge, Fulham Road, London SW6.

Stamford Bridge was initially opened on 28 April 1877 as a running track for the London Athletic Club, when a crowd of 6,000 attended its first meeting. The track had been laid out on a former orchard and market garden. It was close to the Lillie Bridge Athletic grounds where the second FA Cup final was held in 1873. The ground was named after the bridge over the West London Extension Railway that still passes the ground today. When it opened, there was only one small stand and a pavilion in the south-west corner. Access to the ground was excellent, as it was close to Walham Green underground station (now Fulham Broadway) and Chelsea (later Chelsea & Fulham) station on the W.L.E.R. but the latter was closed in 1940. The ground's owner, Gus Mears, planned a new venue for cycling and athletics in 1904, and also wanted to rent it to Fulham FC. Fulham were about to face a court hearing over the safety of their 'orange box' main stand but Mears wanted too much in rent and Fulham's chairman, John Dean, declined his offer. Mears almost decided to abandon the stadium idea and accept an offer from the Great Western Railway who wanted the site for a coal yard but he decided to form his own club instead. The famous football architect, Archibald Leitch, was employed to build the updated ground at Stamford Bridge and work started very quickly. He was also given the task of modernising Fulham's Craven Cottage. The Bridge's main stand looked almost identical to Fulham's new Stevenage Road stand, with 5,000 seats, a paddock, latticework columns and a central gable on the roof. Oval-shaped banking was formed around the track and was made up from soil and clay that was being excavated by Mears' company from the Kingsway tunnel project in central London.

Various names were suggested, including Stamford Bridge, Kensington, and even London FC but they decided on Chelsea in the end. The Chelsea Football and Athletic Company was launched in May 1905 and their annual rent at the Bridge fixed at £2,000. With its opening capacity of 60-70,000 it was England's second-largest venue after Crystal Palace. The first game at the newly revamped ground took place on 4 September 1905 against Liverpool in a friendly and an estimated 6-7,000 attended. Chelsea finished third in the Second Division at the end of their first season, and an average gate of 14,638 was the highest in their division. When Manchester United visited the ground in April 1906, a huge crowd of 67,000 attended the match. After promotion to the First Division in 1907, Chelsea's gates were the highest in the League, and the banking had to be expanded. Another record crowd of 77,952 attended for an FA Cup tie with Swindon in 1911. The Bridge was also used as a neutral venue for cup semi-finals and also for full internationals, amateur internationals, Charity Shield matches and an Amateur Cup final before the First World War. It also staged rugby league (Great Britain against New Zealand in 1908 – the code's first ever game in London), occasional rugby union and athletic meetings.

Stamford Bridge staged three FA Cup finals from 1920-22, but attendances were below capacity due to high ticket costs. Their best crowd was for the 1921 final between Wolves and Spurs when 72,805 attended. The FA Cup final moved to Wembley in 1923. Speedway was introduced at Stamford Bridge in 1928, and for the next four years it regularly drew crowds of 25,000-50,000. Very little money was spent on the stadium in the inter-war years. The Amateur Athletics Association decided to move its meetings to White City in 1932 due to the damage caused to the running track by speedway. Speedway had to leave the Bridge when greyhound racing was introduced in 1932. Although the football club attracted large crowds throughout the 1930s they seemed to always be struggling financially, and greyhound racing company the Stamford Bridge Stadium Limited started bossing Chelsea FC around.

The first major construction at the ground since 1905 was a cover at the rear of the Fulham Road terracing (later to be called the Shed), which was built in 1935. The roof was old fashioned and only covered supporters who stood more than halfway up the terracing. A new ground-attendance record was set when Chelsea drew a crowd of 82,905 for the visit of Arsenal on 12 October 1935. The club needed to build a stand on the west side of the ground, but instead a very strange-looking grandstand was developed on the north-west corner. It had 2,500 seats and was built on stilts above the existing terracing. The stand was probably built for greyhound fans rather than Chelsea supporters. The work was started in 1939 but was soon held up by the Second World War, so it was not completed until October 1945. Regular users complained that the whole structure shuddered when underground trains passed by the back of the stand. To make matters worse some of the seats had restricted views due to the glazed-screen end.

When Moscow Dynamo visited the ground in November 1945 for a goodwill friendly, 74,496 people paid to watch and another 20,000 broke into the ground without paying. Several thousand spilled onto the greyhound track and climbed on the roofs of the stands. Gates remained high over the next decade – which culminated in Chelsea winning their sole League title in 1954/55. The first floodlights were erected in 1957 at a cost of £37,000, and switched on for a friendly against Sparta Prague. A new stand on the west side of the ground was built in the late 1960s, but was again very rudimentary. It cost £150,000 to build and had 6,300 tip-up seats, and basic uncomfortable concrete benches in front that offered a poor view. A roof was built over this to protect the spectators from the weather.

Talks began in March 1971 over the building of a new east stand and architects called Darbourne and Darke were employed to design it. This would be the largest single stand at this time at a British ground. It had three tiers and contained 11,500 seats, cost

Chelsea, May 1983. The Shed End is taken over by Fulham supporters for the visit of Cardiff (Rugby League Division Two).

£1.6 million and was to be the first phase of a £5.5 million scheme to create a completely new 60,000 capacity stadium. The rest was never built as the club were hit by financial problems over the next two decades. Work began on the east stand during June 1972. The Leitch-designed stand and all the outbuildings and extensions were quickly demolished. The weathervane that depicted George Hilsdon (a Chelsea player before the First World War), which had been on the old stand's gable since about 1932, was also taken down and put into store. The stand was bedecked by problems, including the 1973 fuel crisis, the subsequent imposition of the three-day week by the government and pay disputes. This meant the stand was not completed until August 1974 (a year late) and Chelsea's debt had reached £3.4 million. The unloved north stand finally came down in the late 1970s. Crowds plummeted in the early 1980s with Chelsea close to the bottom of the Second Division, and two matches during 1982/83 drew less than 7,000.

A decision that was to create huge problems for the club came soon after the transfer of ownership of the ground to a holding company called SB Property. A new chairman arrived in April 1982, in the shape of Ken Bates. He was said to have paid just £1 for the club, then put in another £200,000 towards keeping it going as they were losing £12,000 a week. Instead of selling their SBP shares to Bates, the Mears, who had owned the club since its formation, sold up to property developers called Marler Estates, who gained a seventy per cent share as part of an overall deal worth £1.25 million. Bates and Chelsea supporters were furious with this decision. Marler dropped all pretence and applied for planning permission in 1985 to redevelop the Stamford Bridge site for housing. The Tory-controlled Hammersmith and Fulham Council gave approval for this development in March 1986. Under the terms of their lease, before any redevelopment could take place at the Bridge, Marler would have to rehouse Chelsea FC to a suitable ground, within a fifteen-mile radius of the Bridge. Marler paid Fulham chairman Ernie Clay £9 million for Craven Cottage. The plan seemed to be to relocate both clubs into either the Bridge or the Cottage, then sell the other ground at a profit. Fortunately for both Chelsea and Fulham, control of Hammersmith and Fulham Council changed from Tory to Labour in May 1986, and their policy was to preserve football at all three grounds in the borough. Marler then bought Loftus Road as well for £6m in February 1987.

New plans were presented to the council in late 1987 for three new two-tier stands to join the existing east stand for a 40,000 capacity stadium. This would occupy around six of the site's near-twelve acres. The remaining space, part of which would be created by the clearance of the oval-shaped banking, would be taken up by a 160-bed hotel and underground car park (behind the proposed south stand), 264 luxury flats (immediately behind the new west stand), a leisure centre (in the north-east corner of the site), and offices and shops around the main entrance on Fulham Road. These plans eventually reached completion in 2001 with the emergence of what was to be called the 'Chelsea Village' – but only after a lot of chopping and changing of the original plans. In November 1991, the independent valuation of the Bridge was set at £22.85 million; less than Cabra hoped, higher than Bates feared. With a slump in the property market, Cabra went into receivership in October 1992 and the new landlords were the Royal Bank of Scotland, the property company's main creditors. They took over the Bridge's freehold and on 15 December 1992 granted Chelsea a twenty-year lease, with an option to buy the site at any time within that period, not for £22.85 million but for £16.5 million. Chelsea fans were ecstatic. Bates was hailed as a hero. The club's problems were not yet over as Bates did not have the money to finance the new development on his own and needed other backers. Matthew Harding came on the scene with the finance that was needed in September 1993. The new north stand was to cost around £7.5 million, of which the Football Trust would grant £2 million. But Chelsea could not raise the balance. Harding was among Britain's 100 richest people and he agreed to put in £5 million towards the new stand in the form of a loan. He also joined the board and invested a further £2.5 million on players.

Work on the north stand started in December 1993. During the summer of 1994 the famous Shed and south bank were demolished to make way for a temporary stand, and behind this an underground car park was built. The north stand was opened in November 1994 and the ground's capacity rose to 31,760. Soon afterwards, Harding paid £16.5 million for the ground's freehold from the Royal Bank of Scotland but Chelsea still had to pay Harding the £1.5 million rent they had been paying the bank.

Harding was killed in a helicopter crash while the north stand was being built. The stand was eventually named after him. A hotel, residential flats, penthouses, restaurants, bars and fitness centre were also built as part of the Chelsea Village. The temporary south stand was also replaced with a permanent structure and the final piece in the jigsaw was the completion of the west stand in 2001. This had been held up by protests from local residents living behind it. The ground is now all-seater with a capacity of over 41,000.

ALEX'S FIRST TIME: Before the days of away travel many supporters in West London would visit Craven Cottage one week and Stamford Bridge the next. I was no exception and was a regular at both grounds during the 1960s. My first match at the Bridge was for a match between Chelsea and Sunderland on 29 August 1964. Chelsea won 3-1 with goals from Ken Shellito, Bert Murray and George Graham before a crowd of 46,710. Chelsea were helped as Sunderland had to field a sixteen-year-old goalkeeper called Derek Forsyth. The enormous west terrace was still in place at this time and meant that the ground could still hold up to 70,000 fans.

CHERTSEY TOWN
Ground: Alwyns Lane, Chertsey, Surrey.

Chertsey Town have had a yo-yo existence in the last decade, going from the bottom to the top of the Isthmian League and back again. Chertsey were formed in 1890 and they soon joined the West Surrey League; their first success came in 1897 when the Surrey Junior Cup was secured. In 1919, the club joined the Surrey Intermediate League where it stayed, uneventfully, until 1939. They played at Willow Walk, Free Prea Road, Chilsey Green, The Grange and The Hollows around the local area before the club's move to Alwyns Lane in 1929, whose football and cricket grounds were donated by a local worthy called Sir Edward Stern. As there were no facilities, players changed at the Bell, a public house some 300 yards from the football pitch. A wooden dressing room was soon built and after the Second World War a substantial grass bank was created behind the Alwyns Lane end goal, until this disappeared altogether in the early 1980s. The suffix 'Town' was added to the club's title in 1950 and club members constructed the impressive brick-built main stand in 1954 that remains in good condition today, and is situated on the church side of the ground. Although Chertsey gained membership of the Surrey Senior League immediately after the Second World War, it was not until 1959/60 that success came with the league championship. This was repeated twice in the next three years.

Gales destroyed a corrugated shelter built behind one of the goals in 1963, just three years after it had been built, and opposite the main stand, a bus shelter-type covered area was created the same year. In the early 1960s the club built a prefabricated clubhouse that was replaced with the present brick-built structure in the late 1970s. Chertsey Town joined the Metropolitan League in 1963, but the increased cost of travel meant that after four seasons the club joined the Spartan League in 1967. The club had little success, but in 1974/75 they were league and League Cup runners-up to Farnborough Town. The club moved to the London Spartan League in 1975/76 and on through the Athenian League until they joined the Isthmian League with a place in Division Two (South) in 1984. They were instantly relegated to the Combined Counties League but won promotion back to the Isthmian ranks at the first attempt.

Chertsey Town reached the quarter-final of the FA Vase in 1987/88, where they lost to Bashley after winning through six rounds. New dressing rooms were built in 1988, and the rooms below the stand were then turned into a physio and kit room. Extensive concrete terracing around the pitch, and a training area and additional turnstiles, have been built in recent years.

The Isthmian League placed the club in new Division Three when it was reorganised in 1991 and they were runners-up in 1991/92. Further promotion came in 1993/94 when they finished as runners-up of Division Two and again in 1994/95 when they entered the Premier Division. The club also reached the quarter-finals of the FA Vase again in 1991/92, but they lost at home to Bamber Bridge at this stage. They did not stay in this heady position for long and they were relegated twice – in 1997 and 2000. Chertsey Town entered the newly formed Division One (South) in 2002/03 but, unfortunately, the club's fortunes remained the same as they finished rock bottom, only accumulating 16 points all season, and conceding a whopping 139 goals in the process. There was improvement the following season as the club again reached the fifth round of the FA Vase before losing to Bideford at Alwyns Lane.

ALEX'S FIRST TIME: My only visit to Alwyns Lane was on 26 October 1982 for an Athenian League match between Chertsey Town and Chalfont St Peter, which the visitors won 5-1. The programme did not have any names for the Chalfont team as the club had failed to notify Chertsey of their side in advance.

Chertsey Town, December 1974. Eight wooden sections offer an elevated view from the stand, with dressing rooms beneath. Opposite was a covered side.

CHESSINGTON & HOOK UNITED
Ground: Chalky Lane, Chessington, Surrey.

The club are making a comeback after years in the doldrums caused by financial problems. Chessington FC was formed in 1921 and entered the Kingston & District League. Within four years they were Division Four Champions. They merged with North Chessington and, after a gradual rise through the leagues, they won the Premier Division in 1961. Chessington FC and Hook FC, who were both playing in the Kingston & District League, merged in 1967 to form Chessington & Hook United. The club moved into intermediate football and joined the Middlesex League in 1967/68, finishing their second season as runners-up to move into the Surrey County League, where they were Division One Champions in 1970/71. They were founder members of Home Counties League in 1972 and this League changed its name to the Combined Counties League in 1978. They left the Combined Counties League in 1984, appearing in the Surrey Premier and Surrey Combination and nearly went out of business due to financial problems.

The introduction of a new management team led by chairman Graham Ellis saw a rebirth of the club and a return to the Combined Counties League in 1997. Chessington & Hook were runners-up in the Combined Counties Premier League Cup in 1998 and gained the Southern Combination Cup in 2002. Their best finish in the Combined Counties League was fifth in 1979/80 and 1980/81 and their best season in the FA Vase came in 1977/78 when they reached the second round, where they lost at Ringmer 3-1. Since the club re-formed

Chessington & Hook United, November 1982. Spectators were reluctant to use the cover on offer, or the three chairs provided. Eventually, this was replaced by the Bill Bateman Stand on the opposite side.

in the mid-1990s, their best seasons in the Combined Counties League came in 1997/98 and 1998/99 when finished tenth, but they have had no success in either the FA Cup or Vase.

ALEX'S FIRST TIME: This was for a Combined Counties Premier Division match between Chessington & Hook United and Sandhurst Town on Tuesday 20 April 2004. Sandhurst won 2-1 on a rainy night before a crowd of forty. This is one of the most rural grounds in the London area and its only cover is a corrugated-iron roof over a standing area. The clubhouse and tea bar are pleasant and the locals are friendly.

CHIPSTEAD
Ground: High Road, Chipstead, Surrey.

Chipstead Football Club was formed in 1906 and they struggled financially in their early days due to lack of gates, surviving mainly on the proceeds of whist drives and other fund-raising events. Changing facilities at the ground did not arrive until 1919. Before this, the teams changed at the local White Hart public house. Chipstead played junior football until 1962, but having finished runners-up in the County Junior Cup the previous year, they then moved into the Surrey Intermediate League and played in the South-Eastern section. The club became founder members of the newly formed Surrey Premier League in 1982.

In the next few years the club had great success, finishing runners-up three times and winning the league cup on three occasions. The club was awarded senior status in 1986 and promoted to the Combined Counties League where once again they found success, winning the league championship in 1989/90. Chipstead made their debut in the FA Vase in 1987 and in the FA Cup two years later. A new clubhouse was opened in 1979 and another major acquisition was made in 1990 with the purchase of floodlights. A small wooden stand with cover for around 100 has been built on the halfway line and the car

Chipstead, July 2004. The original wooden stand on the right has a capacity of twenty-eight on individual chairs.

park was fenced off from the ground. The club acquired some extra land in 1994 that enabled them to have a four-sided ground and improve facilities as funds allowed. A new covered section was erected between the existing stand and clubhouse in recent years.

ALEX'S FIRST TIME: This was for a match between Chipstead and Merstham in the Combined Counties League on the 16 January 1996. Chipstead won 2-0. My lasting memory is of a long walk up from Chipstead station along very dark country roads – where I often had to jump into a ditch to avoid being run over by a speeding car.

CIVIL SERVICE
Ground: Civil Service Sports Ground, Riverside Drive, Chiswick, London W4.

Civil Service Football Club competed in the first ever FA Cup competition during 1871/72. They had no set ground until 1892, when a permanent home ground was secured at Norbury. Three year later they moved to a ground at Chiswick Park, which had been used by the Chiswick Park FC, and from 1901 the club was installed at the White Hart ground, Neasden. Civil Service played at Edmonton for 1902/03, and succeeded in going right through the Amateur Cup to the southern semi-final. The following season, the club moved to Wood Lane, Shepherd's Bush, and in the FA Cup met the professional club Fulham in the third round, holding them to a 3-3 draw at Craven Cottage but losing 3-0 in the replay. Two seasons later, owing to Wood Lane being required for the Great Exhibition, the club migrated to the National Athletic Ground, Kensal Rise, a ground previously used by Queen's Park Rangers.

Civil Service were founder members of the Isthmian League in 1905 but, after the split of the amateur clubs from the FA in 1907, they moved to the Amateur Football Alliance playing in the newly formed Southern Amateur League. The club was playing at

Civil Service, July 1974. Within ten years this magnificent structure with eight rows of benches had been replaced by a steel shelter, and the dressing room underneath by portable cabins.

Stonebridge Park and on the ground of the S.W. Ham CC until 1914 when the war brought about the ending of the club's activities, as practically all its players enlisted with the Civil Service Rifles and were quickly in action after the outbreak of hostilities.

After the armistice, the club was invited to rejoin the Isthmian League and late in 1919 a fine playing pitch was obtained at the Hurlingham Polo ground in Fulham. After three seasons at this venue they moved to share Hampstead Town's ground until 1925, when they moved to the new Civil Service sports ground at Chiswick. This large complex catered for a number of different sports, but the ground occupied a corner of this area by Riverside Drive. Next to this road a large grandstand was built, housing dressing rooms beneath its elevated seating tier. Spectator access was gained via two staircases at either end of the stand. While facilities improved the club's form plummeted and, after finishing bottom of the Isthmian League in 1927/28, they returned to AFA football and the Southern Amateur League, where they remain to this day. The stand became very dilapidated in its final years and was rarely used as few people watched Civil Service matches. The grandstand was eventually pulled down in the late 1980s when it became impractical and too expensive to maintain. It was replaced with two small covered areas and two huts for dressing rooms.

BOB'S FIRST TIME: This was for a Thursday afternoon game between the Civil Service and the Combined Services at Riverside Drive on 30 September 1982. The match was part of the Civil Service FC's diamond jubilee celebrations and a crowd of fifty saw the Combined Services win 2-0. The hospitality was good as free glasses of whisky were offered to all spectators.

CLAPTON
Ground: The Old Spotted Dog Ground, Upton Lane, Forest Gate London E7.

Clapton have a long and interesting history and have managed to survive in an area notorious for the loss of its football grounds. The club was formed as Downs FC in August 1877 and played on Hackney Marshes, using the Downs Hotel (thus their name) as the headquarters. They were renamed Clapton a year later and moved to more private surroundings at Elm Farm, that was close to Lea Bridge Road, in 1886. The club transferred to their present ground in 1888, located on a field on the south side of a public house called the Old Spotted Dog. St Bart's Hospital had used the land before the club took over the ground and at that time the area was rural, with the ground being reached down Upton Lane past farms and fields. Cricket was also played there but disappeared after the First World War, with players of both sports changing in an old barn.

Clapton's popularity was immense and crowds of 3,000 or more would gather for friendlies until they joined the Southern League, when even larger attendances were seen at the Spotted Dog ground. The record attendance was set in November 1898 with the visit of Tottenham Hotspur, when somehow an estimated 12,000 people entered the ground as temporary stands were erected to accommodate the huge crowd. The club entered the FA

Clapton, July 1979. Miraculously the Old Spotted Dog has so far survived developers' ambitions. The main stand had five rows of benches. Opposite was a long, low structure with four rows of planks.

Cup for the first time in 1889/90 and beat Old St Paul's 6-0 in their first match. They reached their first FA Amateur Cup final in 1905 but lost 3-2 to West Hartlepools at Shepherd's Bush.

Clapton were founder members of the Isthmian League in 1905 and are the only club to be of continuous membership, although in recent years they have often only remained by the skin of their teeth. Clapton appeared in six FA Amateur Cup finals, winning five times, and they won the Isthmian League championship twice and were runners-up four times between 1903-1928.

The Spotted Dog was developed between the wars but was never very impressive. A small changing hut improved changing facilities and a corrugated-iron fence was built around the ground (that was by now surrounded by housing on all four sides). Two small stands were built, one with seating for around 300. Clapton lost their ground in 1940 due to wartime use and shared with Ilford at their ground at Newbury Park, but moved back to the Spotted Dog after the war.

Clapton were relegated to the Isthmian League Second Division in 1976 and again in 1982, but won the Second Division title in 1982/83 – their last real success. The ownership of the ground has changed hands many times over the years and the local council and a major brewery have leased the ground to Clapton in recent years. As Clapton's status in the non-League world gradually deteriorated, the ground has fallen into disrepair and the stands were eventually condemned and pulled down when they became unsafe. A fire in the early 1990s saw the demise of the clubhouse, which has subsequently been rebuilt, and a small modern stand was erected in recent years to allow the club to meet the ground grading of the Isthmian League. Clapton have come close to losing their historic ground on a number of occasions in recent years. It nearly became an all-weather sports centre and in 2000/01 Clapton spent most of the season playing home games at other grounds due to poor state of their pitch.

ALEX'S FIRST TIME: Clapton 0 Finchley 1 on 22 March 1988 in the Isthmian League Division Two (North). The Spotted Dog was a very run-down ground by 1988 and it was difficult to imagine past glories. The clubhouse was tatty and the stand was out of use as it was considered dangerous (and was soon pulled down). They continue to struggle for survival, so visit it before it is too late.

COBHAM
Ground: Anvil Lane, Cobham, Surrey.

Cobham Football Club were formed in October 1892 and played in local leagues as a junior side, using a variety of grounds. They gained intermediate status during the 1930s and soon afterwards achieved senior status in 1938 when they were elected to the Surrey Senior League. At this time they were playing at the Cobham Recreational Ground. Cobham became league Champions in 1948/49, narrowly missing a double by finishing runners-up in the League Cup final. They also entered the FA Cup for the first time that season but lost in the preliminary round at Leatherhead, 2-0. The club moved to their current ground at Anvil Lane in 1955 (also known as the Leg O' Mutton Field) and became known by the nickname the 'Hammers'.

Cricket fast-bowler-turned-commentator Bob Willis made occasional appearances in goal in the 1970s and is now a life member of the club. They had their record attendance at Anvil Lane in 1975, when 2,000 watched a charity match against a showbiz team. Cobham were members of Home Counties League in 1977/78 (formed from the Surrey Senior League) that was renamed the Combined Counties League the following season. Cobham had an excellent run in the FA Vase during 1985/86 when they reached the third round before losing at Anvil Lane to Abingdon Town 4-0 (a game that I attended – see below). They had beaten Frimley Green, Horndean and Ringmer to reach this stage.

Cobham, July 2004. Nettles run riot over the close season in the cover behind the goal, which is the only shelter for spectators.

The ground's floodlights were installed in 1997/98 and Woking were the inaugural visitors to play under them in a special friendly match. Cobham came closest to winning the Combined Counties League in 1998/99, when they finished runners-up behind Ash United after leading the table for much of the season. They won 24 of the 40 games and scored 108 goals in the league. Cobham equalled their best run in the FA Vase in 1998/99 when they again reached the third round. They beat AFC Totton, Peacehaven & Telscombe and Stowmarket Town before losing at home to Camberley Town 2-1. The Hammers' most recent silverware was won in 2001/02 when they beat Bedfont 3-2 at Woking to win the CCL Premier Challenge Cup. Their worst season in the Co-Co League was 2002/03, when they finished 21st out of 24 with only 40 points from 46 matches.

ALEX'S FIRST TIME: I managed to turn up late for this one on 14 December 1985. Not realising that Cobham did not have floodlights, I arrived at 2.30 p.m. for a 3 p.m. kick-off only to find it was nearly half-time when I arrived. Abingdon Town easily beat Cobham 4-0 in the third round of the FA Vase before an official attendance of 92 (I counted over 150).

COCKFOSTERS
Ground: Cockfosters Sports Ground, Chalk Lane, Cockfosters, Herts.

Cockfosters is one of the easiest grounds to get to, being opposite the tube station of the same name. They have one of the least developed grounds in the London area. Cockfosters FC was originally formed in 1921 and their ground at Chalk Lane was presented to the club by local landowner Lady Bevan from her family estate. They entered the Barnet League and had success as the club moved up through the divisions. The club merged with the successful Cockfosters Juniors and they joined the stronger Wood Green & District League during the 1930s. Promotion was again achieved through the lower divisions, culminating in 1938/39 when they won the Wood Green League's Premier Division, the League Cup and the Barnet Cup.

Cockfosters finished as runners-up in the Northern Suburban Intermediate League's First Division and gained promotion into the Premier Division in 1947. They were quickly relegated but bounced straight back in 1949/50 as the First Division champions and, in the very next season, they were runners-up in the Premier Division. The late 1940s also saw success in a number of local cup competitions but the club struggled during the 1950s.

The start of the 1960s saw success at the club again and the Northern Suburban League's First Division and Premier Division championship were won in two successive seasons. The club gained entry into the Herts Senior County League for 1966/67 and they won the Division One title that season. Twenty-five seasons were spent in this County League and all but the very first were spent in its Premier Division. During these years they also won the London FA Intermediate Cup twice, the Herts FA Intermediate

Cockfosters, July 2004. Since Bob's visit in 1990 a PVC overhang was added to the clubhouse, plus a backless plastic-roofed structure backing on to the bowling green.

Cup once and the Herts Senior County League Cup (The Aubrey Cup) was won on two occasions. The club changed its name from Cockfosters Athletic to Cockfosters in 1968.

Cockfosters won another treble in 1978/79: the Herts Senior County League's Premier Division title, the Aubrey Cup and the Herts FA Intermediate Cup. They were Champions of the Herts County League again in 1980/81 and 1983/84 and were runners-up in 1982/83 and 1984/85. They gained senior status in 1991 from the London FA and they joined the London Spartan League Premier Division. Cockfosters had their best run in the FA Vase in 1991/92, when they reached the second round after beating 61FC (Luton), Kempston Rovers and Kingsbury Town, before losing at Great Yarmouth Town 2-1. Following the amalgamation of the Spartan League with the South Midlands League in 1997/98, the club were placed in its First Division. Their Chalk Lane ground is opposite Cockfosters tube station and remains a basic ground with few facilities. The record attendance at the ground came in 1968/69 when 408 spectators saw a Herts County League match with Saffron Walden.

BOB'S FIRST TIME: Cockfosters entertained Colney Heath in a Hertfordshire Premier Division match on 3 April 1990 for Bob's visit to the venue. A 'crowd' of only forty-six saw the homesters win 1-0 in a game that was rather bizarrely only thirty-eight minutes each way, a regular occurrence in this league in those days. The ground was called Dacre Field at the time and was very basic, with only a small cover made from wood and no floodlights.

COLLIER ROW & ROMFORD
Ground: Sungate, Collier Row Road, Collier Row, Romford, Essex.

Collier Row Football Club was founded as a junior club and they played in the Essex Olympian League for many years. Their previous names were Hamden United and Collier Row Juniors. The club decided to make progress towards gaining senior status in 1980 and joined the London Spartan League as an intermediate league club. The following year they were given senior status by the Essex County FA and moved into the Premier Division of the London Spartan League. In their first season, Row finished fifth. They won the Premier Division title in 1983/84 with only three matches lost. They reached the quarter-final of the FA Vase in 1984/85 – the run finally came to an end with defeat away to Wisbech Town. The following season saw the club make a concerted effort to obtain Isthmian League status. They knew that they needed to win the League and raise the standard of the ground to achieve this. The title was clinched in the last match of the season after they had managed to attain Isthmian League standard for the ground.

In its first season the club finished ninth in Division Two (North) and they also reached the semi-final of the FA Vase. The record attendance at the ground came on 28 February 1987 when Collier Row met Garforth Town in the sixth round of the FA Vase when 1,053 paid to watch. In 1988 the club won its third promotion in six years when they won a spot in the First Division of the Isthmian League, but they struggled in the higher league and were soon relegated.

The club bought the Sungate site from a local farmer in 1948 and they relocated from their previous ground in White Hart Lane in the village of Collier Row. At this time it was nothing more than an open field with a railway carriage for dressing rooms with baths placed outside – which must have been extremely cold for most of the season. Later a wooden pavilion was built, but was destroyed by fire in the 1950s. The Sungate ground overlooked some pleasant countryside but was typical of many Isthmian League grounds – due to the league's insistence on fully enclosed grounds it was surrounded by an ugly corrugated sheeted fence. A nursery and a car dump were to be found at each end of the ground and, on the far side, a pristine wall with fir trees behind. These replaced a line of mature elms that were killed by Dutch Elm Disease.

The ground has gradually been improved over the years. A new changing-room complex was built in 1982 with floodlights and surrounding rail and concrete standing around the pitch being built a year later. To gain entry into the Isthmian League, a seated stand was built in 1985, which contained seats rescued from a cinema at Butlin's in Clacton. Cattle grazed the pitch until the 1970s, when a goat took over the job. This goat could be bad tempered when club members attempted to remove it from the pitch. The surface was notoriously poor and when I visited, the ground had a makeshift public footpath across it!

Despite this the reformed Romford decided to move to Sungate in the summer of 1996 to merge with Collier Row and take up their Isthmian League status. They had reformed in 1992 and had previously played at Hornchurch until 1995 when they moved to share with Ford United. The league closed the ground in March 1999 due to the poor state of the pitch and the ground's inadequate facilities. Romford finally ended

Collier Row, May 1998. The main stand was originally kitted out with comfy cinema-style seats. The plastic replacements were part of a programme of 'improvements'. The capacity is about 150. (Photograph by Vince Taylor)

their stay at Sungate in December 2001 after the clubhouse and boardroom had burned down the previous year.

ALEX'S FIRST TIME: This was on 6 August 1983 for a 1-1 draw between Collier Row and Finchley. But the match was not played at Sungate as its pitch was in such poor condition – despite it being pre-season – and was moved to the Epping Country Club. We saw the ground on our way and the pitch was bone-hard with very little grass on it, looking as though no work had been done on it throughout the summer.

CORINTHIAN CASUALS
Ground: King George's Field, Tolworth, Surrey.

Corinthian Casuals are the amalgamation of the former Corinthian and Casuals clubs. The Corinthians were formed in 1882 and the Casuals in 1883 and their players were drawn exclusively from the elite public schools and universities. In their early days, many internationals and leading players of the time appeared for them and they were able to compete with most professional sides for ability and talent of their players. They played at various venues in the London area until 1895, after which most of their home matches

Corinthian Casuals, December 1984. Ambitions of transforming Wimbledon Park, with its stand made up of five rows of planks on concrete, into an Isthmian League venue were thwarted when Wandsworth Council vetoed the proposals that Merton Council had agreed to.

were played at the Queens Club, West Kensington until after the First World War. Today, this venue is more famous for its pre-Wimbledon tennis tournament. The ground at that time possessed a tall stand that seemed out of proportion with the rest of the venue.

The Corinthians decided to change their rule of not playing competitive matches in 1923 and entered the FA Cup. They were given an exemption to the first round due to their reputation and high standing with the FA and in 1927 they were drawn at home to First Division Newcastle United in the fourth round. They were now playing at the huge arena at Crystal Palace, Sydenham, which since staging twenty FA Cup finals between 1895 and 1914 had fallen into disuse. Over 56,000 packed into Crystal Palace for the tie, only to see the amateurs go down 3-1 to their professional opponents.

The Casuals initially took their players from Charterhouse, Eton and Winchester Schools and later took from all public schools and university old boys. Their colours were chocolate and pink. Casuals had been founder members of the Isthmian League in 1905, and though they left in 1907, they returned after the First World War. One of the grounds that they played on was the Essex County Cricket Ground at Crawley Road, Leyton, which possessed a large pavilion and two wooden covered stands. The fine old pavilion remains 'in situ' today and was recently the home to London Intermediate League teams Leyton County and Leyton Paragons, although Essex CCC no longer uses the ground.

Casuals then shared Crystal Palace with Corinthians for a spell before becoming the tenants of Kingstonian in 1925 at their former Richmond Road home. They remained there until 1939 but they became homeless and, partly due to the Second World War, they decided to amalgamate with the Corinthians.

Corinthians had lost their headquarters at Crystal Palace and were by now struggling to find a first-class side – their exemption to the first round proper of the FA Cup was also coming under question. They came from a similar background to Casuals and drew on the same diminishing pool of university-based players. Therefore, rather than disbanding, the move seemed the best way of perpetuating the Corinthian ideals. Their first match as the newly named Corinthian Casuals was played in the grounds of Lambeth Palace.

After the war, they were forced to take on a nomadic existence, having short spells at the Polytechnic Stadium at Chiswick, the London University Ground at Motspur Park (Fulham's present training ground) and on the grounds of opponents when these were not available. Their wandering came to a temporary end in 1951 when they secured a lease at Kennington Oval, the home of Surrey County Cricket Club.

The Oval had staged the first FA Cup final in 1872 and the first Home International football match. The pitch was to be found at the Vauxhall End on the opposite side of the ground from the pavilion. The crowds sat mainly in the Vauxhall Centre Stand (now the Fender Stand) and in the seating by the large scoreboard. Corinthian Casuals' home matches had to be crammed in between late September and early March due to the demands of cricket and the need for the outfield to be repaired. Alternative home venues had to be sought from March.

The club left The Oval in 1962 and moved to nearby Dulwich Hamlet at Champion Hill. They drew an attendance of over 7,000 when they played a FA Cup first-round match against Watford in November 1965. They moved to Tooting & Mitcham United's Sandy Lane Ground in 1971 and anybody could now play for the club as long as they remained of amateur status, which meant that they regularly finished bottom of the table. They moved again in 1983 to Molesey's Walton Road ground. They reached the first round of the FA Cup, where they played against Bristol City. The club hired Dulwich Hamlet's Champion Hill and, in one of the last big games before the ground was demolished and rebuilt in a much more modest form, 2,116 saw the two teams fight out a 0-0 draw – but they lost the replay.

They thought they had found a permanent ground at last when they moved to the Wimbledon Park Athletic Stadium in 1984. This had a 500-seat concrete grandstand that had been built in the early 1960s but had no floodlights. Unfortunately, Wandsworth Council owned half the ground and the other half belonged to Merton Council, and neither could agree with the club's plans for the ground. They lost their Isthmian League status before the move and were now playing in the Spartan League. Casuals took the opportunity to take over the King Georges Field, Tolworth ground in 1988 from the ailing local Surrey Senior League club Tolworth, who had run into financial troubles. At last they had their own ground. There was little at the venue at this time but facilities have gradually improved over the years. Soon after their move a cover was put up in front of the clubhouse. Next came the installation of floodlights, and not long afterwards the original cover was replaced by a seated stand combined with a terrace. By the time they reclaimed their position in the Isthmian League in 1997, a covered terrace had been erected at one end, further terracing had been laid opposite it, a turnstile block had been constructed and the whole area was enclosed by a wooden fence. Corinthian Casuals are now also a community club with a whole host of youth teams playing under their colours.

ALEX'S FIRST TIME (Wimbledon Park): I saw a schoolboy match here in 1964 when two of my school team represented Putney Schools against East Ham Schools in the Crisp Shield semi-final. I later saw Beckton United beat the Casuals 2-0 in a Spartan League encounter on 23 March 1985. (Tolworth): This was for a match between Casuals and Waltham Abbey in the Spartan League on 24 February 1990 when the ground was little more than a railed-off pitch in a recreation ground.

CRAY WANDERERS

Ground: Hayes Lane, Bromley, Kent / Oxford Road, Sidcup, Kent.

Cray Wanderers are the second-oldest football club in the world and were formed as long ago as 1860, when a group of railway labourers wanted to kick a ball about in their spare time. They played on a field in Star Lane and were employed by the South Eastern & Chatham Railway, building railways in the Chislehurst area. They had to change in the Coffee Tavern, as there were no facilities on the ground. This is now a listed building located next to the railway viaduct in St Mary Cray High Street. By the 1890s Cray played on open land near Grassmeade called Derry Downs, which had a rickety wooden stand. They were not able to take a gate at Derry Downs so in 1898 moved to an enclosed field owned by a Mr Joynson and transported the stand down to the new ground. Their next ground was Fordcroft – where there was a tragedy on Easter Monday 1900, when during an 'A' team match against Morden Swifts from Deptford, lightning struck the

Cray Wanderers, October 1973. Grassmeade was on its way out: the stand in the middle had lost its four rows of seats and the cover on the right its PVC roof.

ground. The flagstaff on the roof of the stand was hit by a lightning flash and caused an explosion when it hit the stand's iron roof. Many spectators were sheltering inside the dressing room underneath: and one man was killed and over thirty seriously injured. When the landowner decided to sell the land in 1936, this included a paper mill, his house and the football ground and Wanderers lost use of the venue. The site was soon used for building purposes and disappeared under the Tip-Top factory in Cray Avenue.

Cray Wanderers moved to Foots Cray to play at a ground called Twysden. The pavilion was still being built when the first game was played at the ground, against Margate on 28 November 1936. A water pipe laid down the centre of the pitch caused a hump and an uneven surface. The club did not appear from 1939-1944 due to the war. They had to find another ground when peace was declared and moved back to a pitch close to their former ground at Grassmeade after a brief nomadic existence. Cray and the local gas company's sports guild jointly rented Grassmeade from its owners, St Philomena's School. Both had to vacate the ground in 1947 and the following seasons saw Wanderers at their lowest ebb, playing at St Mary Cray Recreation Ground, in junior football. However, the Gas Board Guild had negotiated a lease on a ground at Northfields Farm in 1950, an oval-shaped field next to Grassmeade, and they agreed to share it with Cray. After returfing the pitch and making the ground look presentable, the first match took place against Foots Cray Social on 16 September 1950. They soon lost this ground, however, and were forced to move to a muddy site close to the river, and adjacent to the old Fordcroft at Tothills.

They rented Grassmere permanently from 1955 and were at last able to make some long-term plans for improving facilities. By the mid-1960s, a pitch-length stand and low terracing had been laid behind each goal. A clubhouse and a new lighting system were also built at the attractive tree-lined ground. Unfortunately, they lost this in April 1973 when they were evicted by the school trustees when the ground was sold for housing. It took a couple of years to turn their new Oxford Road ground into something resembling a proper venue. A small covered stand and a clubhouse were erected. The almost-new clubhouse was burned down in 1976 but was quickly rebuilt. One hundred seats were installed in the stand in 1992, and the following year a bus shelter-type cover went up opposite. The record crowd at Oxford Road came during 1979/80 when 1,523 saw a FA Vase quarter-final against Stamford.

Cray Wanderers moved from the Kent Senior League to the Isthmian League in 2004. The local council refused permission for floodlighting on their Oxford Road ground due to complaints from local residents, Due to this, Cray have played their home matches at Bromley's ground at Hayes Lane in recent seasons. However, the ground was in use again as Danson FC moved to Oxford Road during 2002/03 after the sale of their Green Court Road ground.

ALEX'S FIRST TIME: I attended a match between Cray Wanderers and Faversham Town on 8 February 1997 that the visitors won 2-0. It is a shame that Cray are not currently using the ground, as it is a very pleasant ground hidden behind some houses. There is a very large tree by the side of the pitch whose branches overhangs the playing area, a small neat stand on the halfway line and a comfortable clubhouse.

CROCKENHILL
Ground: Wested Meadow, Wested, Eynesford Road, Crockenhill, Kent.

Wested Meadow is one of prettiest grounds in the London area. Surrounded by countryside, it has a very quaint feel to it. The present Crockenhill club was formed in 1946 and offered the use of Wested Meadow. Other Crockenhill teams used the ground before the war, when it was undeveloped with no facilities. During the war it was used as a site for a barrage balloon and had a Nissen hut to guard it. The club started playing in the Kent Amateur League and, by 1951, they had erected a small stand plus dressing rooms, a tea bar, office and a loudspeaker system. The record attendance for the ground of 800 came in 1948 against Maidstone United in the Kent Amateur Cup. The stand remains in-situ today, but now has a new roof, and the canteen has been used as a physio room and a club shop. There are grass banks around the pitch and an interesting entrance, built from corrugated iron. Next to this was a small covered area with railway sleeper terracing, but this was pulled down in the 1980s. The clubhouse was created around the old Nissen hut and the entrance during the 1960s, and was later extended to include an old turnstile, which came from the ground of Thameside Amateurs and possibly dates back to the 1890s.

Crockenhill joined the Kent League in 1968/69 and, after finishing third in 1980/81, won the title for the only time in their history in 1982/83, when they won 19 of their 32 games. They also had good seasons in 1985/86 and 1986/87 – when they finished third and second respectively. The 1987 hurricane damaged the roof of the stand and the clubhouse when a tree fell through them. The stand's roof was not repaired for some time after this. A small terrace has been laid to the west of the stand in recent years and the clubhouse was also renovated. During the 1990s, Crockenhill usually struggled close to the bottom of the table and they were forced to leave the Kent League in 1999 and joined the Kent County League. This was due to the Kent League insisting that all clubs installed floodlights but local residents objected to this, and the local council refused to give the club permission to install them. They played at Erith & Belvedere during 1998/99, but soon returned home.

Crockenhill, May 1984. The cover at Wested seems designed for the vertically challenged. The stand shows what can be achieved with the imaginative use of wood, tin and metal poles.

Crockenhill played in the FA Cup from 1984-1989 without much success. They entered the FA Vase for the first time in its inaugural season of 1974/75 and beat Slade Green Athletic, Swanley Town, and Dartford Amateurs before losing 2-0 to Molesey (at home). They have also reached the third round on three occasions and they last played in the vase during 1996/97. They won the Kent County League title in 2003/04 but chose not to move up the pyramid system.

BOB'S FIRST TIME: Bob visited the ground for the first time in January 1974 and was struck by what a lovely place it was. It had, and still has, a stand made from wood and iron with a wonky tin cover alongside, painted dark green. By March 1977, there was a minuscule and short-lived cover behind one goal. Bob finally saw a match there on 2 May 1984. This was a Kent League match with Cray Wanderers before a crowd of ninety. The stand and dressing rooms had been painted in a garish red, although the cover was still green, but the paint was peeling off.

CROWN & MANOR
Ground: East London Stadium, Burdett Road, Mile End, London E1.

The club was formed at the turn of the century in Hoxton. Under a variety of names, it catered for young people in one of the most notorious areas of London. From this grew the respected Hoxton Manor and the football team gained senior status in 1932 when they joined the Spartan League Eastern Section. In the first year they were Champions and were promoted to the Premier Division. This began a run that earned them the title 'The Wonder Team from Wiltshire Row'. They were the youngest team playing senior amateur football in the South of England at that time. They also had a reputation as the model amateur soccer club and the team that never disputed a referee's decision.

When war came in 1939, they amalgamated with the Crown Club (also from Hoxton) to become Crown & Manor, also from Hoxton, and kept going through the war years with players on leave making up the numbers. This amalgamation took place when financial support was withdrawn from the Hoxton Manor club and the Crown club had their premises demolished by a bomb. The club was admitted to the Middlesex Senior League in 1946/47. When this became the Parthenon League, they won the Premier League championship twice and the League Challenge Cup on one occasion.

After the Second World War, Crown & Manor were constantly searching for a ground of their own. They lost their ground at Cheshunt in 1947 then moved to another one at Hendon, but were forced to move on again in 1952. Crown & Manor moved back to the Cheshunt Cricket Club at Albury Way, Cheshunt again, via Wimbledon, in 1954 and found a new venue at Belling Sports Ground, Turkey Street, Enfield in 1974. Amazingly, the stand was still in place when the ground was visited in 2001, although the remainder was derelict. They were without a ground again in 1984/85, so shared with Cheshunt FC. Despite this, they had their most successful season for years when they won the Spartan League championship – six points clear of runners-up Yeading.

Crown & Manor, March 2002. The stand at Bellings Sports Ground, Turkey Street – one of many former homes – was on its last legs.

The club moved to the East London Stadium at Mile End from 1987 but, after finishing bottom of the Spartan League in 1988/89, with only 14 points from 38 games, Crown & Manor dropped out of that league. They are currently playing in the Middlesex League. The East London Stadium has a stand with 440 plastic bucket seats under a steel roof. There are also five steps of concrete terracing either side of the stand and opposite it. Spectator facilities are some way from the pitch due to it being an athletics stadium.

BOB'S FIRST TIME: This was for a London Spartan League encounter played on 13 April 1987 between Crown & Manor and Brimsdown Rovers, which ended in a 2-2 draw. The fifty-five spectators looked lost in the large stand.

CROYDON
Ground: The Croydon Arena, Albert Road, Woodside, London SE25.

When Croydon Tramlink opened in May 2000, I thought that it would help Croydon to attract a better attendance. I was wrong, despite the ground having its own tram stop. Formed as Croydon Amateurs on 17 April 1953, the club has played at Croydon Arena since their formation, when the ground was formally opened before a game with Pegasus FC. In fact, the club was created to use the stadium, which was essentially built for athletics. The present grandstand has been there since the ground was built and has been modified several times. It presently has 450 seats, all with a good elevated view but some distance from the play. The 'Amateurs' joined the Surrey Senior League, and in

Croydon, October 1976. This covered standing area was opposite the main stand: note the park bench in front and grass banking.

their first season reached the finals of both the Surrey Senior League Challenge and Charity Cups. Croydon lost the Challenge Cup final, but they shared the Charity Cup after a 1-1 draw with Dorking in front of a 1,600 crowd at Croydon Sports Arena. Croydon were elected to the Spartan League in 1963 where they spent just one season, but won their first league title in excellent style, winning 29 of their 34 league games and scoring 123 goals in the process. Croydon immediately stepped up into the Athenian League, and two years later they won the Second Division championship. Croydon were elected to the recently formed Second Division of the Isthmian League in 1974, and the name 'Amateurs' was dropped. Croydon achieved promotion to the top flight of the Isthmian League in 1975/76 without losing a league game all season in 42 matches. Despite this they could still only finish second, four points behind Tilbury.

Croydon had their best league campaign in the Premier Division when finishing fourth in 1985/86 behind Sutton, Yeovil and Farnborough. In the FA Cup, Croydon have only once gone through the qualifying rounds, in 1979/80, when they held Third Division Millwall to a 1-1 draw at Selhurst Park in the second round before bowing out 2-3 after extra time in the replay at The Den.

In the late 1980s the local authority decided to redevelop the Arena, replacing the eight-lane cinder track with a larger, tarmac track. Unfortunately, this meant that the pitch was even further away from the stand, thereby further decreasing the matchday atmosphere. Croydon also spent over a season playing home matches elsewhere, which did not help the club's finances. In the early 1990s there was little stability either on or off the field, when the club experienced five chairmen and eleven team managers, mounting debts and threats of closure. Wages were not paid and the whole team walked out on the club. The club was saved from the brink of folding by local businessman Ken Jarvie with the players of his

Thornton Heath League side, Phoenix Sun, who stepped up nine levels of football to fulfil the club's fixtures. Not surprisingly, some very heavy defeats followed and another place was gained in the annals of the Isthmian League, this time for the most goals conceded.

The arrival of Ken Jarvie sparked one of the most successful periods in the club's history. A nineteen-match unbeaten run (another club record) at the beginning of 2000 saw Croydon storm to their first league title for thirty-four years. In addition, Croydon reached their first cup finals since 1982. A narrow defeat against Conference side Woking in the Surrey Senior Cup final was forgotten about the following night as Croydon beat Purfleet 2-0 to win the Isthmian League Full Members Cup. However, two seasons later, budget cuts and the loss of a number of high-quality players proved crucial, and the club was relegated to Division One (South).

Although the facilities at the Croydon Arena are excellent, the presence of a running track and other athletics equipment causes a distinct lack of atmosphere at the ground. Vandals have struck on a regular basis over the years, including burning down the clubhouse. The first one was built in 1964 and a new one followed, which the FIFA chairman Sir Stanley Rous opened in 1981. Floodlighting was installed in 1970, and was celebrated with a match against Crystal Palace. In 1989, major work was completed on the installation of a new athletics track. New perimeter walls, concrete fences, floodlights and seating went in before Croydon returned.

ALEX'S FIRST TIME: This was for an AC Delco Cup first round match with Bishop's Stortford on 21 September 1987, that went to extra time before Devon Gayle hit a very late winner. Although this ground is the closest to where I live, I rarely make a visit there as you need a pair of binoculars to be able to see what is going on as you are so far from the pitch and there is little atmosphere when watching a match.

CROYDON ATHLETIC
Ground: Mayfields, Mayfields Road, Thornton Heath, Surrey.

Croydon Athletic has developed from two clubs: Wandsworth FC, who were formed in 1948, and Norwood, who were created a year earlier. Wandsworth had played at a number of grounds, including: Kimber Road (Wandsworth), Wisley Gardens (the famous gardens near Cobham), Moorfax Sports Ground and London Road (Mitcham). Norwood had played on park pitches at Wandle Park and Lloyd Park in the Croydon area and 1986 played on the club's present ground at Mayfields, Thornton Heath. The merger was mutually beneficial as Wandsworth FC did not have a permanent ground but had senior status, while Norwood had a ground.

The two clubs merged in 1986 to form Wandsworth & Norwood FC and the new club took Wandsworth's place in the London Spartan League. The club changed its name to Croydon Athletic in 1990, which reflected better the area that they played in. The Mayfields ground was formerly called the NFC Sports Ground. Over the next few years it became fully enclosed and a small stand with a corrugated iron roof was also built. Before being

Croydon Athletic, January 2004. Built in 2003, this magnificent cantilever stand holds over 300. There is also cover at one end and opposite the stand.

enclosed, the ground was overlooked by the local cemetery. Floodlights were added in 1990 but the clubhouse was small and described by the club as a 'glorified scout hut'.

The team got off to a flying start in 1993/94, finally finishing in the runners-up position of the Spartan League. However, they were unsuccessful in their bid to join the Isthmian League – despite many ground improvements, including building an extension to the clubhouse. Athletic were crowned London Spartan League Champions in 1994/95, with striker Marc Flemington scoring 54 goals, but the ground was still not up to standard. Covered terracing was built opposite the main stand and open terracing behind one goal. Big improvements were also made to the dressing rooms. As a result, the club entered the Isthmian League in 1997 having extended the stand to hold 163 seats. They soon gained promotion to the new Division One (South), playing in the same league as the likes of Dulwich, Tooting, Carshalton and Bromley. A cover was erected over the terraces behind the goal in memory of a former player, Paul Muir, who died as an innocent victim of senseless street violence. There is a plaque to Paul's memory.

The club embarked on its most ambitious ground development project in 2003 – thanks largely to a grant from the Football Stadia Improvement Fund who awarded them £150,000 to build a new and impressive 302-seat stand. The club were able to do other improvements on the ground, including a new turnstile block. They also levelled the playing surface, having installed both a drainage and sprinkler system, and reseeded the pitch.

ALEX'S FIRST TIME: Mayfields has changed out of all recognition since my first visit on 3 October 1987. The clubhouse was very small but homely and I had a chat with a man over the wall who worked at the next-door cemetery. An unfortunate player broke his leg in this match between Wandsworth & Norwood and Edgware in the Spartan League. Play was held up while we waited thirty minutes for the ambulance to turn up and take him off to the local Mayday Hospital. I had previously seen Wandsworth play Ulysses on their former ground, close to London Road near Mitcham Junction Station. There was little on the ground and only seventeen spectators were present.

CROYDON COMMON
Ground: The Nest, Selhurst Road, South Norwood, London SE25.

Croydon Common were formed as an amateur club in 1897 and their first ground was a park pitch on the Whitehorse Road Recreation Ground, which still exists today. Their first competitive matches were in the Croydon Charity Cup from 1899. They joined the Surrey FA in 1903, entered County competitions for the first time and their fans began calling the club 'The Robins'. They moved up another step when they joined the Southern Suburban League Division Two in 1906 and now played home matches at the Crescent in the Selhurst area. The following year a new professional club was formed using the Croydon Common name and ground. They played their first game in the Southern League Division Two against Southend United, losing 3-0 at the Crescent on 14 September 1907. Croydon Common also joined the South Eastern League that was partially made up of Football and Southern League clubs' reserve teams.

The Robins subleased The Nest from the London Brighton & South Coast Railway in 1908, and it was home to the club for the rest of its existence. The Nest had been built some years earlier on the site of Selhurst Wood. The twenty-one-year lease was signed on 15 September 1908, the parties being The Croydon Common Football & Athletic Company Ltd, The London Brighton & South Coast Railway Company and the Ecclesiastical Commissioners for England – who actually owned the land and leased it to the Railway Company. The lease stipulated that the ground could only be used for soccer or athletics, or for 'the holding of Flower Shows and School treats'. The Church Commissioners would not allow football and other sports to be played at The Nest on Good Friday and Christmas Day. The ground was quite basic, having only earth banks surrounding the pitch. Bushes known to the supporters as 'The Jungle' topped these banks! A cinder athletics track ran around the pitch and there was a small stand with seats on the northern side of the ground, but this burned down in November 1907. A longer new stand was quickly erected in its place. The ground was surrounded by countryside, but the main Victoria to Brighton line ran past on the south side. The entrance to the ground was opposite Selhurst Railway Station.

The club were Champions of the Southern League Second Division in 1908/09 and 1913/14, but on each occasion were relegated the following season. Had they survived the First World War the club may have joined the newly formed Third Division (South), as most of the First Division sides of the Southern League became founder members. However, with increasingly poor attendances due to the war and mounting debts,

Croydon Common – The Nest, September 1923. Crystal Palace took over The Nest in September 1918. Here, Fulham's Arthur Reynolds beats a Palace forward to the ball while Alec Chaplin looks on in the 1-1 draw on 15 September 1923. (Photo courtesy of Alex White)

Croydon Common were wound up in February 1917. One of their debtors was the Railway Company who sublet The Nest.

Following the demise of Croydon Common, the Railway leased the ground to Crystal Palace FC and they played there from 1918 until the newly built Selhurst Park was ready in 1924. After leaving the ground in 1924, Crystal Palace sublet it to a local side named Tramways FC. The Southern Region's Selhurst Depot was built on the site in the next few years and The Nest completely disappeared in the process.

CRYSTAL PALACE
Ground: Selhurst Park, Whitehorse Lane, South Norwood, London SE25.

A short-lived football club called Crystal Palace was formed in 1861 by members of its exhibition staff. They played a role in the formation of the Football Association in 1863 and they reached the semi-final of the very first FA Cup in 1872. A football ground was created next to the Crystal Palace Exhibition site in 1895 (see next section on the Crystal Palace Grounds) and the FA Cup final was played there until 1914. The owners decided to form their own professional club to play at this venue. This new club was called 'Crystal Palace' and started playing at the Crystal Palace grounds in September 1905, as members of the Southern League Second Division. The club was soon

Crystal Palace, July 1975. Five rows of seats in the stand at Herne Hill Stadium accommodated 214 people. Thousands more could sit on the wood benches on both sides at this cycling venue.

promoted to the First Division and crowds were often over 10,000, but this must have looked small in such a vast ground, capable of holding 120,000. The stadium was taken over by the Admiralty in 1915 and Crystal Palace were forced to move to the Herne Hill cycle and athletics ground, home of amateurs West Norwood. The FA Amateur Cup final had been staged there in 1911. This ground is still in use today as a venue for cycling and the occasional non-League side, and has not changed a great deal over the years.

Palace moved to The Nest at Selhurst in 1918. This was formerly the home of Croydon Common (The Robins) who had folded in 1917. Palace regarded the move as temporary, because in February 1919 they began the process of buying and developing a nearby site that would become Selhurst Park. Palace became founder members of the Football League Division Three in 1920 and the site's purchase was completed in January 1922 at a cost of £2,570. The Nest was opposite the entrance to Selhurst Station and there was one stand, shallow banking around three sides and just one entrance for the whole ground (see section on Croydon Common). Selhurst Park was formerly a brickworks, situated in a natural hollow, and belonged to the London Brighton & South Coast Railway Company. The new ground occupied fifteen acres and was within walking distance of three railway stations: Norwood Junction, Selhurst and Thornton Heath.

The new ground was opened in August 1924 and The Nest soon became a railway depot that still covers the site today. Only one stand with minimal terraces around the three sides of earth banking was built and even these were not completely ready, due to labour disputes, when the ground was opened. The partnership of Archibald Leitch and Humphries, a Knightsbridge building contractors, prepared the ground at Selhurst Park. The main stand at Selhurst was a typical Leitch structure and looked almost identical to ones built at Craven Cottage and Stamford Bridge in 1905. However, Palace had less money so their stand lacked exterior brick detailing or the familiar pedimented Leitch roof gable. Palace were relegated at the end of their first season at Selhurst Park, but crowds improved a great deal at the new venue. The ground was used for a Home International match between England and Wales in March 1926.

A new board of directors took over in 1950, and they had plans to rebuild Selhurst Park into a huge modern stadium capable of holding over 100,000 spectators, but nothing ever came of those plans. The terraces were not fully concreted and were topped by either grass banking or rough earth. The first primitive floodlights, mounted on poles and on the stand roof, were first used in September 1953 and the lights were replaced in 1961 with four corner pylons costing £18,000. They managed to persuade European Champions Real Madrid to play Palace in a floodlit friendly in April 1962.

During the 1960s, Palace rose from the Fourth to the First Division and the ground needed modernisation to cope with the larger crowds that were attracted to Selhurst Park. These were the first major improvements at the ground since it was built in 1924. The uncovered Park Road side was converted into a new stand that was called the Arthur Wait stand, after the club's long-serving chairman. This had a large shed-like roof that covered the existing banking, and 5,000 seats were placed at the rear with terracing at the front. The roof's fascia was painted in red and blue stripes but this was later covered in adverts. The stand was ready in August 1969 for the start of Palace's first ever season in the top flight. The club did not stay there long, however, and found themselves soon back in the Third Division.

In the late 1970s, Palace fought their way back to the First Division again and a record crowd of 51,482 somehow squeezed into Selhurst Park for the visit of Burnley in May 1989, for the match that clinched the Second Division Championship. The main stand paddock was converted to seating that brought the total at the ground up to 11,508 but reduced the ground's capacity to 38,366.

In September 1985, Palace and Charlton Athletic became the first League clubs in Britain to agree upon a long-term ground sharing arrangement. This arrangement helped improve Palace's financial situation as Charlton stayed for six seasons and paid Palace ten per cent of gate receipts plus half all the running costs. Palace were relegated again in 1991 and to help solve their financial problems, the open Whitehorse Lane End terracing was partially sold off and redeveloped into housing and a supermarket. The club offices and club shop were incorporated into the new complex and a smaller terrace was built to replace the original one, and thus reduced the ground's capacity by a further 7,000. As Charlton departed in 1991 they were replaced by Wimbledon, whose Plough Lane ground was not deemed suitable for top-flight football. The deal was eased by the fact that Palace's chairman Ron Noades had also been the Dons' owner in the 1980s. Wimbledon agreed a seven-year deal to share Selhurst Park – much to the chagrin of many of the Dons supporters. This move would later lead to even greater acrimony within the Wimbledon club between its owners and supporters, when the owners decided to move the Dons to Milton Keynes in 2003 (see Wimbledon).

Crystal Palace, August 1979. At this time Selhurst had two large open ends. The Holmesdale can be seen to the right of the Arthur Wait Stand.

The Taylor Report, instigated after the disasters at Valley Parade and Hillsborough, would mean that Palace would need to make significant changes to improve Selhurst Park. The first development was to improve the very basic Arthur Wait stand and this began during the summer of 1990. At a cost of £400,000, the lower section was converted from terracing to seating and 5,080 seats plus additional facilities for disabled spectators were put in place. The contractors used a combination of concrete and polystyrene blocks to create the new surface on which the seating was placed. A double row of thirty-two executive boxes with balconies were installed above the open Whitehorse Lane End terracing in 1991 and a new car park was laid behind the main stand, replacing a school. During 1992/93 a new three-storey hospitality block was built at the rear of the main stand and the number of boxes was increased to forty-eight. Also, 2,500 seats were bolted to the terraces at the Whitehorse Lane End. A 'goalpost' supported roof was placed over both the boxes and seats. This brought the cost of the Whitehorse Lane development up to £2.3 million and Selhurst Park had a capacity of 30,115, including 18,300 seats, by August 1993.

The club's next development was at the Holmesdale Road End, but this was fraught with major difficulties due to objections from local residents that the new structure was blocking their view and the sheer size of the project. The new stand at the Holmesdale Road End cost £5.7 million to construct and looks completely out of proportion with the rest of the ground and, due to its enormous size, towers above the rest of Selhurst Park and can be seen for miles around the ground. It is a double-deck stand and was built between May 1994 and August 1995. Huge amounts of London clay had to be removed to make sure the new stand had proper foundations. The stand's roof is designed to look like a 'drooping beak' to protect spectators from the elements. The stand offers excellent views and holds 5,341 seats on the lower tier and 2,806 in the upper tier. The back of the stand has been carefully matched to fit into its location.

It was announced in February 2004 that National Athletics Stadium at the Crystal Palace would be taken over by the London Authority, who would make funds available to renovate the by-now dilapidated stadium. There was immediate speculation that the football club may move back to their original ground, where they played on their formation in 1905.

ALEX'S FIRST TIME: This was before the Arthur Wait stand was built and the ground was very basic. Spectators were allowed to stand on the grass-and-ash banks that topped the concrete terracing. I saw Crystal Palace play Ipswich Town on Boxing Day 1965 in the old Second Division and they won 3-1 thanks to two goals from Alan Stephenson, who would soon be sold to West Ham United. I sat in the main stand as a guest of a school friend and his family.

THE CRYSTAL PALACE GROUNDS
Ground: National Athletics Stadium, Crystal Palace Park, London SE20.

The Crystal Palace was originally built to house the 1851 Great Exhibition, held in Hyde Park. At the end of the exhibition it was decided to move this to a site on the side of Sydenham Hill in South London where the Crystal Palace was rebuilt at the top of the hill. Joseph Paxton, the Palace's designer, also made plans for a park with ornamental gardens, terraces and fountains. A football ground was not built until 1895 and came about for two reasons. Firstly, the Football Association decided that the FA Cup final should return to London and secondly, the Crystal Palace Company decided to fill in the large fountain basins, thus creating two huge arenas for various sporting and recreational activities. The most southerly of these became the football ground.

The ground was laid out with the goals positioned at the north and south ends. Around the playing area was a roped-off area known as 'The Ring'. On the east side, the ground rose rapidly away from The Ring to the trees. At the back of this area, the Crystal Palace Company had already installed a switchback railway as a fairground attraction. On match days, spectators would stand on the bank and, as the railway was closed, they could also stand on this area. On the bank opposite was the pavilion, which was a small pitched-roof structure of wooden construction. It was here that guests of honour would sit and where the FA Cup was presented to the winners. On either side of the pavilion were two multi-span stands, bringing the total seating accommodation to 3,000, including space for the press. On the southern end of the ground, there was

The Crystal Palace Grounds, May 1950. (Aerofilms, ref. 7888)

more accommodation for 3,000 inside the ring. The banking behind this was where the vast majority of the crowd stood, but the view here was poor and only a lucky few could see anything of the game. This was the ground as it was when over 42,000 saw Aston Villa beat West Bromwich Albion in the 1895 Cup Final. By 1901 over 110,000 watched Tottenham Hotspur take on Sheffield United in the final. When the FA gave the Crystal Palace Company more security with a five-year agreement in 1905, the company made a number of improvements to the ground. Large stands and rows upon rows of small gravel terraces were built upon the once-green banks that surround the field. They rose gradually from the bottom of the slopes at intervals of about six inches, supported by strong timber, while the surface was sprinkled with a layer of gravel, which allowed better drainage. The old stands on either side of the pavilion were replaced by two new and larger modern stands that accommodated 5,000 people. This encouraged the Crystal Palace Company to start its own football club in 1905 (see Crystal Palace Football Club) and they joined the Southern League. The FA Cup final was played at the Crystal Palace until 1914 and the Crystal Palace Football Club was also forced to vacate the ground in February 1915 and move to the Herne Hill Cycling Grounds after the Admiralty commandeered the ground. As well as FA Cup finals, Inter-League matches and Home Internationals were also played at Crystal Palace, including some England versus Scotland matches.

In the inter-war years, amateur football, in the guise of Casuals and Corinthians Football Clubs, took over at the Crystal Palace ground, both taking up residence in 1922. Casuals played their last game their on 2 May 1925 in an Isthmian League encounter with Oxford City. Corinthians appeared there regularly until 1933 and played their last game at the Crystal Palace two days before the fire, which burned down the huge glass building known as the Crystal Palace on 30 November 1936. The England amateur international side, FA Amateur Cup finals and Varsity matches were also played at this venue in the inter-war years. Speedway was introduced for a while from 1928 when changes were made to the ring and in the late 1930s the arena was used as a paddock for the motor-racing circuit.

After the Second World War, junior football was periodically played on the main pitch. Football, notably the Arthur Dunn Cup final, was also played on the adjacent cycle track that had several stands on the Eastern side. In the late 1950s the site was closed, with access impenetrable until the ground was finally swept away in the early 1960s to build the National Sports Centre. This was opened in 1964 and soon hosted the first ever all-seated match in Britain when Crystal Palace FC met West Ham United in a friendly on 19 August. A host of other sports were also played on its reopening and I remember visiting the site and watching rugby league there. In later years the London Crusaders Rugby League side played at the venue for a while. The ground was by now essentially an athletics stadium, but Crystal Palace FC played the occasional friendly match at the venue and their reserve side appeared there regularly from 1999.

ALEX'S FIRST TIME: This was for a reserve match between Crystal Palace and Southampton on 26 January 2000. The game ended in a 1-1 draw but the crowd of about 100 looked totally lost in such a vast arena. The pitch was some way from the stand, which made it difficult to feel involved with what was going on.

DAGENHAM & REDBRIDGE
Ground: Victoria Road, Dagenham, Essex.

Victoria Road was first used as a football ground in 1917 by the Sterling Works side, whose factory was situated alongside the ground. It was not fully enclosed until the summer of 1955, when Briggs Sports, the existing users of the ground, moved out to Rush Green Road to be replaced by Dagenham FC. Briggs moved to their new ground in Rush Green Road, merging with Ford Sports to become Ford United.

Dagenham FC were formed in 1949 and the local council offered them the use of The Arena. A 300-seater concrete grandstand was built on the east side of the ground in October 1950 and three months later Dagenham had their largest crowd at The Arena when 7,000 attended an FA Amateur Cup tie against Walthamstow Avenue. After the club left The Arena, it continued to be used for local cup finals and schools matches for over thirty years, but it has fallen into disuse recently. Both the stand and dressing room block on the opposite side of the ground have been demolished, though some of the terracing near to the site of the old stand can still be seen. Dagenham moved to Victoria Road during the summer of 1955 and they levelled and reseeded the pitch and extended the banking and the terracing. The only cover was a tiny wooden stand, which was steep and narrow, and there were a few rows of seating, on the far side of

Dagenham & Redbridge, September 1989. The much-refurbished stand holds about 650 people. By 2000 an additional stand had been built to the right. There is a substantial covered area opposite, stretching the length of the pitch.

the ground. The main stand, with a capacity of 800, was built that autumn and was opened on 7 January 1956 by J.W. Bowers, the chairman of the Essex County FA. The first match was an Essex Senior Cup tie with Harwich & Parkeston and the score was 6-0.

During the summer of 1956, the turnstile block at the Victoria Road side of the ground was added, and the men's toilets situated at the Victoria Road end were also built. Two summers after this, the cover over the opposite side from the stand was erected, at a cost of £1,400. The first floodlit match at Victoria Road was Dagenham *v.* Woodford in the FA Youth Cup on 26 September 1957 and the first senior match was a friendly against Rainham Town on 19 March 1958.

Dagenham FC worked their way through the Metropolitan, Delphian, Corinthian and Athenian Leagues before joining the Isthmian League in time for the 1973/74 season. They reached two FA Amateur Cup finals, losing in 1970 to Enfield (5-1) and Skelmersdale United (4-1) in 1971. They also reached two FA Trophy finals, in 1977 (losing 2-1 to Scarborough) and 1980 (losing to Mossley 2-1). Having been consistently near the top of the Isthmian League, Dagenham were invited into the Alliance Premier League (Conference) in 1981 but were relegated back to the Isthmian League at the end of the 1987/88 season.

Redbridge Forest was formed out of the remnants of the Ilford and Leytonstone Clubs (see their sections). They merged in 1979 to produce Leytonstone-Ilford, who in turn merged with Walthamstow Avenue in 1988 to form Redbridge Forest. The Victoria Road ground changed little until the arrival of Redbridge Forest in 1990 to ground-share with Dagenham. They paid for a new stand to be erected in the corner of the ground to increase the seating capacity and replaced the grass banking at the Pondfield End with concrete terracing that brought the ground up to Conference League standards. Redbridge Forest and Dagenham merged in July 1992 and in 1995 they replaced the crumbling pitch perimeter wall with a new brick-built one and two years later rebuilt the toilet block at the Victoria Road end of the ground. By 2001, the original wooden stand was past its best and a new 800-seater stand replaced it. It was used for the first time for the Essex Senior Cup final against Canvey Island on 4 August 2001; just twelve weeks after the old stand saw its last game. New turnstile blocks were built in 2001 and the club replaced the eight floodlights that used to sit on the sides of the ground with four corner ones. The improvements made have brought the ground up to Football League 'A' graded standard and the capacity is now 6,000. The club-record attendance is now 5,949, set against Ipswich Town in the FA Cup on 5 January 2002. The club came close to gaining entry to the Football League but were pipped in controversial circumstances by Boston United, whose manager was later banned for making illegal payments to players.

The ground has been chosen to host some important matches over the past five years, including a women's full international match between England and Sweden and UEFA youth international matches between England and San Marino and Cyprus.

ALEX'S FIRST TIME: This was for a an Isthmian Premier League match between Redbridge Forest and Aylesbury United on 20 September 1989, which the visitors won 2-1. I remember that the original wooden stand was painted in a bright red colour.

DANSON FURNESS/ALMA SWANLEY
Ground: Green Court Road, Crockenhill, Kent.

The history of Danson is complicated and linked to the histories of Furness and Alma Swanley. The Furness club was formed as Furness Withy FC in 1968, following the merger of several shipping company sides. They began playing at Brackley Road, Beckenham and other grounds used include the Dock Labour Board ground in Chislehurst, now called Flamingo Park, and the Castaways Ground in Southwood Road. In 1982 the parent company withdrew support and they became Furness. Furness played in the South London Alliance prior to 1991 and in that year merged with Danson (Bexley Borough) to form Danson Furness United, playing at the Danson's ground at Crook Log Ground, Brampton Road, Bexleyheath until a ground-share agreement with Alma Swanley came about in 1992.

Danson had previously played at Randell Down Road from 1941 until 1953, when they moved to Eltham Road. They had been at Crook Log since 1960. Danson (Bexley Borough) were formed in 1941 and joined the Kent League in 1987/88 but usually struggled close to the bottom of the table.

Alma Swanley were formed in 1963 as Alma United, and played at Swanley Recreation Ground. They were named after a public house called 'the Alma' on the A20 near Swanley. The club initially played in the Dartford & District League before progressing to the reserve sections of the Greater London and Metropolitan London Leagues. They achieved senior status in 1973 and joined the London Spartan League in 1975/76,

Danson-Furness/Alma Swanley, April 1976. Swanley Recreation Ground was packed for the clash of ground-sharers Alma Swanley and Swanley Town. A PVC roof on wooden beams offered shelter for spectators.

before moving to the Kent League in 1982/83. They won the Kent Senior Trophy in 1976 when they beat local rivals Swanley Town 3-2 in an exciting final. The club won the Kent League title in 1985/86 with 75 points from 34 matches and were third two seasons later. They reached the quarter-final of the FA Vase in 1980/81 after beating Uxbridge, Bowers United, Cheshunt and Coventry Sporting before being knocked out by Windsor & Eton in a replay after a 2-2 draw at Swanley before an attendance of 700. Despite finishing fifth in 1993/94, Alma Swanley folded at the end of the season.

Danson Furness United took over the tenancy of the Green Court Road Ground. They were Kent League Champions in 1995/96 after finishing as runners-up the previous season. Their record crowd came during their championship season when 1,150 saw a match with Dartford. After 1997 they were known as Swanley Furness but in 1998 they dropped into the Second Division of the Kent League, as they did not have any floodlights. They were called Danson Furness by 2002 and were due to move to Cray Wanderers' ground at Oxford Road during 2002/03 after the sale of their Green Court Road ground.

ALEX'S FIRST TIME: I visited Green Court Road on 20 May 1985 for a match between Alma Swanley and Tunbridge Wells in the Kent League. The visitors needed to win their last two matches to take the title and easily beat Swanley 3-0 before 120 spectators. They were victorious over Ramsgate in their last match to take the title.

DARENTH HEATHSIDE

Ground: Heathside Club, Horton Road, South Darenth, Dartford, Kent.

The club was formed as Heathside Sports FC in 1951 and played in the Dartford League. They played at Bexley Hospital from 1957 and moved to Heathside in 1972. This was the former home of Horton Kirby Paper Mill, which at one time housed bowls, cricket and football. Cricket ceased at the ground when the football club bought it, as they put up a barrier around the cricket pitch. This was later updated when Darenth joined the Kent League. The original clubhouse is still in use and a small 140-seater stand was built next to it during the late 1970s. Darenth moved to the Greater London League in 1968 and on to the Metropolitan League three years later. They joined the London Spartan League in 1975 and the Kent League in 1978 and were runners-up of the Second Division at the end of their first season. Their best seasons in the Kent League came in 1979/80, 1985/86 and 1988/89 when they finished in fourth place. The record attendance at Heathside was in 1976 when they played Jimmy Hill's International XI in a charity match when a crowd of approximately 900 attended.

The club entered the FA Cup for the first time in 1986/87 but lost 6-0 at Welling United in the first qualifying round. They had a better record in the FA Vase and reached the third round in 1988/89, before losing 1-0 at Hailsham Town after beating Redhill, West Wickham and Malden Vale on the way. The ground also has floodlights and there is a

Darenth Heathside, April 1976. By 1985 a brick stand with four rows of benches had replaced the tin shelter provided at the then-Heathside Sports Ground.

huge railway viaduct passing the ground that rather overshadows the small venue but gives it a distinct feel. The ground is also surrounded by countryside and is quite picturesque. Darenth Heathside sadly folded during the summer of 1995 and no football club currently uses the ground. They had struggled at the bottom of the Kent League during their last four seasons.

ALEX'S FIRST TIME: This was on 27 December 1988, when I did a double-header and saw Croydon play Bromley followed by Darenth Heathside playing Danson in a Kent League Division One encounter watched by just sixty-five fans.

DARTFORD
Ground: Sharing Gravesend & Northfleet's ground during 2003/04.

Members of the Dartford Working Men's Club formed Dartford FC in 1888 and for the first few seasons played only friendly fixtures. After reaching the final of the Kent Senior Cup in 1894, Dartford became founder member of the Kent League in 1894/95. They initially played on a pitch laid out behind Westgate House for a short spell but when this was needed for a new housing and road scheme, they moved to Lowfield Street. This was called Mr Potter's Meadow and this became home in 1891; at some point a small stand was built for officials. They moved to Summer's Meadow in 1894 and a grandstand was built in September 1895 at a cost of £90. They took the major step of joining the Southern League Second Division in 1896/97 and finished as champions at the end of their first season, but poor results after this led to financial problems and Dartford FC was wound up in 1900. A new club called Dartford United was formed but lasted just one season and, after this, amateurs Dartford Rangers became the senior club in the town. This outfit were soon known as Dartford FC, and played on Summer's Meadow, where some dressing rooms were built. The ground was quickly improved with fencing at the town end and more changing accommodation.

The club stayed at Summer's Meadow until the outbreak of war in 1914 when they disbanded. After Dartford reformed in 1921, they bought five acres of land in Watling Street for £1,000. A corrugated fence surrounded the site, the ground had an enclosure and substantial banking and this cost around £600. Six tennis courts were also placed in this area. A large all-seater stand was quickly built at a cost of £2,900 and opened on 19 November 1921 before a crowd of around 4,000. Unfortunately, the stand, dressing rooms, offices and boardroom were destroyed by fire in February 1926. A fund was set up by the club and supporters to rebuild the stand, and this was opened in March 1927. It had seating for 1,000 and the club had learned their lesson, building it with steel instead of wood. Also included within the confines of the stand were dressing rooms, offices, recreation rooms and baths.

Darts played in the Kent League and won the League Cup in 1923/24, before switching to the Southern League for 1926/27. The club won many trophies during the next decade. Dartford won the Southern League (Eastern Section) title in 1930/31 and 1931/32 and the overall championship by beating Western Section winners Exeter City 7-2 away in 1931 and Yeovil 2-1 at home in 1932. Dartford became the first club outside the Football League to reach the FA Cup third round proper in successive seasons. The Darts lost 3-2 to Derby County at the Baseball Ground in 1935/36, and the following season lost 1-0 at home to Darlington at the same stage. They had caused an upset in November 1935 when they had won 3-0 at Cardiff City in the FA Cup first round.

A 150-foot long covered enclosure was built opposite the stand at Watling Street in 1930, and more turnstiles were added at the main entrance. Dartford closed down during the Second World War and the ground was lucky to escape enemy bombing as it was close to the docks. Terracing was laid at the Watling Street end in 1947 and the Supporters' Club raised the money for an extension to the covered side in 1949. The stand's enclosure was terraced in 1950 and the popular side cover was completely terraced with new turnstiles in 1955. Watling Street's record attendance came in 1948 when Dartford played Leyton Orient before 11,004 in the FA Cup first round.

Dartford switched on new £6,000 floodlights in October 1963, and surplus land, including the tennis courts, was sold off to Brent School so that they could enlarge their playing fields. Other improvements during the 1960s included a revamped car park. The wooden fencing around the pitch was replaced with a brick-built wall, and the terracing on the popular side was also improved.

Dartford also reached the second round of the FA Cup in 1950/51, 1961/62, 1965/66 and 1968/69. They won the 1973/74 Southern League championship and reached the FA Trophy final that season but lost 2-1 to Morecombe at Wembley Stadium, after beating Ashford Town (Kent), Minehead, Banbury United, Weymouth and Macclesfield Town in the semi-final. They won the Southern Division of the Southern League in 1980/81 but lost the championship decider against Midland Division Champions Alvechurch on penalties, after drawing 3-3 on aggregate. They also reached the FA Trophy semi-final that season where they lost to Bishop's Stortford, 3-2 on aggregate. Dartford had a season in the Alliance Premier (now Conference) in 1981/82 but were relegated straightaway. Dartford gained a fourth Southern League title in 1983/84, which resulted in a return to the Alliance (by now the Gola League). This time the Darts stayed two seasons, finishing third in 1984/85. Dartford reached two more FA Trophy semi-finals during the 1980s, losing to Burton Albion in 1987 and two years later Macclesfield Town gained revenge for their 1974 defeat at the same stage.

In the wake of the Hillsborough disaster of 1989, Dartford needed to make decisions about their Watling Street ground. They either had to relocate to a new ground or improve their existing one. They decided to stay at Watling Street but the costs of changes to the ground led the club into debt due to crippling interest charges. Maidstone United had sold their own ground and needed a suitable home so they could seek Football League status. The Dartford directors made a decision that they would later regret when they agreed to ground share with Maidstone. United got into the League but did not last very long and went bankrupt. The cost of ground improvements that Maidstone had carried out were passed on to Dartford and they were forced to sell the Watling Street ground to pay off the creditors. Dartford

Dartford, October 1973. The wood and tin main stand held about 900 on wooden benches. Opposite was a twelve-step covered terrace.

withdrew from the Southern League after only four games of 1992/93, but the club's Supporters Association came to the rescue. The continuing existence of the youth team enabled the club to maintain both its senior status and full membership of the FA.

A ground-sharing arrangement was made with Cray Wanderers in 1993 and Dartford became members of the Kent League. They finished their first season in sixth position with an average crowd of over 300, despite the travelling involved. Dartford moved in with Erith & Belvedere for the start of 1994/95. The Darts were involved in a long battle with Furness for the First Division title in 1995/96, but they lost out at Furness in the last fixture of the season, when the home side clung on for a 1-1 draw to deny Dartford on goal difference. They returned to the Southern League (Southern Division) in 1996/97 and finished fourteenth at the end of their first season. A fire at Erith & Belvedere in September 1997 meant that both clubs had problems completing their home fixtures and the following season Dartford found a new ground-sharing arrangement with Essex-based Purfleet FC. In October 1998, the local council promised the club a piece of land within Dartford's borough, on which they could build a new home of their own. The land was previously used as the Stone Lodge rifle range and was situated just off the M25. However, by 2003/04 they were ground sharing with Gravesend & Northfleet with no new ground seemingly on the horizon after the Department of the Environment threw out their plans for the site. Things looked up in May 2004 when the local council offered to build a new £2m stadium for the club.

ALEX'S FIRST TIME: Only 937 attended an Autoglass Trophy match between Maidstone United and Fulham on 23 October 1991 at Watling Street. Fulham won easily, 6-2, and Andy Cole, who later went on to find fame with Manchester United, had an outstanding match for Fulham, while on loan from Arsenal, and set up many of the goals.

DULWICH HAMLET

Ground: Champion Hill Stadium, Edgar Kail Way, East Dulwich, London SE22.

Dulwich Hamlet had the most outstanding non-League ground in the London area from 1931-1991. This was their former Champion Hill ground that could hold crowds of over 20,000 with its pitch-length stand and deep concreted terraces around the rest of the pitch. Dulwich Hamlet have played in and around the Champion Hill area of Dulwich since their inception in 1893, following the cricket club members' decision to form a football club. Initially, a piece of ground in Woodwarde Road was used for practice games but there were no facilities of any kind and the players changed in the Reading Room in Dulwich Village. They had to carry the posts and flags from here to the ground. When the pitch became unplayable, pitches in Dulwich Park were often sought. A new ground at College Farm in Burbage Road was used from 1895, but after one season Hamlet were on the move again to Sunray Avenue where they stayed for six years. The club had two grounds from 1902, the reserves playing at Sunray Avenue while the senior side moved to the Freeman's ground in Champion Hill. A stand, capable of holding 250 people, was built during the close season of 1906 and on the Constance Road side some three-tiered standing boards were laid down. However, Hamlet moved to Champion Hill for the first time in 1912. There were dressing rooms, a stand and the pitch had a fence around it by the start of the First World War. The ground was in continuous use throughout the hostilities. New dressing rooms were constructed and a new pitch barrier and rough terracing was cut into the banking around the ground in 1918.

Between the two wars, Dulwich Hamlet had their greatest successes and attendances were often into five figures. They won the FA Amateur Cup four times, the London Senior Cup twice, the Surrey Senior Cup five times, the London Charity Cup seven times, and the Isthmian League championship three times. In the same period, sixteen of their players were capped by England at amateur international level and another four players by Wales. The huge crowds caused considerable problems so new seating was installed in the enclosure and the terracing on the north side was completed, with six more steps created opposite in 1920. Thanks to the club's supporters' club, covered accommodation was also increased at the cost of £1,000. Today, the approach road to the new ground is called Edgar Kail Way. He was their star player during the inter-war period and was a very skilful amateur player who obtained more publicity than all the other Hamlet men put together.

A new ground was planned in the late 1920s next door to their existing ground by the forward-thinking club committee This would be capable of holding 20,000 or more, and as the 1930s approached fund-raising was underway and work had commenced to raise the ground level, create banking and lay paths. The new ground was finally ready in October 1931 and the secretary of the FA, Sir Frederick Wall, performed the opening ceremony. A vast covered enclosure holding 2,000 and a seated stand with a capacity of 2,400 were built on the new ground and some 16,200 people saw the first game against Nunhead. Profits were ploughed into further ground improvements, including increasing the banking, adding crush barriers and replacing the wooden fences around the pitch with iron railings. A record crowd of 20,744 attended the FA Amateur Cup final

Dulwich Hamlet, May 1990. The main stand, opened in October 1931 by Sir Frederick Wall, held 2,400. Opposite was an enormous covered terrace. (Photograph by Alex White)

played at Champion Hill in 1933 between Kingstonian and Stockton and numerous amateur internationals and other important games were played there. The crowds went into decline after 1950 during a less successful period of the club's history, but the ground continued to be used for important representative matches.

The next major structure, a new clubhouse, was built in 1964 and later that year on 28 October, Chelsea were the opponents when new floodlighting was switched on for the first time in front of a crowd of 4,000. With the massive reduction in attendances from the early 1960s, the ground went into decline and the massive terracing and pitch-length stand began to deteriorate due to lack of care and attention. Part of the ground was sold off for use as a nightclub and squash club but debts continued to rise. Part of the stand was condemned as unsafe, as were large areas of the terracing, which led to them being declared unusable. The outer wooden wall surrounding the ground was creaking with age and the whole ground had become a millstone around the club's neck with attendances down to a couple of hundred by the late 1980s. There had been little money to maintain the stadium and vandals continued to do a great deal of damage at the ground. Three sides were closed for the 1989/90 season, as the club could not raise the money to obtain a safety certificate from Southwark Council. The last game took place at Champion Hill in May 1991.

Sainsbury's offered to pull the old ground down and build the club a new smaller one as well as a supermarket for themselves. There is a now an impressive grandstand that also houses the main facilities, including bars, offices and dressing rooms, as well as a health club. There is also a gable clock and fascia board attached to the large building behind the stand. The club was given only a ten-year lease and may lose the ground when this comes up for renewal.

ALEX'S FIRST TIME: My first visit to the original Champion Hill ground was for a FA Cup first-round tie between Corinthian Casuals and Bristol City which ended in a 0-0 draw on 19 November 1983. Due to the threat from some Millwall fans the local police kept us in the ground at the end of the match. However, when the dilapidated fencing started to creek under the strain of the crowd the police decided to let us take our chances. I saw the first game on the rebuilt ground on 3 October 1992 when Hamlet beat Hendon 2-1 before a crowd of 752. It does not have the atmosphere of the original ground but meets the club's needs better.

EAST HAM UNITED
Ground: Ferndale Sports Ground, East Ham Manorway, Beckton, London E6.

East Ham United were formed in 1933 as Storey Athletic and their first ground was at Tilletts Farm. They took the place of an earlier club of the same name who were founded in 1880 and played their home games at White Barn Lane from 1892-1914 when they folded. Around 1948 Storey Athletic moved to the Ferndale Sports Ground in Pennyroyal Avenue near Cyprus Place in Beckton and changed their name to East Ham United around 1953. That November they attracted their record crowd when they played Sutton United in the FA Amateur Cup when 2,400 attended the match.

East Ham United joined the Essex Senior League in 1978/79 and finished fifth in 1979/80. Otherwise it was one season of struggle after another until 1994/95, when they finished ninth. Their only recent entry in the FA Cup ended in a 7-0 home defeat against Sudbury Wanderers in September 1995. They also entered the FA Vase for the first time in 1976/77 and amazingly reached the quarter-finals before losing 4-0 at home to Sheffield after beating Basildon United, Edgware and Epping Town on the way. They did not enter the competition every season but also reached the fourth round in 1979/80 where they lost to Leyton Wingate but received a record defeat in the competition in 1995/96 when they lost 10-0 to Wealdstone in the first qualifying round.

The Ferndale Sports Ground had a difficult history and was seen as one of the least appealing venues by the opposition as it was a dreary ground in a depressed area. The ground was often vandalised and the club usually struggled to attract crowds. There was a small-seated stand with four rows of seats, behind which were the dressing rooms. It had a wooden roof that was held up by five narrow pillars made of wood. Attempts were made to improve the ground: new floodlights were installed in 1983 and two years later the pitch and fencing was improved. A new entrance in Pennyroyal Avenue was created in 1986 and a new dressing-room complex was built in 1989. After years of struggle they gave up the ghost in the summer of 1999 and amalgamated with neighbours Barking. The Ferndale had been compulsorily purchased by the London Docklands Development Corporation and the last game was played at the ground in December 1999 without a single paying customer in a match with Brentwood. The site is to be redeveloped for housing (see Barking).

East Ham United, March 1985. Becton Gasworks provides a dramatic backdrop to the stand, which was a tin roof attached to the dressing rooms with three rows of benches. Opposite was timber-and-earth terracing.

BOB'S FIRST TIME: This was on 23 March 1985 for a match between East Ham United and Witham Town, which the visitors won 4-0 in the Essex Senior League. It was mainly the enthusiasm of Rueben Gane that kept the club going, despite very poor attendances, and this match only attracted eighteen paying spectators. Behind one goal was the vast Beckton Gasworks and along one wall was the club's name in huge letters. In front of the dressing rooms was a veranda with benches and there were rudimentary floodlights along each side of the ground. This area of London has changed enormously in recent years.

EDGWARE TOWN
Ground: White Lion Ground, High Street, Edgware, Middlesex.

Workers for the construction and engineering firm William Moss & Sons, based in Cricklewood, formed Edgware FC in 1939. The firm had taken over the White Lion sports ground located in the High Street in 1932, being formerly used by Edgware Rugby Club. The ground was named after the public house that was situated by its entrance. Edgware joined the West Middlesex Combination and became Champions for 1939/40. This league was renamed the Middlesex Senior League for the following season and Edgware won the title in 1943/44 and were joint winners (with Twickenham) the following season. Edgware moved to the London League in 1945 and won the Western section but lost to Woolwich Polytechnic, the Eastern section winners, in the championship play-off. Edgware also reached the final of the Middlesex Senior Cup but lost 2-0 to Wealdstone. The club joined the recently formed Corinthian League in 1946. A record attendance of about 8,500 attended a FA Cup tie with Wealdstone at the White Lion ground in October 1947. There was another large attendance in October 1949 when an estimated 7,100 saw another FA Cup tie against Wealdstone that was televised in full by the BBC. A grandstand was built around 1946 and the banked areas were also soon in place. The terracing opposite the main stand was covered at around this time and the area behind the goal nearest the pub was also terraced, although in later years it reverted to grass banking. A hard standing area has now been placed here.

In 1953/54, the club finished runners-up to Carshalton Athletic in the Corinthian League, but at the end of 1962/63, this was disbanded and Edgware were placed in Division One of the Athenian League. Edgware finished third in the 1963/64 season and were promoted to the Athenian League Premier Division. Difficulties with the new pitch were to cause the club serious financial difficulties in the next few seasons and in 1964/65 and 1966/67 many home matches had to be played on opponents' grounds. Two successive relegations meant that by 1968/69 the club had dropped to the Athenian League Second Division and were also heavily in debt. Edgware added the 'Town' to their name in 1970 and merged with local junior side Brent Green, who provided several club officials. The Middlesex Senior Cup final was reached again in 1973/74, but Hendon won 4-1 on aggregate over two legs. Edgware finished second in 1981/82 in the Athenian League but were not promoted to the Isthmian League due to their ground being considered of unsuitable standard. Floodlights were installed in 1979 and the old wooden stand was destroyed by fire, to be replaced in 1984 by an impressive concrete and metal structure of identical size that has seating for 220.

Edgware Town, October 1972. There were six rows of wood seats in the elevated tin-and-wood stand. Opposite was cover stretching most of the length of the pitch.

The Athenian League disbanded in 1985 and Edgware were placed in the Premier Division of the Spartan League. The 'double' of Spartan League and cup was achieved in 1987/88, but again promotion to the Isthmian League was denied due to the inadequate ground facilities. However, after winning the Spartan League again in 1989/90, Edgware's application to join the Isthmian League was at last approved. Edgware found some success in the FA Vase when they reached the last sixteen, losing to the holders and eventual losing finalists, Guiseley. Wealdstone moved to share the White Lion Ground in August 1995, ending a nomadic temporary period in which they played at Vicarage Road and Yeading, forced by the demise of their own Lower Mead ground. The White Lion public house was demolished in 1997 and replaced by a hotel called the Premier Lodge. Its construction meant the demolition of the club's offices, that were replaced by new ones as well as a new turnstile block. The club has struggled in recent years owing to financial difficulties and at the end of the 2000/01 was relegated to Division Three of the Isthmian League; Edgware also survived the trauma of losing their clubhouse to fire in the summer of 2003.

ALEX'S FIRST TIME: This was not for an Edgware match but for a Isthmian League Division One (North) encounter between Wealdstone and Slough Town on 18 January 2003. The home side won 3-2 before an attendance of 432. I had previously been to a wedding reception in the old clubhouse before it burned down. The ground is interesting and well worth a visit.

ENFIELD
Ground: The Stadium, Southbury Road, Enfield, Middlesex.

It was a very sad day when Enfield lost their Southbury Road ground. Formed as Enfield Spartans in 1893, their first ground was at Bailey's Field in Baker Street, where they had a stable for a dressing room. The Spartans entered the Tottenham & District Junior Alliance in 1894/95, followed by the North Middlesex League in 1896. The club moved to the larger Tucker's Field that was a basic field at Canonbury Road. This was roped off and at one time was home to Stamford Hill FC. The Spartans moved to Cherry Orchard Lane in 1900 and the team used the George Hotel as a dressing room. They changed their name to Enfield FC and found immediate success when the North Middlesex Premier Division championship was won in 1901/02 and 1902/03, with the club suffering just one League defeat in those two seasons.

The second title win prompted Enfield to apply for senior status and join the much-stronger London League. Enfield was invited to become a founder member of the Athenian League in 1912 and two years later they won the Middlesex Senior Cup for the first time, defeating Uxbridge Town 2-0 at Tufnell Park. Enfield suspended activity during the First World War and on resumption spent a season each in the Middlesex and London Leagues, returning to the Athenian fold in 1921. With the use of volunteer labour, a small wooden stand complete with a few rows of planking for seats and some weather boarding for protection was erected. They also put duckboards around the pitch. At the Baker Street end a form of wooden terracing was created which gave an elevated view, and at the far end of the field, near the stand, were the dressing rooms. Cherry Orchard Lane was merely a muddy unmade road in those days, which ended in a path that led past the old ground in Bailey's Field and through a rusting iron gate that had an old hut to keep the gateman dry. A screen was put up along the alley by the pitch to prevent spectators obtaining a free view.

The team had a excellent season in 1934/35 when they won the London Senior Cup by beating Metropolitan Police 2-0 in the final at Leyton, were runners-up in the Athenian League and reached the semi-final of the Amateur Cup, to be narrowly beaten by Wimbledon on Dulwich Hamlet's ground. The much-loved Cherry Orchard Lane ground was lost to housing development. However, on 5 July 1936, Enfield Urban Council began work on a new ground within Enfield Playing Fields. It was not ready until the October and tenancy for the first season cost the club £200. The contractors were Cearns of Stratford and when work finally finished the ground was opened for an FA Cup tie with Golders Green on 31 October. It had an impressive 120ft-long stand with 750 seats and a further covered area for 400 standing spectators. Dressing rooms and offices, plus a large clubroom, were incorporated and at this time the rest of the ground was flat standing and the pitch was not fenced off.

During the war Enfield competed in the Herts and Middlesex League with only moderate success, but when the Athenian League was re-formed, and some of their best players returned from overseas, they quickly got into their stride. Little of note occurred at Southbury Road until 1958 when a new lounge bar was opened before a friendly with Arsenal. The Athenian League championship finally came to Southbury Road in 1961/62 in some style, as every home League game was won. A record crowd of over 8,000 watched a match with Tottenham Hotspur on 10 October 1962 to mark the opening of the floodlights. The championship was retained by a margin of 7 points in 1962/63, dropping just six points during the season, and the Isthmian League decided to increase its constitution and invited Enfield to join.

The Starlight Nightclub was built next to the ground in 1974 as a way of raising funds. Enfield finished as Champions of the Isthmian League seven times. Enfield's best season in the Isthmian League was undoubtedly 1977/78, when they finished a massive 31 points clear of their nearest challengers. The club continued to improve the ground and new crash barriers were placed behind the goals in 1980 and the stand-side terracing was extended. New floodlights and a club shop soon followed and more terracing was laid along the Gayler Road side with barriers, including segregation, and both ends were re-surfaced in 1988. The club joined the Alliance Premier (Conference) League in 1981/82 and were Champions in 1982/83 and 1985/86 but were relegated in 1989/90. They won the Isthmian League title in 1994/95 but the club were very disappointed when the news came through that they had failed to meet the stringent financial criteria laid down by the Vauxhall Conference so could not be promoted. Enfield's cup record is equally impressive and they won the FA Trophy in 1981/82 and 1987/88, the FA Amateur Cup in 1966/67 and 1969/70.

Enfield, November 1973. The stand held 620 on ten rows of benches. There were covered terraces on the opposite side and at both ends.

The Gayler stand side of the ground was flattened so that a temporary stand could be erected in 1997 to increase the seating levels so that Saracens Rugby Union Club could also use the ground. This was very basic and mainly made of plywood with a canvas cover but could hold 2,000 spectators. Sadly, with the club in financial difficulties, Southbury Road was sold off for redevelopment. The planning committee of Enfield Council granted permission on 10 May 1999 for Southbury Road to be sold to Building Construction Company for around £4 million. The meeting itself saw stormy scenes as Enfield supporters vented their anger on the committee members. The site of the football ground has now been turned into a leisure development and housing. The supporters were so angry that they decided to break away from the parent club and form their own club, Enfield Town. They went to play at Brimsdown Rovers and joined the Essex Senior League. Enfield FC has struggled on, playing on the ground of Borehamwood, with crowds rarely over the hundred mark.

ALEX'S FIRST TIME: This was for the London Senior Cup final between Kingstonian and Hampton on 2 May 1987. The K's won 2-1 before a crowd of over 350. With its excellent stand and impressive terraced areas, the loss of Southbury Road was a great one.

EPPING TOWN
Ground: Stonards Hill, Fairfield Road, Epping, Essex.

Epping Town were founded in 1888, and for half-a-century they played in minor football, principally as members of the Woodford League, the Walthamstow & District League, and the South-West Essex League. Epping Town were granted senior status in

1936 when they were accepted as members of the Spartan League. The club's earliest grounds were rudimentary and were mostly nothing more than unenclosed fields. The first, at Epping Plain, was located opposite St Margaret's Hospital on the edge of the forest. Just before the First World War, they moved to the Bell Field, next to the Bell Inn public house, which had no facilities for either spectators or players. The club's headquarters and dressing rooms were located some distance away at the Duke of Wellington Public House, which ensured a long walk to the playing area. There were football pitches on this site until the 1960s, but the Bell Inn was pulled down and a motel has been built on the site. The club moved to Bury Lane in the early 1920s. This ground was initially little more than a pitch on a large open field, but the club were able to move up into senior football when a pavilion was built to enable them to offer minimum facilities. The Bury Lane ground is now part of a large open area, with the Epping Cricket Club opposite.

Due to the hard work of a dedicated band of committee members, Epping were able to move to a new ground at Stonards Hill in 1949. The ground was not totally enclosed as the public had access to the area because it was council owned. The playing pitch was railed off and eventually the club built a half-pitch-length three-step concrete terrace. On this terrace a basic seated stand was built in 1964 to accommodate around 250 spectators, plus cover was added for a further 400. A clubhouse and changing rooms were located at the car park end.

The post-war football boom helped Epping to attract crowds of 3,000-4,000 to Stonards Hill for local derby matches against Harlow and Bishop's Stortford. Epping joined the Parthenon League in 1953 for one season then moved onto the London League. Nine seasons were spent in this competition and the club became the last ever Champions of the competition in 1963/64. Epping joined the newly formed Greater London League in 1964. Support for the team at this time was relatively good, and for a Charity match against Tottenham Hotspur in 1968 the biggest crowd seen at the ground for many years was present. They never reached the first round proper of the FA Cup, but the team had its best run in the 1973/74, where in the final qualifying round they lost 2-1 at home to Chelmsford City before an attendance of approximately 1,800. The club's floodlights were installed in April 1974 and in their first match under lights they beat Ulysses 4-0.

Epping Town joined the Athenian Second Division in 1974 and the team had their greatest triumph when they became the Champions in 1975/76, finishing two points above Epsom and Ewell. The club easily held their own in the upper division, finishing sixth of eighteen clubs and reaching the fifth round of the FA Vase. They joined the Isthmian League in 1977, but struggled and were now on the way down. The present ground was clearly not good enough for the increasingly stringent ground grading rules of the Isthmian League and the club sought a move to a ground with better facilities without success. The local council proved unhelpful in the quest. An acrimonious split developed between the club's board and its management and players during 1984/85, that led to the latter walking out of the club in mid-season. The club was left in dire straits with a fixture backlog to catch up on, and few quality players left. The board had to act swiftly and new players were signed on, but at this time of the season the choice

Epping Town, March 1979. This tin structure, decorated in club colours, was the only spectator accommodation, with four rows of benches on the right and four concrete steps on the left of the picture.

was limited, and the replacements were woefully inadequate. With the club at the foot of the table as match after match was lost, the frustrations that built up finally reached breaking point in a match at Leyton Wingate. The match ended in turmoil when an Epping player (who was also a director) allegedly struck out at some opposition players. The incident got out of hand and the police were called but the culprit had left the ground before any action could be taken. Due to past misdemeanors (including financial irregularities) and unresolved disciplinary matters, the league's management body decided that enough was enough and informed the club that they had lost their Isthmian League status and their record for the season was struck from the records. Epping Town Council then refused to allow the club to play at Stonards Hill during 1985/86 and the club folded soon afterwards. Stonards Hill was still in use in recent years, although the main stand and covered enclosure had been removed. In their place, near one end of the concrete terracing, there was a small and very basic corrugated steel enclosure. Eppingdale used the ground for a while in the Essex Intermediate League. They were formerly known as Coopersale and at one time played on an adjacent pitch.

BOB'S FIRST TIME: Epping entertained Corinthian Casuals in an Isthmian League Division Two match on 31 January 1984 and drew 1-1 before 120 spectators. All the spectator facilities were on one side of the ground.

EPSOM & EWELL
Ground: West Street, Ewell, Surrey.

Epsom & Ewell's West Street ground was one of the prettiest grounds in the London area until it was sold for redevelopment in 1991. Ever since this happened, they have continually been trying to find a site for a new ground without success. It had a rural feel to it, despite being surrounded by houses, and boasted a comfortable stand and a welcoming clubhouse. The club was founded in 1917 as Epsom Town FC and on reaching senior status they joined the Southern Suburban League and won the league championship at the first attempt without losing a game. The club progressed and in 1922/23 they reached the final of the Surrey Junior Cup, losing 2-1 (after a 1-1 draw) to Caterham Mental Hospital. Epsom Town were winners of the Surrey Senior League in 1925/26 and 1926/27 and were elected to the London League in 1927, winning the title at the first attempt. They reached the final of the Surrey Senior Cup again, losing 3-2 to Redhill in 1928/29. After beating Woking, Nunhead and Leytonstone, all clubs from the Isthmian League, Epsom Town reached the first round proper of the FA Cup for the only time in their history in 1933/34, where they faced Clapton Orient from Division Three (South) but lost 4-2 at Orient's former ground at Lea Bridge.

Epsom Town remained in the London League until 1949, and were runners-up four times between 1931 and 1938, changing their name to plain Epsom FC in 1937. During the 1920s, the club played at a ground in Horton Lane, Epsom but by the outbreak of war in 1939, were playing at West Street in Ewell. During the period of the war, the club decided to stop playing and the West Street ground was let to a side that played under their former name of Epsom Town. Epsom FC reclaimed their West Street ground in 1945. Epsom joined the Corinthian League in 1949 but rarely challenged for the title. The club merged with Ewell FC and Stoneleigh FC in 1960, changing their name to Epsom & Ewell FC They were elected to Division One of the Athenian League for 1963/64 and finished bottom of the table with only 9 points from 26 games, conceding 104 goals. The following season they finished bottom of the table again and were relegated to Division Two. This was the year in which the first rumours circulated that Epsom's West Street ground was to be sold to property developers and in 1966 the borough council rejected planning permission for ninety-nine flats to be built on the West Street ground.

Over 700 saw Epsom narrowly lose 2-1 to Tooting & Mitcham at West Street in an Amateur Cup tie in 1969. They were not re-elected to the Athenian League when they finished bottom of the table again at the end of 1972/73. Former Fulham player Pat O'Connell was then appointed manager and the club was accepted back to the Surrey Senior League and this heralded a turnaround in their fortunes. Epsom & Ewell were League runners-up and League Cup winners in 1973/74 and the following season they were League Champions and again won the League Cup. Their greatest triumph though came in 1975 when they reached the final of the inaugural FA Challenge Vase competition. Reigate Priory, Horley Town, Worthing, Eastbourne Town, Hornchurch, Addlestone and Stamford were all beaten before Epsom & Ewell lost to Hoddesdon Town 2-1 in front of a 10,000 crowd at Wembley Stadium. The Athenian League quickly offered the club its place back in Division Two and the club were promoted to Division

Epsom & Ewell, September 1975. The stand built in honour of Robert T. Bradshaw (d. 1928) had five rows of wooden benches. Behind one goal was a small tin-and-wood shelter.

One at the first attempt. Millwall signed two of Epsom's players, Trevor Lee and Phil Walker, during 1975/76 and they immediately became first-team members and helped Millwall gain promotion to the Second Division of the Football League.

New floodlights were installed in 1976 and the club was elected to the newly formed Isthmian League Division Two. Epsom & Ewell also purchased the freehold of their West Street ground. They finished their first season in the Isthmian League as Division Two Champions and a new clubhouse was built in 1978. Epsom gained Isthmian League Premier Division status in 1984 when they finished runners-up to Windsor & Eton, but two seasons later they had been relegated back to the Second Division. They had one of their best crowds in recent years for the visit of Chelsea on 10 March 1987 for Tommy Tuite's Testimonial, when a crowd of 1,800 entered West Street.

Epsom & Ewell finished just below the halfway mark in 1990/91, and so became a founder member of the newly formed Third Division. They played their last game at West Street in 1991 after selling the ground to a building company and moved to share with Banstead Athletic. Their greatest asset had disappeared and they have been struggling to survive ever since. At the end of January 1994, a site for a new ground was purchased at Banstead Road, Ewell, but the local council rejected their planning application. They had plans passed on another site in the borough in 1997/98, but there were problems over the completion of the purchase. The move to a new ground is still unresolved and Epsom & Ewell continue to share with Banstead Athletic at their Merland Rise Ground. The Isthmian League reorganisation in 2000/01 resulted in the club gaining a place in its Division One (South).

ALEX'S FIRST TIME: It was a lovely August afternoon and the West Street ground looked very pretty. Epsom & Ewell beat Wokingham Town 2-1 in a pre-season friendly before a crowd of about 100. Unfortunately, the value of the land tempted the club to sell the site without fixing up a new ground to play at.

ERITH & BELVEDERE
Ground: Park View, Lower Road, Belvedere, Kent.

The present Erith & Belvedere club were formed in 1922 following the restructuring of Belvedere and District FC, a club founded towards the end of the First World War. The Deres lost 3-1 to Chatham in their first Kent League match on 26 August 1922. There was also a club called Erith FC who were formed in 1885 and appeared in the inaugural FA Amateur Cup in 1893. It was amazing for such a new club to reach the FA Amateur Cup final in 1924, where they lost 3-0 to Clapton at The Den, and the following season Erith & Belvedere played Third Division Reading in the FA Cup but lost 2-0 at Erith. They built a new stand in 1924 out of the proceeds of their cup run. Apart from two seasons (1929-31) in the London League, the Deres remained in the Kent League until the war. Their best finish was third in 1928/29. They reached the final of the FA Amateur Cup again in 1938 but lost again, 1-0 to Bromley. The crowd at The Den for the final was 33,346, the largest ever for a Deres match.

The Deres joined the South-East Combination during the war years and did well in wartime competitions (local industry was important to the war effort so they lost few players to the Forces). They won the Kent Senior Cup in 1941/42 and the South-East Combination League and cup double. They dropped only 1 point, scored 253 goals in 44 games, and had a 64-game unbeaten home run ended only by an Army side fielding four full internationals. The Deres were founder members of the Corinthian League and won the Memorial Shield (League Cup) three seasons in succession (1948-50) and remained in the Corinthian League throughout their existence. Their record crowd at Park View came in 1949 when 5,573 watched an FA Amateur Cup tie with Crook Town. The club moved to the First Division of the Athenian League in 1963 and were promoted to its Premier Division in 1971. They won the Athenian League Cup in 1974. The club chose to return to the Kent League in 1978 and in 1981/82 won the title. They moved up a level and joined the Southern League, but it was an uphill battle at this higher status. They did, however, finish ninth in the Eastern Section in 2001/02.

Erith & Belvedere, July 1972. The stand was integral with the dressing rooms and social club, with seven rows of planks and two rows of plastic tip-up seats. Opposite was cover stretching the length of the pitch.

A fire destroyed the seventy-year-old stand at their old ground at Park View, Belvedere in 1997 and this put the club's existence in danger. The ground was generally in a poor state by this time anyway. They were forced to move and share with Welling United and decided on an unusual arrangement to develop one side of the ground that they could call their own. At the start of 2003/04, their long-awaited new clubhouse and dressing rooms were finally in place. They also had their own modern stand, giving them a fully fledged HQ of their own at the Park View Road ground.

ALEX'S FIRST TIME: The only match that I saw at their former Lower Road ground at Belvedere was a London Senior Cup semi-final. This ended in a 3-3 draw after extra time. Erith & Belvedere's opponents, Hampton, arrived over an hour late after their coach broke down and the match finally ended at half past six.

ERITH TOWN
Ground: Erith Sports Centre Stadium, Avenue Road, Erith, Kent.

Another ground that is essentially an athletics stadium, the main stand does not have a roof so expect to get wet. The club was formed as Woolwich Town in 1959 and played on a Sunday in the London Metropolitan Sunday League. They were senior section champions of that league three times in 1965/66, 1970/71 and 1974/75. They changed their name briefly to Woolwich Heathway in 1989 but soon returned to being called Woolwich Town. The club played at Flamingo Park, Sidcup until 1991 but after this shared with Greenwich Borough FC at Harrow Meadow. They switched to Saturday football in 1990 and joined the South-East London Amateur League and, after finishing as champions, moved on to the London Spartan League for 1991/92, competing in the Second Division. The club gained senior status in 1990 after they amalgamated with R.E.M.A. Charlton and gained promotion to the First Division in 1992. They were runners-up in 1994/95 and were also beaten finalists in the London Intermediate Cup

Erith Town, July 2004. A first-floor balcony offers the only shelter for football spectators.

that season. Woolwich Town acquired the sole use of Erith Sports Stadium in October 1995. The ground has 1,006 seats alongside an athletics track, but these are uncovered. Behind the seats is the glass-fronted balcony of the Erith Sports Centre, from where spectators can watch the football and athletics. The club gained senior status from the Kent FA in 1995 and were promoted to the Premier Division of the Spartan League. Their best season in the Premier Division was 1993/94, when they finished fifth out of sixteen clubs. Woolwich Town joined the Kent League in 1996 after making two appeals to the FA in an attempt to move across the pyramid system. They changed their name to Erith Town in 1997 as they were now playing in that town. The first three campaigns in the Kent League were a struggle and they finished close to the bottom of the table each season. They improved a great deal in 1999/2000 and finished in seventh place. They have never gone beyond the first qualifying round of the FA Cup but have reached the second round of the FA Vase on three occasions. In 1999/2000 they lost at Corinthian Casuals 1-3, in 2002/03 they lost at Arundel 1-0 and in 2003/04 they lost at Harwich & Parkeston 2-0.

BOB'S FIRST TIME: This was for a London Senior Cup first-round match between Woolwich Town and Hillingdon Borough. Borough won the game 2-1 after extra time before a then-record attendance of 116. The match was played on the 13 November 1995, just after the club moved to Erith Sports Stadium.

ETON MANOR
Ground: Wadham Lodge, Kitchener Road, Walthamstow, London E17.

Eton Manor is a soccer club, formed as part of a big organisation that was set up for Hackney working boys. Mr Gerald Wellesley and a group of Old Etonians founded the club in 1901 and the first headquarters were in a converted coffee house in Hackney. Field-Marshal Lord Roberts officially opened the new headquarters in 1913, in Riseholme Street, Hackney Wick. This was a magnificent building that housed its many hundreds of members. The football club competed in various local leagues until 1933, when they attained senior status and were elected to the First Division of the London League. They also played at the Wilderness Ground for the first time with a match against Clapton FC. After winning the championship in their first season, they were elected to the Premier Division. Membership of the London League continued until the close of 1958/59. During that time the club won the League championship four times, were runners-up twice and were finalists in the Essex Senior Cup in 1938, where they were beaten by Romford. The reserve team won the reserve section twice, also the Reserve Section Cup. Eton Manor joined the Aetolian League in 1959, then moved on to the Greater London League in 1964, before moving to the Metropolitan League in 1969. They joined the Essex Senior League in 1975 where they still play today. Their best season in this competition appears to have been 1978/79 when they finished third.

Eton Manor, May 1982. By 1982 Temple Mills was looking derelict with little evidence of having hosted a senior football club.

During the 1950s they ran seven boys' soccer teams, five old-boy sides and three rugby fifteens. Cricket, lawn tennis, squash and boxing are also big club activities. There were two celebrities involved in the organisation. These were Nicky Gargano, a middleweight boxing international, and Reg Jennings, an amateur squash champion. The organisation had 1,200 members – 400 under eighteen, and 800 over eighteen during the 1950s. The club prides itself on its reputation for sportsmanship and gentlemanly conduct on and off the field of play, and new members are expected to do their utmost to live up to these traditions. The club has an unbreakable rule that nobody can become a member after his sixteenth birthday. This makes recruiting of new players from other clubs impossible but leads to a sense of loyalty to the club, which is unsurpassed anywhere in football. Every player playing today came to the senior section from the boys' club at the age of eighteen.

Eton Manor played at the 'Wilderness', a giant sports complex in Ruckholte Road, Leyton, until 1968. This was surrounded by a huge wall with a statue of a discus thrower over the main entrance and a lintel within the ground stating 'A game's a game at Eton Manor'. This was primarily an athletics track, which was surfaced and opened around 1949. Floodlit meetings were held there from the 1960s. The bends were reported to be a bit tight but it was a very popular track in its day. An all-weather track was put in place around 1959 and was the first use of this type of surface at a British venue. It had a series of wooden shelters and stands dotted around its running track. This disappeared under what is now the Lea Valley (formerly Eastway) Sports and Leisure

Centre by Quarter Mile Lane and Temple Mill Lane. After leaving the Wilderness, Eton Manor played at the G.U.S. Sports Ground, Clapton and shared with Walthamstow Avenue from 1978. In the early 1980s they played at the Norwegian Seamans' Ground in Jenkins Lane, Barking but in 1985 found a more permanent home when they moved to Roding Lane, Buckhurst Hill. This had a smart clubhouse and dressing rooms but the pitch was riddled with problems caused by flooding from the river Roding. The clubhouse had an overhanging veranda and there was a set of training lights on each side of the pitch. Their record crowd was 600 when Leyton Orient visited to open the new floodlights on 25 January 1989. The club was homeless again in 1994, as they did not have the money to renovate the ground up to Essex League standards. They shared with Stansted then Purfleet at the Thurrock Hotel. They used East Ham United's ground during 1995/96 and then moved in with Barkingside from 1998-2000. They were sharing Leyton Pennant's Wadham Lodge Ground from 2000-04 and they moved to Burnham Ramblers' Leslie Field ground, Springfield Road, Burnham-on-Crouch, Essex for season 2004/05.

BOB'S FIRST TIME (Norwegian Ground): This was on 28 April 1984 with an unusual kick-off time of 11 a.m. on a Saturday. Eton Manor played Canvey Island (1-1) in the Essex Senior League before a crowd of twenty-five. The ground had a roped-off pitch, a social club and a set of eight floodlights. (Roding Lane, Buckhurst Hill): Bob saw the same opponents meet in the Essex Senior League on 11 May 1985 and Canvey Island lost 2-1 before another small crowd of only thirty-seven.

FARLEIGH ROVERS
Ground: Parsonage Field, Harrow Road, Warlingham, Surrey.

The club was formed as Farleigh & Chelsham United in 1922 by local lads who kicked a ball about on Farleigh Common. Their first pitch was on this common and was bordered by a road and Moorcroft House. The first changing facilities were very basic, being an old barn that was shared with animals and a hollow tree. They moved to their present ground at Parsonage Field in the mid-1920s and, thanks to their club president, William Coker Iliffe, who owned the land, paid a nominal rent of only £1 per annum and the players changed at the local church hall. The club changed its name to Farleigh Rovers in 1929 and in March 1959 bought the ground for £300. They built a concrete building in 1971 that held the changing rooms and other facilities.

They won the Surrey County Intermediate League in 1981/82 and joined the Surrey County Premier League and won its title in the first two years. Farleigh Rovers joined the Combined Counties League in 1984/85 but they often found themselves at the wrong end of the table. They finished eleventh in their first season and eighth in 1988/89. Their best season was 1990/91 when they were sixth with 52 points. They left the Combined Counties League in 1994 and moved to the Surrey Premier League where they played until 2003, when this league became the lower division of the

Farleigh Rovers, July 2004. The tin veranda with twelve seats is a relatively recent addition.

Combined Counties League. Farleigh Rovers entered the FA Vase for the first time in 1985/86 but lost to Molesey in the extra preliminary round. Their record in this competition was poor and they only won two matches before bailing out in 1994.

ALEX'S FIRST TIME: I saw Farleigh Rovers play Corinthian Casuals in a Surrey Senior Cup fourth qualifying round tie at Vicarage Field on 7 December 1991. This is a pretty ground surrounded by countryside, but it's very difficult to get to by public transport since they stopped running buses up to Warlingham Park Hospital.

FELTHAM
Ground: Feltham Arena, Shakespeare Avenue, Feltham, Middlesex.

Feltham FC was known as Tudor Park when they were formed in 1946. Tudor Park played at Rectory Park in Hanworth, then at the Remo Depot in Feltham and finally played on the Glebelands playing fields before moving into their present home, the Feltham Sports Arena in 1962. For their first three seasons, Tudor Park were members of the West Middlesex Sunday Football League but in 1949/50 became affiliated to the Middlesex County FA and played Saturday football under the county's jurisdiction as members of the Staines & District League. The club was elected into the Hounslow & District League in 1955/56 and in turn were elected to the Parthenon League.

When the council opened the new Feltham Arena in 1962, Feltham FC moved in and the club has remained there ever since. It was built as a running track and had a pavilion with changing rooms as the only facility until the huge 1,300-seat stand was added in 1966. The rest of the ground was slightly banked to give an elevated view all around. It remained virtually unchanged until fire regulations forced a drastic reduction in the capacity, with half the seating being removed, although it is still possible for 600 people to either sit or stand should the capacity ever be needed. The stand lost its roof in recent years so spectators have to face the elements without any protection.

Feltham, January, 1987. For once a plastic pitch was a boon for football, as evidenced by the larger-than-usual arena attendance. There was standing room at the top of the stand behind the fourteen rows of plastic benches.

The club changed their name to Feltham in 1963 after being granted senior status by the Middlesex County Football Association. The local council insisted it be included in their title if they were to use the arena. Feltham had their first taste of senior football in the Surrey Senior League in 1963/64, in which they had a successful five-season spell. The club replaced Petters Sports in the Spartan League in 1968 and at the end of season 1972/73 they were promoted to the Second Division of the Athenian League. They had their record crowd during 1972/73 when 1,938 attended the Arena for a Middlesex Senior Cup match with Hampton. Feltham, along with fifteen other member clubs, resigned to join the newly formed Second Division of the Isthmian League in 1977 and the club was promoted to the First Division in 1980/81. They were relegated to the newly formed Division Two (South) at the end of 1983/84 and transferred to Division Three in 1992 after the league had been restructured. A merger with Hounslow of the Southern League was made in 1990 and the side competed under the name of Feltham & Hounslow Borough until the end of the 1994/95 season, when it was decided to change the name back to Feltham.

Feltham still played on an artificial pitch during 2003/04 that was originally laid in November 1984 and funded by Hounslow Council, the Sports Council and the GLC – but the Arena lost its running track at this time. The club continued playing on it in the Isthmian League until 1995, when regulations instructed them to add another 300-seat stand on the opposite side of the ground as well as replace the perimeter fencing. As the ground is council-owned and with an average crowd of around only sixty, it was not considered feasible and the club have dropped into the Combined Counties League. In their first season in the Combined Counties League, Feltham finished eighth, followed the next season by fourth, and were winners of the League Cup after defeating Godalming & Guildford 5-1 in the final. The grandstand had lost its roof by this time due to asbestos being found in it. Feltham left the run-down arena in 2004. They plan to develop a new base at Green Lane, Hanworth and plan to share with Egham Town during 2004/05.

ALEX'S FIRST TIME: Everywhere else was off in the London area due to freezing weather when I visited the Feltham Arena. The match was on due to the artificial pitch being playable. I remember shivering along with another 114 spectators and enduring a 0-0 draw in an Isthmian Division Two (South) encounter with Horsham on 8 February 1986.

Finchley, December 1974. The all-tin covered side with four concrete steps is complemented by a stand on the opposite side.

FINCHLEY

Ground: Summers Lane, Finchley, London N12.

Finchley Football Club was formed in 1874 when it had its headquarters and changing rooms at the Railway Hotel in Ballards Lane. Their first ground was at Long Lane, which they used until 1884 when they moved to a well-appointed ground at the back of the Green Man pub in Whetstone. This was home for a further ten years until their next move to the Woodhouse Lane ground in 1894, which was on the corner of Woodhouse Lane and the Great North Road. The changing rooms were then at the Park Hotel, later known as the Tallyho Hotel. The club moved again to a ground at the Swan and Pyramids, playing their first game on 19 September 1899. This ground had wooden railings enclosing the pitch, but after only two years it was required for building land, which meant Finchley had to move on again. They moved to Cobley's Farm, which is close to Finchley Memorial Hospital. This ground was known as Fallow Corner and many years later became part of the Holloway Grammar School sports ground.

Fallow Corner remained home until 1914 when the club closed down due to the First World War. The club was reformed in 1920 and played at Long Hill for a season before finding a new ground at Station Meadow in June 1921. This was a former home of Saracens Rugby Club. This was easily the best ground that the club had played on up until this time and had wooden huts with an old copper boiler for the bath. There was a large wooden stand with seating and a hedge bordering the ground. The Gun Meadow remained home until 1929 when the club rejoined the Athenian League and work began on a new ground at Summers Lane. The ground was located on land that had been bought from the Ecclesiastical Commissioners. The stylish concrete stand was opened on 20 December 1930. It had nearly 600 seats, yet within a year it had been converted to a two-sided stand to accommodate rugby on the adjoining ground. This is the same stand that still exists today.

Summers Lane began hosting differing events such as boxing, baseball and summer fêtes. Major cup finals and representative matches were also held there, sometimes in front of crowds as large as 5,000. The ground record was broken in 1950 when Bishop

Auckland visited for a quarter-final FA Amateur Cup tie as 9,555 crammed into the ground, but Finchley lost the match. Two years later Crystal Palace were the visitors for an second-round FA Cup tie that officially attracted 7,000 – although many got in free. Finchley pulled off a great shock by beating Palace 3-1 but lost at Shrewsbury Town 2-0 in the next round. This was their best ever run in the FA Cup but they did reach the first round in 1946/47 and 1953/54. Finchley were Athenian League Champions in 1953/54 and also runners-up in 1956/57, 1963/64 and 1965/66.

The Supporters' Club paid for new terracing around the ground and in 1960 new entrances were built. Two years later West Ham United were the visitors when on 10 October 1962 new floodlights were used for the first time. Finchley had their best run in the FA Amateur Cup in 1964/65 where they lost to Hendon 4-1 at the semi-final stage. Finchley joined the Isthmian League in 1973 but did not set the world on fire and were relegated to Division Two in 1981. They returned as runners-up to Division One in 1984/85 but were relegated again two years later. They also had their best season in the FA Vase in their promotion year, reaching the fourth round before losing to Steyning Town 2-1. Due to financial problems and Wingate's desire to play on a ground where they could add refurbishments and call it their own, Finchley merged with Wingate to become Wingate & Finchley in 1991. For further details see the section on Wingate & Finchley.

ALEX'S FIRST TIME: I visited Summers Lane on 28 March 1989 for an Isthmian League Division Two (South) match between Finchley and Petersfield United. A crowd of 110 saw a 1-1 draw. I remember buying an excellent club history of Finchley in the rather dingy bar under the stand. The main stand was impressive with its back-to-back views looking over the football and rugby pitches.

FISHER ATHLETIC

Ground: Surrey Docks Stadium, Salter Road, Bermondsey, London SE16.

Fisher Athletic were formed when Michael Culiton, the headmaster at Dockland School, announced that a club was to be set up to provide sporting facilities for underprivileged youths of Bermondsey in 1908. This organisation included the famous boxing club. Fisher was linked to the Roman Catholic Church and was named after the martyr, Blessed John Fisher. However, the football club folded in 1964 and their main achievements had been winning the London Intermediate Cup in 1959/60 and the Surrey Intermediate Cup in 1961/62. Fisher Athletic were reformed in 1966 and played in the Kent Amateur League before joining the London Spartan League in 1974. At this point the club played at a poorly equipped ground at London Road, Mitcham.

They were always keen to return to their base in London's docklands and Fisher were able to relocate to their current Surrey Docks Stadium in 1982. They won the Spartan League championship for the second successive time that season and the new facilities enabled them to join the Southern League. Fisher won the Southern League Southern

Fisher Athletic, April 1978. The ground in Carshalton Road on Mitcham Common opposite the Goat pub was pretty basic. In the background is the future home of Ikea on Purley Way.

Division title at the first attempt with 23 wins from their 34 games. The following season they were narrowly pipped for the Premier Division title by Dartford. However, they beat Conference League champions Maidstone United 1-0 at Gillingham in the Kent Senior Cup final.

The highlight of 1984/85 was in reaching the first round of the FA Cup in only their second season in the competition. They were rewarded with a home draw against Third Division Bristol City, and lost 0-1 before a record crowd of over 2,000. That season the club won both the London Senior Cup and the Bill Dellow Southern League Cup. The following season Fisher finished third in the Southern League Premier Division. After a great struggle that ran to the final match, the club was successful in winning the Southern League Premier Division championship in 1986/87 to earn promotion to the Conference. However, they had to convince the new league's inspectors that the stadium was up to their standard. After spending a total of £100,000 on a new 400-seater stand and raised terracing all round the ground, new toilets, new turnstiles and a players' treatment room, they were elected to the Conference League. The record crowd at the Surrey Docks Stadium came on 4 May 1991 when Barnet were the visitors. Barnet gained a victory to allow them to enter the Football League as Champions and this attracted an attendance of 4,283.

Fisher's success came to an end in 1992 when they were relegated back to the Southern League and then to the Southern Division, generally finishing in mid-table. They were renamed Fisher '93 in 1993 and this was changed to Fisher Athletic (London) in 1996 but in recent years have reverted back to Fisher Athletic again. A new limited company was formed during 1997/98 and the club was rewarded with a long-term lease on their stadium. On the final day of 1999/2000, Fisher beat Newport IOW

2-0 to be crowned Eastern Division Champions, but success was short-lived and after just one season in the Southern League Premier Division they were relegated back into the Eastern Division. Season 2001/02 saw a good run in the FA Cup, reaching the fourth qualifying round before losing 3-1 at home to Forest Green Rovers.

It came as a surprise when Fisher Athletic announced in May 2004 that they would be ground-sharing at Dulwich Hamlet for the next two seasons while the Surrey Docks stadium is knocked down and rebuilt. The stadium and surrounding locality are to undergo a massive redevelopment in the next few years.

ALEX'S FIRST TIME: On a very wet night in late December 1983, I saw Fisher beat Gosport Borough 3-2 in a Southern League Premier Division match. I also attended the match that attracted the record crowd against Barnet in May 1991. Most of the crowd had an excellent view of proceedings, despite the size of the attendance.

FORD UNITED
Ground: Ford Sports Club, Rush Green Road, Romford, Essex.

Ford United's roots lie in the car industry that was the main employer in this part of Essex. The present Ford United FC dates from a 1958 merger between two older clubs, Ford Sports FC (Dagenham) and Briggs Sports FC, both of which were founded in 1934. The latter actually began life as Briggs Motor Bodies FC and entered a team in the London League from 1935 and moved to the Spartan League from 1945. Ford Sports (Dagenham) also played in the Spartan League between 1938-1948 and 1950-1958 and first played in the FA Cup during 1934/35, where they lost at Romford. Briggs Sports played at Dagenham's Victoria Road Ground from 1934-1952 and were a very successful cup team – they even reached an FA Amateur Cup semi-final during 1953/54 where they played in front of 58,000 people at St James' Park, Newcastle but were beaten 5-1 by Bishop Auckland.

Ford United's ground was the Ford Sports & Social Club in Rush Green. Before this they played at Kent Avenue, Dagenham until the Ford Company decided to build a new factory on the site. They opened their Rush Green Ground on 14 May 1955 with a game between the Combined Area XI and West Ham United. A 600-seater stand was built with glass-screen ends flanked by large terracing either side of the stand and on the opposite side from the stand. The ground attracted a crowd of 10,000 for the visit of Bishop Auckland in a FA Amateur Cup tie in 1957, but interest waned after this. Ford Sports and Brigg Sports amalgamated in 1958 to form Ford United. The newly merged club joined the new Aetolian League in 1959/60 and became the first champions, a feat they repeated in 1962. They switched to the Greater London League from 1964 until 1971, when they joined the Metropolitan London League. In 1974 they moved on to the Essex Senior League. They were champions in 1992, runners-up in 1994, and remained in that league until earning promotion to the Isthmian (Ryman) League in 1997, on the back of another Essex Senior League title and a much-improved ground.

Ford United, July 2004. The distinctive all-concrete stand has 320 seats. Either side are concrete terraces. Opposite is concrete terracing the length of the pitch with a bit of cover in the middle.

Ford United won Division Three in 1998/99, scoring 110 goals in 38 games in the process and continued their rapid rise in 2000, when they romped to promotion again. 1997 saw the first major ground improvements for over forty years at Rush Green with the club hoping to gain admission into the Isthmian League. The club spent £40,000 to fence off the ground and individual seats were also placed in the stand. Some of the terracing was also covered and off-field facilities were also upgraded. Ford United's greatest moment came in 1998/99, when they overcame Wellingborough, Barton, Woodbridge, Welwyn GC and Lowestoft to set up an FA Cup first round tie at Preston North End. The Lancashire club won 3-0 before an attendance of 10,167, but it was still a great achievement by Ford United. In the same season, they also reached the FA Vase fifth round (last sixteen) before losing to eventual finalists Bedlington Terriers. The Isthmian League forced Ford United to leave their Rush Green Ground in 2001, as they were only able to gain one-year leases on the ground from the Ford Motor Company, which did not meet the league regulations. Since then they have been playing at Barkingside's Oakside ground (see Barkingside). They changed their name to Redbridge FC in May 2004 in an attempt to attract greater local support.

ALEX'S FIRST TIME: This was for an Essex Senior League match between Ford United and Southend Manor on 3 May 1989 with the home side coming from one goal down to win 3-1. I was very impressed with the main stand, which seemed to be easily the best thing on the ground.

FULHAM

Ground: Craven Cottage, Stevenage Road, Fulham, London SW6.

It looked as though Craven Cottage had gone forever until Fulham's surprise return to the ground in 2004. The impressive and newly refurbished ground can now hold an all-seated crowd of 22,000. Fulham were formed in 1879 when the Reverend James Cardwell asked his Sunday School teacher to found a football team. His name was Tom Norman and he called it after their church, the St Andrew's Cricket & Football Club. The club's first home ground was at Star Road, Fulham and was commonly known as the 'Mud Pond' and measured only 85 x 65 yards. St Andrew's were playing at Eel Brook Common by the start of 1883/84 and this still exists as an open space today. The following season they moved to a ground at Lillie Road close to St Andrew's church and Tom Norman later stated in a local newspaper that this was on the site of the present Queen's Club, which is now famous for lawn tennis. This was not the same Lillie Bridge ground that was used for an early FA Cup final.

The club moved to Lower Putney Common at the start of 1885/86. This was little more than a football pitch on the common with no spectator or player facilities. The following year, the club acquired a pitch at Ranelagh House. This was close to the Thames between Putney Bridge Station and the Hurlingham Club. The players changed at the Eight Bells pub, which was owned by Fulham's centre forward Jack Howland, and they walked under the railway arches to get to their pitch. The club changed name to Fulham St Andrew's in 1886 to distinguish it from other clubs in the area known as St Andrew's. Unfortunately, the Ranelagh Club were forced to move to Barn Elms, Castlenau during the summer of 1888 when the land was acquired for new housing. Barn Elms was south of the Thames and therefore located on the opposite bank of the river from the present Craven Cottage ground. Fulham were invited to join them in this move but the pitch was some way from the club so the players changed at the nearby Red Lion pub. Despite not playing in Fulham, the club changed their name to plain Fulham in December 1888.

Barn Elms was some way from Fulham and support was poor, so the club was on the move again at the start of 1889/90 when they moved to a ground called Purser's Cross (or Roskell's Field) situated close to the present Parson's Green station. Players had to be careful, as there was a tree on the pitch. The players changed at the Rose & Crown public house in Parson's Green Lane. Purser's Cross had its fair share of postponements in 1890/91 and the club gave up the ground and moved back to play on Eel Brook Common again on 7 February 1891. Fulham rented the Half Moon Ground for 1891/92. This was a properly enclosed ground and was located on the opposite side of Lower Richmond Road from the present Half Moon public house in Putney. The club could take a gate but there were no facilities on the ground, which was shared with the Wasps Rugby Club. Attendances began to rise and the club entered, and won, the newly formed West London League in 1892/93. Fulham bought the Craven Cottage ground in 1894, but it took two years before it was ready for use. In the meantime, they lost the use of the Half Moon Ground at Putney in 1895 and the site was built upon soon afterwards. Fulham used the ground of rivals Stanley FC for most home games during 1895/96. This was situated at the Captain James Field at Halford Road, Walham Green.

Fulham Football Club actually obtained a lease on the Craven Cottage ground in 1894 from the Church Commissioners and paid an annual rent based on takings from the gate. This was later amended to a basic flat rate that changed little over the years: Fulham paid £2,000 per annum in the early 1980s. The original Craven Cottage, a riverside home belonging to the gentry, was burnt down in May 1888 and was a ruin for many years, with the grounds very overgrown and neglected. The original building stood roughly where the middle of the playing pitch is now situated. The ground's level was raised and flattened with excavations from the Shepherds Bush Railway (being built at this time) to avoid flooding. Banking was also raised on three sides using road sweepings, courtesy of the local council. These banks were not properly terraced until 1905, and consequently became very muddy when it rained. However, prior to 1903 attendances rarely rose over 4,000 so this was not a great problem.

The first game played at Craven Cottage was a reserve match against St Mary's Recreation on 3 October 1896, but the first team played their inaugural game on the site a week later against Minerva in the Middlesex Senior Cup. The completion of the ground had been delayed by a trade dispute between the club and the contractors; this went to court before being resolved. A stand was built on the Stevenage Road side in 1903 and was quickly nicknamed the 'Rabbit Hutch'. The Rabbit Hutch had seats for 300 supporters in four distinct blocks. It was forty yards in length, very tall and narrow, and covered by four gabled roofs with two canopies added to cover the standing area to the front. The original wooden dressing rooms, built in 1896, were situated behind the stands. In 1905 the club hired Archibald Leitch to remodel the ground. The club had rejected a move to the newly opened Stamford Bridge and felt that they needed to upgrade their own facilities to match those down the road. Chelsea had recently been formed to use the Stamford Bridge ground and had entered the Football League. Fulham were still playing in the Southern League at the time. The banks were properly terraced on three sides and an impressive new full-length stand was built on the Stevenage Road side. Many of the other stands built by Leitch have either been pulled down or have been altered out of all recognition. The Cottage is unique. In its early years players, including Jimmy Sharp and Wattie White, lived in a flat upstairs. It also contained dressing rooms, a boardroom and offices. Its balcony, from which you can now sit and watch a game, was not added until about 1925. The Cottage was modernised in 1933 and again in the mid-1970s, but its character remains unchanged.

Craven Cottage was selected for an international fixture between England and Wales in March 1907. The biggest attendance, meanwhile, came in October 1938 when 49,335 squeezed into the ground for a Second Division fixture with Millwall. From the 1920s to the early 1960s advertising hoarding stretched down the whole of the riverside terracing and many will remember the words 'Fulham Football & Athletic Club' on the centre gable of the Stevenage Road stand. The terracing at both the Putney and Hammersmith ends was extended upwards in 1959 when the club entered the First Division. These top sections were out of use in the early 1990s as they were deemed unsafe. The top of the Hammersmith End was strengthened in 1997 and executive boxes were placed there. Former Anderson air-raid shelters, which hail from the Second World War, could be seen under the Putney terrace.

Floodlights did not come to the Cottage until September 1962. Fulham's close proximity to the Thames did not help as the Port of London Authority had objected to earlier attempts to install lights. The Hammersmith End was roofed in 1965 and just before this an electronic scoreboard, which doubled as a refreshment hut, was installed by the halfway line on the riverside terrace. This rather complicated system was later housed in the roof of the Hammersmith End – but was never easy to understand. The Riverside stand was opened in February 1972; the opening was marked with a friendly against Benfica, Eusebio and all. This stand does not improve the look of the ground but it offers a good view of a match, although it looks a little incongruous alongside the rest of the stadium.

The arrival as chairman of Ernie Clay in 1977 heralded the beginning of a period of complicated financial and development difficulties for the club. Under his leadership the finances deteriorated after their near-miss at promotion to the top flight in 1983. He forced his managers to sell off their best players and gates dropped to around the 4,000 mark, while debts accelerated to over £3 million. During this time the Cottage also hosted rugby league in an abortive attempt to raise income levels. Ernie Clay bought the land from the Church Commissioners in 1985 for £932,000 with money raised from property developers Kilroe. This was seen by many as an attempt by Clay to cash in on the enormous property value of Craven Cottage due to its desirable position on the banks of the river. Clay quickly submitted plans for luxury flats to be built at the Putney End and behind the Riverside Stand, but after these were rejected Clay sold the club and its ground to Marler Estates in the summer of 1986. Marler Estates suggested a ground share with Chelsea and then a merger with QPR so that the ground could be released for development. Fortunately for the fans, the Hammersmith & Fulham Council stuck firmly behind their interests by blocking Marler's attempts to gain planning approval. The Stevenage Road façade and the Cottage were granted listed status in an attempt to thwart any development.

The Jimmy Hill-led consortium came onto the scene in 1987, buying the right to use the club name (Fulham 1987) and leasing the ground from Marler for three years. In an attempt to protect the ground from redevelopment, the council sought a compulsory purchase order to buy Craven Cottage. Just before the public inquiry was due to begin, the Jimmy Hill consortium dramatically took Cabra's side in return for cash for the ailing club and an extra three years on the lease. There was an angry backlash from the fans but Jimmy Hill later interpreted the situation as a 'no lose' move that would see the club protected whichever way the inquiry went. The public inquiry eventually rejected not only the planning application by Cabra but also the CPO by the council!

The last game at Craven Cottage was due to be an encounter with Bradford City on 2 May 1992 but sadness turned into joy as it was announced that the club were staying put for another season. The club had even been in talks with Chelsea to share Stamford Bridge and own part of the ground. The gods were with Fulham, however, as within months Cabra had been wound up as the property bubble burst and its main creditor, the Royal Bank of Scotland, became Fulham FC's new landlord. The bank granted the club a ten-year lease with a £7.5 million option to buy the ground, but the sting in the tail was that unless the club came up with the money by June 1996, it would be charged a huge annual rent. A new scheme named Fulham 2000 was launched in February 1994

Fulham, May 1986. The Cottage has miraculously survived the redevelopment of Fulham's home.

with the aim of raising funds from supporters to assist in keeping the club going and help keep them at Craven Cottage. The following year more plans were submitted for flats to be built around a newly designed ground.

Things changed dramatically with the arrival as chairman of Harrods owner Mohammed al-Fayed in May 1997. Part of this deal was to finalise the purchase back of Craven Cottage from the Royal Bank of Scotland. Fulham quickly rose from the Second to the Premier Division and were given the special dispensation that operates for newly promoted clubs that allowed them to play for one season at the top level with terraces. In the meantime there were plans for a new state-of-the-art 32,000-seat stadium. After a long process, planning permission was finally granted in January 2002. However, the club had now changed its mind and the proposed new stadium was now deemed too expensive to be pursued. Fulham had already moved to share Loftus Road while the new stadium was to be built and the club announced that they would be staying for another season. Most supporters feared the worse but in December 2003 it was announced that Fulham would be returning to Craven Cottage on a short-term basis with £5-6 million being spent on new seating at the Hammersmith and Putney Ends that will also be reroofed. The Stevenage Road stand will also be fully decked out with new seating and new floodlights installed.

ALEX'S FIRST TIME: Fulham are my club and my favourite ground is Craven Cottage so I am hoping that we go on to stay at the Cottage for many more years. My first match at the Cottage was a 5-0 home defeat against Wolves in pouring rain on a cold December day back in 1962. For some unknown reason I still decided to go back for more punishment. My main memory of this game was Alan Hinton hitting a hat-trick for the visitors and racing my friends up and down the terracing.

Greenwich Borough, September 1998. One man, his dog and a few others occupy the only spectator accommodation

GREENWICH BOROUGH
Ground: Harrow Meadow, Eltham Green Road, Eltham, London SE9.

Greenwich Borough's main claim to fame is that it discovered Crystal Palace, Arsenal and England star Ian Wright. The club was formed as Woolwich Borough Council in 1928 and played in the South London Alliance until 1975. They won the Premier Division five seasons on the trot from 1960-66 and in 1973/74 and were also runners-up on six occasions. Greenwich Borough joined the London Spartan League in 1975 and were champions of the Senior Division in 1979/80. Their ground was opened on 4 December 1978 with the visit of Charlton Athletic and this was watched by a crowd of 2,000. At this time, there were two pitches at Harrow Meadow, one floodlit and the other with a small covered area. They were league champions in 1979/80, finished fourth in 1980/81 and won the League Cup in 1983, when they beat Malden Vale 4-1 in the final. The following season, they reached the semi-final of the Kent Senior Trophy before losing 3-0 at Deal Town.

Greenwich Borough joined the Kent League in 1984/85 and finished as champions in 1986/87 and 1987/88. They finished three points ahead of Crockenhill in 1986/87 with 78 points and also won the League Cup by beating Sittingbourne 3-1 in a replayed final in 1986/87. The following season they were champions again with 83 points, 13 points clear of runners-up Faversham, and scored 111 goals. Their best season in recent years was when they finished third in 1998/99. Greenwich Borough won the First Division Cup in 1998 by beating Herne Bay 1-0 in the final and also put a floodlighting system in for the first time that year on the new pitch. Their best run in the FA Cup came in 1993/94 when they reached the third qualifying round after beating Eastbourne United and Croydon, before losing at home to Molesey. They entered the FA Vase for the first time in 1980/81, reaching the third round where they lost 2-1 at Burgess Hill Town after beating Whistable Town, Shoreham and East Ham United. They went one better in 1989/90 when they reached the fourth round, where they lost to Harefield United 4-5 at Harrow Meadow, after a 1-1 draw. They beat Ash United, Alma Swanley, Cray Wanderers, Hounslow and Whistable Town on the way to the fourth round. Their most famous former player is Ian Wright, who went on to play for, among others, England, Crystal Palace and Arsenal.

BOB'S FIRST TIME: Bob visited Harrow Meadow on 31 August 1982 for a friendly match between Greenwich Borough and Sevenoaks that had been listed in that day's *Daily Telegraph*. Greenwich won 5-0 before a non-existent crowd. The ground had two pitches and the match was played on the one further from the dressing rooms, which had floodlights. The Kent League insisted on the club playing on the pitch closer to the dressing room, so Bob did a revisit on 6 May 1988. Greenwich Borough beat Faversham Town 3-0 in a Kent League fixture played before forty-four spectators. Directly behind one goal was a curiously angled cover with three rows of planks on scaffolding poles that offered some seating to spectators.

HAMPTON & RICHMOND BOROUGH
Ground: The Beveree, Station Road, Hampton, Middlesex.

The Beveree is one of the most pleasant grounds in the London area. Hampton Football Club was founded in April 1921 following a meeting involving four local clubs. They decided to play their matches at Gloucester Road, but this had a reputation of having a rather poor playing surface. The club spent its early years in the South West Middlesex League and the Kingston & District League. Hampton moved to an enclosed ground on Priory Road during the summer of 1923. This proved short-lived and they started 1927/28 playing at Mark Hole Recreation Ground and, during the 1930s, they played at the Hatherop Recreation Ground.

Hampton played at The Beveree for the first time during 1949/50, but only on a temporary basis. The Beveree was named after the large house that still overlooks it today and in whose grounds the pitch was first laid out. This house was built around 1825 on the site of a seventeenth-century house named Rose Villa. Its owner left the ground to the council in the 1940s and it was converted into a football ground. The venue was earlier used for athletics meetings, polo and fêtes and it was only in recent years that a high wall was built to separate the house from the ground. Hampton played at The Beveree until the early 1950s when the council invited Hampton and Twickenham Town to tender for the lease on the ground. Twickenham pushed Hampton off the ground by offering double the rent. It helped that their chairman was also the local mayor.

Hampton were forced to play on Hatherop Recreation Ground for seven years until Twickenham lost the tenancy of The Beveree. Twickenham eventually dropped into local football and folded soon afterwards. During the early 1960s the pitch was railed

Hampton & Richmond Borough, August 1986. Seven rows of concrete steps provided standing room next to the main stand. By 2003 a 100-seater stand had been built behind one goal at the clubhouse end.

off and a small covered area stood on the site of the current stand. It was frequently underwater and that meant it was rarely used.

When Hampton obtained the lease on The Beveree they were also granted Senior Status by the Middlesex County Football Association and they stepped up into the Surrey Senior League. They lost their first game at home to Cobham 3-1 on 22 August 1959. They won the championship in 1963/64, losing only two games. Old stables were used as changing rooms until 1962 when an army building was acquired from a local airport. This has been modernised on a couple of occasions since but is still in use. During the 1960s a small 200-seater stand was built to replace the old shack while a large clubhouse and floodlighting both appeared. The club successfully applied to join the Spartan League, where they won four championships in their seven-season spell in the League.

Hampton became the first club from the Spartan League to have floodlights erected in 1965. A match between a Spartan League XI (including several Hampton players) and an England Amateur XI took place to mark the switching on of the lights. After this success, Hampton were elected to the Second Division of the Athenian League in 1971. Their spell in this league lasted only two seasons as in 1973 they left to become one of the founder members of the new Second Division of the Isthmian League. They reached the final of the Middlesex Senior Cup for the first time in 1972 but lost to Hendon. The club remained in the Isthmian League until their first ever relegation in their seventy-year existence in 1990. Following divisional splits, the club dropped for a second consecutive season into the Third Division in 1991. However, promotions followed in 1992, 1996 and finally in 1998 into the Premier Division.

In 1977/78 the club reached the final qualifying round of the FA Cup after overcoming Ilford in the third game of an epic third qualifying round encounter. Hampton entertained Barnet in the fourth qualifying round and went down 1-2 with goalkeeper Alan Cooling scoring the Hampton goal from a drop kick. Their best performance in any of the national cup competitions came in the FA Trophy in 1984 when they reached the first round proper, where they were beaten by Maidstone 2-0.

The turnstiles at The Beveree were brought from Hurst Park Race Course when it closed in the 1960s. In recent years, The Beveree has been terraced all around the ground and in 1999 the club opened a new stand behind the south goal.

ALEX'S FIRST TIME: I visited The Beveree for a pre-season friendly between Hampton and Sutton United on 6 August 1985. The visitors won 2-0 before a crowd of 176. The Beveree is a pleasant ground tucked away behind Hampton village. It has a rural feel, especially before the club built a higher wall between the ground and the old house.

HANWELL TOWN
Ground: Reynolds Field, Perivale Lane, Perivale, Middlesex.

There was a team called Hanwell in the 1880s that played in the London League Division One during 1898/99, finishing fourth out of nine clubs. Another club called Hanwell Corinthians played in the Hellenic League Division One from 1957-61 and were runners-up in 1958/59 with 34 points from 24 games. They left the league in 1961 and appear to have no connection with the present Hanwell Town club.

The present club was formed in 1948 and moved to their ground at Reynolds Field in June 1981 from the nearby Ealing Central Sports Ground at Horsenden Lane. They played in the Dauntless League and the Harrow, Wembley & District League until joining the Middlesex League in 1970 and winning its League Cup at the first attempt. They were given senior status in 1983, joined the Senior Division of the Spartan League and finished as champions at the end of their first season. Hanwell were promoted to the Premier Division and finished a creditable fifth in 1984/85. After their successful first season, Hanwell mostly finished in mid-table but did make sixth place during 1987/88.

The pavilion at Perivale Lane is impressive and the one structure incorporates the clubhouse and an overhang over a balcony where spectators can watch the game in comfort. A rail was placed around the pitch and new dressing rooms were built in 1984. Floodlights were introduced in 1989. Tottenham Hotspur were the visitors when they officially switched them on before a record crowd of 600 in October 1989. That month, 850 also attended a Middlesex Senior Cup game with Enfield.

Hanwell won the London Senior Cup in 1992 and 1993 and were finalists the following season. They defeated Corinthian Casuals 4-3 in a replay in 1992, beat Brimsdown Rovers 4-3 the following year but lost to Ford United 2-1 in 1994. During 1992/93, Hanwell Town finished fifth in the Spartan League and the following season lost to Willesden Hawkeye in the final of the Spartan League Cup. Hanwell Town were founder members of the Spartan South Midlands Senior Division in 1997 and finished as runners-up in 1998/99 on goal difference to Holmer Green. They were promoted to the top division where they finished a creditable third in 2001/02.

Hanwell Town, August 1984. A wood veranda in front of the dressing room and social club provided the only shelter.

Hanwell have had limited success in the FA Cup but they reached the second qualifying round twice, in 1988/89 and 1997/98. In the FA Vase, their best seasons were in 1985/86, when they lost 5-0 at Southall in the third round, and in 2002/03 when they lost at the same stage 6-0 at AFC Sudbury after beating Ely City, Greenacres and Dereham Town.

ALEX'S FIRST TIME: I saw Hanwell Town play Northwood on a pleasant summer evening in August 1989. The match ended in a 1-1 draw before an attendance of ninety in the Spartan League Premier Division. I watched the match from the balcony of the pavilion/clubhouse.

HAREFIELD UNITED
Ground: Preston Park, Breakspear Road, North Harefield, Middlesex.

Harefield United are one of the oldest clubs in the world, having been formed as long ago as 1868. Before the Second World War they played in the Uxbridge & District League, but they joined the Great Western Combination League in 1946. They remained in this league until 1964 when they moved over to the Parthenon League, which became the Middlesex League in 1968. The Hares moved up into the Athenian League in 1975/76, appearing in the Second Division. Their best finishes in this league were sixth in 1976/77, 1981/82 and 1983/84. They were elected into the Isthmian League Division Two (North) in 1984/85 and soon consolidated their position, finishing fifth at the end of 1988/89, their highest ever position. When the league was reorganised in 1991/92, Harefield moved to the Second Division but they were relegated to the Third Division in 1993.

Harefield United, April 1979. The 110-seater stand remains substantially the same today. Opposite has been built cover with a steel roof and no back.

Harefield decided to leave the Isthmian League in 1996 and became founder members of the Spartan Midland League Premier Division One (South). They joined the Senior Division in 1998 and finished as runners-up of the First Division in 2002/02, when they won 25 of their 38 league encounters and ended the season with 81 points. They continued to do well in the Premier Division, finishing fourth in 2002/03 and fifth the following season.

Honours have been rare at Harefield but they were Parthenon League Champions in 1964/65 and won the Division One Cup in 1965/66. They were Middlesex League Champions in 1966/67 and from 1968-71 and won the League Cup in 1967 and 1969. They also won the Middlesex Premier Cup in 1986.

Harefield first entered the FA Cup in 1979/80 where they lost 4-1 to Walton & Hersham in a preliminary round tie at Preston Park. They have only ever reached the second qualifying round of the FA Cup but have fared better in the FA Vase. They reached the quarter-final in 1989/90, beating Sun Sports, Tiptree United, Bracknell Town, Greenwich Borough and Bashley along the way before losing at Yeading 2-0. They recorded their record crowd for the tie with Bashley when 430 spectators attended the match. Harefield have also reached the fourth round on three other occasions. They have been playing on their current ground since 1963 and before that they performed at Taylor's Meadow in Harefield from 1930 (this is an open field that is still used for football today).

ALEX'S FIRST TIME: This was for a fourth-round FA Vase tie between Harefield and Greenwich Borough, which ended in a 1-1 draw. The match took place in March 1990 before a crowd of 180 and Harefield won the replay 5-4, eventually losing to Yeading 2-0 in the quarter-final. A basic ground, Breakspear Road had a small covered area and a 110-seat stand opposite.

HARINGEY BOROUGH

Ground: Coles Park, White Hart Lane, Wood Green, London N17.

Haringey Borough started life way back in 1910 as Tufnell Spartans, formed when the reserves decided to break away from their parent club Tufnell Park. They have a very complicated history, which is mixed up with histories of two Edmonton clubs as well as Tufnell Park, a major amateur club before the Second World War. Edmonton's first ground was originally known as the Houndsfield Road Recreation Ground but changed its name to the Henry Barrass Sports Ground in 1927. It cost over £18,000 to develop and was built mainly by unemployed labourers on a government scheme. To begin with the ground was basic with a cinder running track surround, a large grass bank on the north side (with a pavilion) and crash barriers. Edmonton FC and Lower Edmonton FC were the initial tenants, but the rent was prohibitive and their tenure only lasted one season. As the ground was underused, there were plans to build a grandstand for £10,000 but the cost was too great. The ground's name was slightly amended to the Henry Barrass Stadium in 1950.

A new club called Edmonton Borough, formed in 1947, took over the venue. They were playing in the London League at this time. Due to lack of building materials during the Second World War, cover was not provided until 1950 when a basic steel sheet and scaffolding structure was built as cover for 500 spectators at a cost of £1,000. Tufnell Park had lost the use of their own ground in Holloway in 1938, and had then played at Hendon's Claremont Ground and then at Albury Ride in Cheshunt. Attendances were poor at Cheshunt, so they decided to return to North London and merged with Edmonton Borough under the title Tufnell Park Edmonton FC in time for the start of 1950/51. Improvements needed to be made on the ground, as it was to be used for Isthmian League matches, and a grandstand was finally built. The north bank was given a roof over newly concreted steps. A bid to install floodlights was made in 1953, but the application was turned down.

Tufnell Park Edmonton were elected into the Delphian League in 1954, where they remained for six seasons. In 1960, the club changed its name to Edmonton FC and moved to the Athenian League in 1963. A new licensed clubroom was opened just inside the Houndsfield Road entrance in 1967. Tufnell Park (Edmonton) vacated the ground when the lease ran out in 1972, and moved on. The new Edmonton and Haringey club moved to Coles Park, the home of the Haringey club. The new name remained for just one year before the club reverted back to plain 'Edmonton', then two years later became 'Haringey' and finally adding a suffix of Borough to the title in 1976. This has remained as the club's name – except for one season when they called themselves Tufnell Park again in 1995/96 when there was a vague hope that they might return to their original home at Junction Road. Haringey Borough still uses the Tufnell Park colours of green and white today and compete in the Spartan South Midlands League.

Haringey Borough, March 1975. At the other White Hart Lane six wood sections provided seating for the crowd, with dressing rooms and social club behind.

BOB'S FIRST TIME: On 14 April 1983 Bob saw Ambrose Fleming Old Boys lose to Highfield 3-2 in a London Spartan League Premier Division match at the Henry Barrass Stadium. This was played on a Thursday evening before a crowd of thirty – who looked completely lost in such a vast bowl. The ground had grass banking all the way round, a large cover on one side and a stand with ten rows of benches on the opposite side. He also saw a match at White Hart Lane on 12 October 1982 when Haringey Borough drew 2-2 with Marlow in the Athenian League. At this time, a small wooden stand was tacked on to the front of the social club. When he revisited the ground in February 1997 to see Islington St Mary's lose to their landlords Haringey Borough, the wooden stand had been replaced by a 264-seater concrete-and-steel stand that was more than adequate for the crowd of just nineteen.

HARROW BOROUGH
Ground: Earlsmead, Carlyon Avenue, South Harrow, Middlesex.

Harrow Borough were called Roxonian FC when they were formed in 1933. They moved to a ground on Northolt Road and a new pavilion was started with an all-round verandah, dressing rooms, baths and showers, a kitchen and lounge. The club played their first match on 9 September 1933 at their new ground on the Earlsmead Estate. A local builder who was connected to a club called Roxeth United supplied the materials free for the new pavilion, which was built by members of the new club. After only four months the club were informed that the ground would be used for other things and that they would have to move to another part of the estate. This second ground cost £1,625 to build and an appeal was set up to try to raise funds for the project. This sports ground would include a football pitch, two cricket teams, and a quarter-mile cinder track in addition to tennis courts and a pavilion. The purchase of the new ground and

Harrow Borough, September 1973. Apart from a veranda in front of the social club, then on the opposite side, this was the entirety of spectator facilities. The lights are about to go up. No post-and-rail around the pitch in those days!

pavilion was completed in 1938. The members who attended the Annual General Meeting in 1938 made the decision to change the club's name to Harrow Town. Several tons of earth had been dumped at the pitch's side to a create banking for the spectators, and soon afterwards a covered stand was presented to the club by a local landowning family. The new stand had seating for 250, with standing room for 100 and was still in use in the late 1990s.

Earlsmead regularly had crowds of 2,000 in its early days, but today attendances are usually around the 300 mark. Further work was done to drain the pitch, and more dressing rooms were added in 1939. While many other local amateur sides closed for the duration of the Second World War, Harrow Town managed to keep going, playing friendlies throughout. The record attendance for the ground of 3,000 was recorded in October 1946 when local rivals Wealdstone were the visitors for a first qualifying round FA Cup tie. The Supporters' Club were granted a licence to build a steel-and-concrete pavilion for indoor training in September 1948, which they paid for themselves and, two years later, more cover was erected. The club changed their name to Harrow Borough in 1965 but the ground was by now in urgent need of improvement. The main pitch was moved and levelled in 1969, and concrete posts and steel tubing surrounded the pitch. The second pitch at the lower end of the ground was sold off to developers and the funds were used to redevelop Earlsmead to a more modern stadium. Work began with floodlights being erected, concrete terraces being built on all four sides of the ground with one-and-a-half sides covered and a fine new clubhouse being erected behind the goal.

Harrow had to play all of their games away from Earlsmead while building work was taking place during 1973/74. The ground reopened for the start of the 1974/75 season, and since then extensions have been built onto the car park. The original shelter on the ground lost its roof due to fire regulations. Borough's finest hour in recent years came in 1983/84 when they took the Isthmian League title. The old main stand disappeared in 1997 to be replaced with a new concrete-and-iron structure. This was partially financed with a grant from the Football Trust.

ALEX'S FIRST TIME: I visited Earlsmead for the first time on 5 December 1989 for a match between Harrow Borough and Erith & Belvedere in the third qualifying round of the FA Trophy. The match went to extra time but finished as a 2-2 draw. I remember the old wooded stand but little else about the ground, except that the floodlights were not very good – which made the venue feel a little gloomy.

HAYES
Ground: Church Lane, Hayes, Middlesex.

Eileen Shackle, the teenage daughter of a wealthy land agent, is probably the most unusual person to have formed a football club. This happened in 1908 when she founded what was to become Hayes FC. She encouraged the local youngsters to form a football team that was originally known as Botwell Mission. This was named after the mission church that was built in memory of her grandfather. This building still exists today as part of the Hayes Library in Golden Crescent. Their first ground was situated close to where Pump Lane meets Station Road, at the end of Coldharbour Lane, and was known as Botwell Common. The club changed its name to Hayes FC in 1924 (some sources say 1929).

Hayes played in the Uxbridge & District Junior League before the First World War. Albert Knight was the club's very first captain in 1909 and was one of the seven footballing Knight brothers who appeared for the club. Sadly, he was killed at The Somme. The club joined the Great Western Suburban League in 1919 and won the Middlesex Senior Cup in their first senior season. They regularly won their league's title during the 1920s with crowds of up to 3,000 often watching matches. Over 5,000 saw the Middlesex Senior Cup final against Southall in 1924 when the two sides shared the trophy. The club moved to a new ground in Church Road in 1920 called Cox's Meadow. It was opened on 26 August with a Whites *v.* Stripes trial, and the first competitive match was against 2nd Scots Guards in the Great Western Suburban League. The first structure of any significance was a grandstand, which was erected in 1925. Hayes were elected to the Spartan League and were runners-up in 1925/26 before winning the title two years later. Hayes reached the Amateur Cup final in 1931, which was played at Highbury, but they lost to Wycombe Wanderers 1-0.

Hayes FC became a member of the Athenian League and were runners-up for the championship in 1931/32 and 1949/50. The clubhouse at Church Road, Hayes suffered a direct hit during an air raid in 1942, which completely destroyed it as well as the club's records. The banked ground was terraced slowly after the Second World War and remained more or less unchanged until the late 1990s. The record attendance at Church Road was set in February 1951 when 15,370 saw an Amateur Cup tie with Bromley. The Athenian League title was won on goal average in 1956/57 over Finchley and they reached the semi-final of the Amateur Cup, losing to Bishop Auckland before

Hayes, October 1976. The only change in the stand has been the replacement of wooden benches with seven rows of plastic tip-up seats. Opposite is a fifteen-deep covered terrace and open terraces behind both goals.

a large and very partisan 40,000 crowd at St James Park, Newcastle. Lean years followed through the 1960s but the club was invited to join the Isthmian League at the turn of the 1970s. Although their league form was indifferent, some good FA Cup encounters occurred, the first giant-killing coming with a home win over Bristol Rovers in 1972, before going down to Reading in the next round after a replay. The greatest cup wins came against Fulham at Craven Cottage in 1991 and when they beat Cardiff City in a replay at Brentford's Griffin Park. The Isthmian League title was won on the last day of 1995/96 by the narrowest margin, with a 3-0 win at Carshalton Athletic to move up to the Conference League. Hayes did well until their relegation in 2002 and have struggled to attract the same crowds in the Isthmian League. The club have plans to build a new ground at Hayes Athletic Stadium and sell their Church Road ground for redevelopment.

ALEX'S FIRST TIME: I was impressed with Hayes' Church Lane ground on my first visit. It was a cold January evening in 1987 and Yeovil Town were the visitors for a FA Trophy first-round replay that went to extra time. The game ended 2-2 and Hayes had a player sent off after sixty minutes, so did well to hold out against a strong Yeovil side that included former Spurs star Graham Roberts.

Hendon, April 1972. By September 2001 the back of the covered side at Claremont Road had been cordoned off for safety reasons. Opposite is a stand, with open terraces behind both goals.

HENDON
Ground: Clitterhouse, Claremont Road, Cricklewood. London NW2.

This ground is likely to disappear in the next couple of years, which would be a great loss to London football. The present Hendon FC was formed as Hampstead Town in 1908. Their first ground was the National Athletic Stadium in College Road, Kensal Rise. This had been previously used by QPR. It is not established whether Hampstead Town played on the main pitch that had grass banking all around and a stand or whether a secondary pitch was in use (see QPR for more information about this ground). Hampstead moved to a new ground called at Avenue Ground in 1912. This was situated between the present College Road and Liddell Gardens in Kensal Rise. There was a pavilion on the ground and an entrance and pathway that led from the local railway station. This ground was built on land belonging to a Mr Dickers, who owned Cowenlaw Farm. At this time it was surrounded by tennis courts and had an entrance from Cricklewood Lane. Town played their first match at the ground on Saturday 21 September 1912 and beat local rivals Kilburn in a London League game. There was a small stand on the ground and Civil Service FC sometimes used this. The area was becoming engulfed with new housing and the club was probably saved from extinction when the Hendon UDC offered the club a piece of land for an annual rent of £255 per year in May 1926.

Work began on the new stadium, which once formed part of Clitterhouse Farm. The farmhouse and outbuildings have survived. The former have been converted into flats and the local council uses the latter for storage. William Harbrow Ltd constructed the grandstand with glass screen ends for possible extension at a later date. However, the stand is virtually unchanged today except that the original bench seats have been replaced with bucket seats obtained from Vicarage Road, Watford in 1993. The dressing rooms are under the stand along with the physio room that was originally a hospitality area. At this time the club changed its name to plain Hampstead. A paling fence surrounded the pitch and a high fence went around the outside of the ground. The pavilion at the Avenue Ground was transported to Claremont Road and the interior modernised. Also, a massive covered terrace was built and named the Gordon Raymond Stand in memory of the club chairman.

The club changed its name to Golders Green in 1933 and this moniker was painted on the roof of the stand, until it was removed when it became a landmark for enemy bombers during the Second World War. The banking was terraced with railway sleepers and the Claremont Road Ground was officially opened on Saturday 18 September 1926 before an FA Cup tie with Berkhamsted. It was clearly a major event as 3,500 attended, paying receipts of £383 17s. In 1946, there was another change of name to Hendon.

There were more changes to the ground after the war and the banking was converted into concrete terracing over many years and a brick-built structure was erected behind the southern end replacing a wooden hut for supporters. Today, the tea bar and Supporters' Club shop stand on the site of the original old wooden clubhouse, demolished when a modern version was built just outside the ground. The first floodlighting system at the ground was switched on when Wolverhampton Wanderers were the visitors on 25 September 1962, attracting a crowd of 4,500. The first match under them was actually a week earlier for a cup game against Finchley. The original pylons still stand although eight lamps now power the system, which was upgraded in 1971.

Claremont Road has seen gates of 3,000-plus for rugby league and Gaelic football matches in recent years, but the highest recorded attendance for football is the 9,000 who watched the FA Cup first-round tie with Northampton Town in 1952. The club played in the Athenian League from 1919 to 1963 and gained three league titles and five runners-up places. In 1963 they were elected into the Isthmian League, where they have remained ever since. The club finished runners-up in their first season, then went one better a year later and won the championship. Hendon FC have won the FA Amateur Cup three times in five finals, and a capacity crowd of 100,000 watched their 1955 final with Bishop Auckland. The club have recently produced plans to move from Claremont Road to the Copthill Stadium, stating that their present ground would cost too much to modernize. The loss of this ground would be a great one.

ALEX'S FIRST TIME: I saw a Middlesex Senior Cup final at Claremont Road that had been held over from the previous season. The match took place between Wealdstone and Hendon on 26 August 1985, and there was a report on the game in the following day's *Daily Telegraph*. Unfortunately, this was mainly because two players were sent off and eight booked in an explosive match. Wealdstone eventually won the cup with a 4-2 victory before a crowd of 650.

Hillingdon Borough, March 1977. Spot the join in the stand at Leas Stadium. A total of 1,276 seats were supposedly available on ten rows of benches. Cover was provided on the other three sides of the ground.

HILLINGDON BOROUGH/YIEWSLEY
Ground: The Leas Stadium, Falling Lane, Yiewsley, Middlesex.

Founded as Yiewsley in 1872, the club were champions of many junior leagues before the First World War. They acquired senior rank on securing admission to the Great Western Suburban League in 1919, but suffered a setback three seasons later when that competition failed to maintain its status. They played in several junior and intermediate leagues, including the Uxbridge League, South-West Middlesex (champions 1937 and 1938), Middlesex County Amateur League (League Cup winners 1939), West Middlesex League, Middlesex Senior League, Great Western Combination and the Spartan League (champions Division One (West) 1949/50). They entered the Premier Division in 1950/51. They were founder members of the Delphian League the following season, finishing third in their first campaign, and reaching the semi-final of the London Senior Cup.

Yiewsley played on a ground called Evelyn's until 1954, when they crossed the road to play at the Leas Stadium. The site was a rubbish tip before it became a football ground. Their chairman, Alfred Ernest Whittit, a local businessman from Sunderland, installed floodlighting on the ground so that players could gain experience by turning out in midweek against clubs from reputedly stronger leagues. The club became Corinthian League champions in 1956/57 but resigned from this league in June 1958 on gaining admission to the Southern League, having decided to become professional. The terracing behind each goal and opposite the stand was covered while a long and low covered stand was also built to improve the ground. They changed their name to Hillingdon Borough in 1964 to give themselves wider appeal after a local government reorganisation in which the borough they played in was renamed. Five years later a crowd of 9,032 somehow squeezed into the Leas Stadium for a second-round FA Cup tie with Luton Town.

Hillingdon Borough also finished runners-up of the Southern League Premier Division in 1968/69 but were relegated in 1974. They bounced straight back as runners-up the following season. They reached the FA Trophy final at Wembley in 1971 but lost to Telford United 3-2. They missed out on a fourth-round home tie with Leeds United in 1973 when they lost to Sutton United in the third round. The club was relegated again in 1979 and seemed to go in decline from this point: Hillingdon Borough was wound up in 1985 due to massive debts. As they had lost their ground they merged with Burnham to become Burnham & Hillingdon, but this name disappeared in 1987 when the club reverted back to its original name of Burnham. At its end it still boasted a capacity of around 14,000, with 1,000 seats and cover for 8,000-9,000, with a clubhouse and car park used latterly as a lorry park. The Leas Stadium lay empty for a couple of years before it was demolished in January 1988 and housing built on the site. Hillingdon Borough were reformed in 1990, after the demise of Ruislip Park, and were founder members of the Spartan South Midlands League. They currently play at Ruislip's old ground at Breakspear Road, Ruislip.

BOB'S FIRST TIME: This was for a Southern League Premier Division match between Hillingdon Borough and Bedford Town. Bedford Town had won 1-0 at The Eyrie the previous day (Easter Monday) and Hillingdon reversed the result with a hotly disputed goal from Reeve. The ground at this time had spectator accommodation on all four sides with lots of corrugated iron. The main stand looked as though it had been built in two stages, with a newer section added on to the front of the original stand. Ten rows of benches provided 1,276 seats. A curious set of twelve low floodlights pylons, six on each side, was erected around 1960. The fence around the ground was in an oval shape and the standing areas behind the goal were a long way from the pitch, suggesting the ground may have been initially built for greyhound racing or speedway.

HORNCHURCH
Ground: The Stadium, Bridge Avenue, Upminster, Essex.

Hornchurch reached the top of the Conference League South in October 2004 but shortly after lost their main backer, which went bankrupt. Hornchurch were formed as Upminster in 1923 and were elected to the Romford League. They played at the Recreation Ground, now known as Upminster Park. The dressing rooms stood where the local library is now situated and the ground had entrances along a pavement lined by hedges. As the ground was not enclosed, the club experienced difficulties with taking gate money, and this eventually led to them moving to a new stadium in 1952, where they remain today. After four seasons in Spartan League football, they were elected to the Premier Division in 1952, and a year later secured admission to the Delphian League. They reached the semi-final of the Essex Senior Cup in 1956/57, only to be beaten by Grays Athletic, the eventual winners.

The Upminster club merged with local rivals Upminster Wanderers to call themselves Hornchurch & Upminster in 1961. Several years after this they became known as plain

Hornchurch, January 1974. Two rows of wood seats were provided in this tiny structure in front of the dressing rooms. Cover was provided to the left, and a seated stand opposite

Hornchurch. Hornchurch's present home, The Stadium, was built as a council-owned athletics track on the site of an old rubbish tip and opened on 1 November 1952 when Brentwood and Warley were the visitors to Upminster FC. Floodlights were installed at the ground in September 1965. The record attendance at the ground was set in October 1966 when they played Chelmsford City in a FA Cup tie in a fourth qualifying round tie. The club also won the Athenian League Division One title in 1966/67.

Hornchurch joined the Isthmian League Division Two in 1975 and were always in its lower divisions until 2003, when they joined the Premier Division after a couple of seasons of success. They were Third Division runners-up in 2001/02 and Division One (North) runners-up the following season. They also had a good run in the FA Vase during 2000/01 when they reached the fourth round before losing at home to Berkhamsted Town 1-2 in a replay. Up until this time, Hornchurch had been perennial strugglers but were transformed into non-League high fliers after the arrival of new cash-backers at Bridge Avenue in 2001. A well-known double-glazing firm has invested heavily in the club, both on and off the pitch. New seats have been installed in the main stand and a section of covered terracing has been erected, while the former wooden officials' stand has made way for a modern replacement. There are plans to erect a new standing cover on the Bridge Avenue side of the ground. They also plan to upgrade the dressing rooms, convert the clubhouse into a restaurant and introduce a pitch-side sports bar. The club wish to bring the stand closer to the pitch by relocating the athletics track, which currently surrounds the pitch, to land at the south of the Bridge Avenue site. This is presently used for training by both the football and athletics clubs. Havering Council currently owns the ground.

Hornchurch had their best ever run in the FA Cup during 2003/04 when they beat Billericay Town, Carshalton Athletic and Paulton Rovers to reach the first round for the first time. Here they beat Darlington 2-0 at The Stadium but in the next round they lost narrowly 1-0 at home to Tranmere Rovers. They also had an excellent run in the FA Trophy that season and challenged for the Premier League title.

BOB'S FIRST TIME: This was for an Isthmian League Division One clash between Hornchurch and Chesham United on 24 January 1984. The match ended in a 1-1 draw before eighty spectators. The original wooden stand was still in place in front of the dressing rooms and had been built in August 1953. Opposite this was a stand made from asbestos sheeting with four rows of seats and terracing on either side.

HOUNSLOW
Ground: Denbigh Road, Hounslow, Middlesex.

When Hounslow lost its Denbigh Road ground in 1991, to all intents and purposes it was the beginning of the end for the club. Founded as long ago as 1884 after a meeting at the local town hall, the first Hounslow Town club played at a ground called Mr Newman's Field. Besides moving their headquarters from the George Hotel to the Nag's Head, Hounslow laid down a new pitch in Teales' Field in 1887, and for the first time made an admission charge of 2d per person. They secured a better pitch at Platts Field, Lampton Road in 1890, but, finding the rent too high, returned to Teales' Field four years later. The defection of their best player, F.E. Bullock, to Ilford and eventually on to Huddersfield Town and England, and the retirement of their experienced manager, J.H. Saunders, caused the club's fortunes to dwindle, and in 1907 Hounslow closed down.

They started up again in April 1921, competing in the Great Western Suburban League and played home games at a ground at Tiverton Road. Crowds were usually between 500-700 and in September 1927 they negotiated with the local council to use the ground at Denbigh Road and were allowed to enclose the ground so a proper gate could be taken. They joined the Spartan League for 1929/30 and a new stand was built by the council at a cost of £500. The council threw them off the ground for 1934/35 due to non-payment of rent but they were back the following year after a season at the Harlington Corner Stadium. A clubhouse was opened in 1937 and after winning the Spartan League (Western) championship in 1946/47 they joined the Corinthian League.

The record attendance at Denbigh Road was 8,546 for a FA Amateur Cup tie with Wycombe Wanderers in 1953. Hounslow Town reached the FA Cup first round in 1954 but lost to Hastings United 4-2 in a televised match. They joined the Athenian League in 1955/56, but the greatest day in their history came in April 1962 when they reached the final of the FA Amateur Cup, and fought out a 1-1 draw with Crook Town before 43,000 fans at Wembley Stadium. They lost the replay at Ayresome Park, Middlesbrough 4-0. The money from this cup run helped pay for new floodlights in 1965 at a cost of £4,000. Hounslow joined the Southern League in 1977, were relegated to the Hellenic League

Hounslow Town, December 1976. Two thousand five hundred was the stated capacity in the twenty-step covered area. Opposite was a 320-seat stand, with open terraces behind both goals.

in 1984 but returned to the Southern League and stayed there from 1985-87. They were then hit by severe financial problems and ran up huge debts with the local council and a big brewery. Hounslow lost their Denbigh Road home during the summer of 1991, when the local council decided to build a school on the site. This was an impressive but run-down ground at the end with a stand and terraces on three sides. Hounslow owned the lease on the ground until the 1980s, when they had to surrender it to the local council. The club merged with neighbours Feltham and, to all intents and purposes, ceased to exist – although the club was called Feltham & Hounslow Borough until 1994. There is a team called Hounslow Borough playing in the Hellenic League but this is not connected with the former club. This club was previously called Harrow Hill Rovers.

ALEX'S FIRST TIME: This was for a match played on 15 April 1987 between Hounslow and Penhill, which the visitors won by 3-1 before an attendance of 150. It was an impressive if run-down ground with a match played on a bone-hard end-of-season pitch with little grass on it. If you never visited Denbigh Road then you missed a treat.

ILFORD

Grounds: Lynn Road, Newbury Park, Essex. Since 1996: The Cricklefields Athletic Stadium, High Road, Ilford, Essex.

The demise of Ilford's Lynn Road ground was a great loss as it was full of character, including its impressive main stand. Initially called Ilford Alliance in their first two seasons of existence, Ilford FC was founded in 1881. They played at various grounds in the south-west Essex town before moving to the Ilford Sports Ground in 1888, which was located close to the town centre in Wellesley Road. It was a large ground that also housed cycling and athletics facilities. There was little on the site except for a tall gabled pavilion, but it was used during Ilford's two seasons in the Southern League from 1894-96. The club then played in the London League and the South Essex League. Ilford were forced to leave the Sports Ground in 1904 when it was required for new housing, but the club soon found some undeveloped land at Newbury Park to the north of Ilford. They played their first match at Lynn Road, Newbury Park in September 1904, when they beat Clapton 2-1. The newly built stand and dressing rooms were ready for use in November. The stand held 400, but initially did not have a roof, and was situated at the south of the ground. Founder members of the Isthmian League, they won the championship in 1907, 1921 and 1922, and won the London Senior Cup six times. Ilford share with Leyton the time record for FA Cup replays when in 1924/25 the clubs met, in all, five times in a third qualifying round tie that took nine hours and forty minutes to decide; Leyton were the ultimate winners.

The freehold of the ground was obtained in 1922 for £3,000 and a 600-seater stand was erected on the north side of the ground later that year. It had a long low roof supported by many struts. There was a clock on its centre gable, so it became known as the 'Clock Stand'. The original 1904 stand was demolished during the summer of 1928 and was replaced by a much larger structure. This cost £4,250 to build and was constructed by East London building firm W.J. Cearns Ltd. It also contained dressing rooms and a clubroom, with 850 seats in elevated tiers, while the large pitched roof provided cover for 950 standing spectators in a paddock section at the front of the stand. Ilford's greatest hours were in 1928/29 and 1929/30, when they won the FA Amateur Cup and the London Senior Cup twice running. They had a great forward line of Vic Potter, Vic Welsh, Reg Dellow, Fred Drane and George Peploe, with Dellow, Welsh and Peploe each playing for England at amateur level.

A crowd of 13,000 saw England play Luxembourg in an amateur international at Lynn Road in 1948 and other large attendances saw France play India and Yugoslavia against Turkey in Olympic matches at the ground later that year. The record attendance for the Lynn Road Ground came in 1952 when 16,400 spectators watched the final of the English Schools Trophy between Ilford Schools and Swansea Schools. Ilford returned to prominence again in 1957/58 when they reached the Amateur Cup final only to be beaten 3-0 by Woking at Wembley after a terrifically hard fight. In reaching the final they defeated Eastbourne 2-1 at home, Bungay Town 4-0 away, Wycombe Wanderers 2-1, Vauxhall Motors 3-0 at Ilford and Crook Town 1-0 in the semi-final at Sunderland.

Most of the banking around the ground had been concreted by 1951, giving Newbury Park an 18,000 capacity with 1,400 seats. The covered accommodation was increased when a roof was erected over the terracing at the Ley Street end in 1957. Floodlights were introduced in 1962 and the ground retained the white wicket fencing that spanned the four sides of the ground until its demise. The last big match at Lynn Road took place in November 1974 against Southend United in the FA Cup, before a crowd of 3,500. The crisis came following Ilford's relegation from the Premier Division in 1977. It was then that the Lynn Road ground was sold off to developers. The main stand was dismantled ready for transportation to the new site and the 'clock stand' was put up for sale. The ground fell into disrepair and was eventually built on.

Ilford, September 1972. Six rows of wood benches were provided in the smaller stand at Ilford. Opposite was an imposing structure with twenty rows of seats. All sides of the ground had concrete or wood terracing with one end covered.

Ilford shared with Walthamstow Avenue during 1977/78, then Leytonstone for 1978/79. Ilford eventually amalgamated with their tenants to become Leytonstone/Ilford FC. They played at Leytonstone's Granleigh Road for a number of seasons when their proposed ambitious new complex near Fairlop failed to materialise. The club was eventually swallowed up into the club that is now Dagenham & Redbridge (See Leytonstone, Walthamstow Avenue & Dagenham).

Ilford reformed in 1987 and joined the London Spartan League Division One the following year. They had a nomadic existence until they moved to the Cricklefield Athletics Stadium in 1989. They were playing in the Essex Senior League at this time. Prior to this, they had played at the grounds of East Ham United and Barking. A grandstand with 221 new tip-up seats and some terracing was built opposite the stand on the renovated ground. The ground, which is just off Ilford High Road and opposite the Cauliflower public house, has had its problems – at one time the pitch was too short and the dressing rooms were 100 metres from the pitch. These difficulties were remedied by money from the Lottery funds.

BOB'S FIRST TIME: Bob never saw a match at Lynn Road but did visit it on 16 September 1972. It was one of the most impressive non-League grounds in London. The Herbert Dunnice Memorial gates brought you in behind the main stand and dressing rooms. This towering structure had twenty rows of seats. Opposite this was a smaller stand with six rows of benches. Behind one goal was a ten-step covered terrace and at the opposite end were ten concrete steps plus six wooden ones. Bob saw the newly reformed Ilford play their first match at the Cricklefield Stadium on 25 October 1989 when 204 spectators saw Ilford lose 1-0 to Walthamstow Trojans in the Spartan League.

Kingsbury Town, February 1974. Eighty spectators were catered for on four rows of benches. By 2004 the stand had been extended both ways to hold 160, and a little bit of cover erected behind one goal

KINGSBURY TOWN
Ground: Silver Jubilee Park, Townsend Lane, Kingsbury, London NW9.

Kingsbury Town were founded under the name of Davis Sports in 1927 and made steady progress in junior football, winning Division Two of the Willesden & District League. They were elected to the Middlesex Senior League in 1943, winning the League's Charity Cup in three successive seasons, and were then elected to the Parthenon League in 1949, when that competition expanded. They became champions in 1951/52 and won the league title again the following season. Kingsbury played for many years without much success and in 1967 they disbanded to amalgamate with another local side to form Kingsbury Town FC. They played in the Spartan League before joining the Athenian League in the early 1970s. However, they returned to the London Spartan League in 1978 after a few unsuccessful seasons and they spent another three years at this level before rejoining the Athenian League in 1981. Kingsbury Town joined the newly created Vauxhall (Isthmian) League Division Two (North) in 1984 and finished in seventeenth place at the end of this first season, but twelve months later were promoted as runners-up to Stevenage Borough, just one point behind the champions and 15 points clear of Heybridge Swifts, who finished in third place.

Kingsbury ran into problems in 1986 when the Isthmian League closed their ground for a while. It has a surprisingly rural feel, despite being in the middle of a heavily built-up area. The Silver Jubilee Park is fenced/hedged off and has all of its facilities along one side of the ground. It is not clear when the club first moved to the site but 1943 and 1952 have both been mentioned. The area was used as an anti-aircraft station and the Nissen huts left over were used for changing rooms until one of them burned down. The ground had a small amount of cover, which eventually blew down in the 1970s and was subsequently rebuilt and lengthened in 1978. The focal point of the ground is the brick-built clubhouse that was erected during the 1970s. The playing surface is enclosed by a post and rail, which, due to Isthmian League regulations, is infilled by a red fence, but the grassy banks are not concreted. A record crowd of 1,500 watched a friendly with Tottenham Hotspur in 1980, to mark the switching-on of new floodlights. Four years later a new 200-seat stand was built. A concrete walkway was added in 1985, terracing was built behind each goal in 1987 and the stand was reroofed in 1989. Brent Council owns the ground, which remains a fairly basic arena.

BOB'S FIRST TIME: This was on 28 September 1982 when Kingsbury Town played Ruislip Manor in an Athenian League match. Kingsbury won 2-0 before an attendance of ninety. The facilities were all on one side of the ground with a seventy-five-seat stand and a small cover adjacent to the social club and dressing room complex.

KINGSTONIAN/AFC WIMBLEDON
Grounds: Kingsmeadow Stadium, Kingston Road, Norbiton, Surrey.

The present Kingstonian FC were formed in 1919 after an amalgamation of the Old Kingstonians and Kingston Town. Kingstonian's history dates back to 1885 through these two clubs. The club was called Kingston and Surbiton YMCA Football Club when it was founded. It was renamed the 'Saxons' in its third season. The name changed again in 1890 to Kingston Wanderers, but after just three years it changed again to Kingston-upon-Thames AFC. After they moved from their first ground at Dinton Road to the pitch where the reserves played in the 1950s at Richmond Road; a split occurred, and the local enthusiasts had their choice on Saturdays of watching either 'Kingston Town' or 'Old Kingstonians' (with headquarters at Norbiton). The original ground was close to what was to become the East Surrey Barracks sports ground.

The club had crossed the road in 1919 and was playing on the second ground at Richmond Road – that boasted a pavilion. As the land had previously been used for allotments, much work was needed to prepare the pitch. Rumours abounded that Kingstonian had folded when at the end of the 1919/20 season the ground was leased to Leyland Motors. A ground-share agreement did not work out and eventually Kingstonian bought the field next door, and later the original ground, for a combined sum of £5,000. A timber stand was erected, and opened by the Lord Mayor in January 1922, and soon after a wooden perimeter fence went up around the pitch. The banking, which was later to be converted into concrete terracing, was built, and dressing rooms and an addition to the stand were in place by 1926. The latter was purchased from the Surbiton Horse Show Society in the county and built on the end of the main stand, where it remained until the end.

The club secured admission to the Athenian League only to finish twice at the bottom of the table. Their fortunes, however, took a turn for the better, and in 1923/24 they won the championship and topped the table again in 1925/26 with a record number of points. Their greatest achievement was in 1933, when they won the FA Amateur Cup. They beat Portland, Leyton, South Bank, Dulwich Hamlet, and Whitehall Printeries (3-0) in the semi-final played at the West Ham Stadium. They beat Stockton in the final, after drawing 1-1 at Champion Hill, when they won the replay at Darlington, 4-1.

Kingstonian were also Isthmian League champions in 1933/34 and 1936/37. By the mid-1960s floodlights had been in use for some while, and new dressing rooms were in place for the match officials. The final structure of any significance to go up was Kingstonian's third clubhouse, which was placed behind one of the goals instead of terracing. Crowds of up to 5,000 were regular occurrences in the 1940s and 1950s but the only honour that came the club's way in these years was the Surrey Senior Cup, which they won by beating Walton & Hersham at Selhurst Park in 1952, after being beaten by Dulwich Hamlet in the final two seasons previously. The ground-record attendance was set in 1955 when 11,000 attended for an Amateur Cup tie against Bishop Auckland.

Covered terraces were put in on the Latchmere Road side in 1957 and floodlights erected in 1961. With the ground beginning to show its age, and with the prospect of a financial windfall on its sale, Richmond Road was sold for redevelopment and the funds were used to build a brand new arena. The wooden stand had become a potential fire hazard by this time and the last game at the ground was in January 1988 against old rivals Bromley, which attracted 1,126 people. After a year-and-a-half at Hampton, they moved to their new Kingsmeadow Stadium at nearby Norbiton. The new ground was built on the site of the old Norbiton Road Sports Ground and was opened for a league match against Slough Town in August 1989. The stand houses most of the clubrooms, bars, restaurants, changing rooms etc. The rest of the ground is very flat with the bare minimum of elevation to the terracing, making it extremely uncomfortable if faced with a large crowd. However, there have been some improvements made to the terraced areas since the ground was built, especially behind the goal at the Surbiton end of the venue. The record attendance for the new ground

Kingstonian, January 1988. The main stand at Richmond Road held about 1,120 spectators. The middle section was opened in 1922. The bit on the right was obtained from the Surbiton Horse Society in 1925/26. Opposite was a covered shelter erected in 1957. (Photograph by Alex White)

is 4,582 for a pre-season friendly with Chelsea on 22 July 1995. Due to massive financial difficulties, Kingstonian were forced to sell their ground to the newly emerging AFC Wimbledon in 2003 and then became their tenants.

ALEX'S FIRST TIME (Richmond Road): I visited the old ground in September 1983 when barely 150 spectators paid to watch an Isthmian League match with Tilbury. I also attended the last match at the ground when Bromley were the visitors in January 1988. I was a student in Kingston for three years during the 1970s but never visited the ground – although I wish I had as it had old world charm, especially as regards the pitch-length wooden stands. (Kingsmeadow): I visited the new ground for the first time on 7 November 1989 to see the K's beat Bromley 4-2 before a crowd of 350. It wasn't the same as their former ground but had a pleasant atmosphere and the clubhouse was big and inviting.

LEYTON
Ground: Hare & Hounds Ground, Lea Bridge Road, Leyton, London E10.

Leyton are the oldest football club in London and the second-oldest surviving amateur club in the country. Their history is complicated and the reader should also see the sections on Leyton Wingate, Leyton (Waltham) Pennant and Wingate & Finchley for a fuller story. This section looks at the club up until 1975 when they amalgamated with the Wingate club to become Leyton Wingate.

Leyton FC was formed in 1868 as the Matlock Swifts and first made their mark in amateur football in the early 1890s. They achieved senior status in 1895 and they went on to win the Essex Senior Cup four times in five years and they also the London Senior Cup in 1903/04.

Leyton, March 1972. The wood cover with six concrete steps disappeared about a year later. By 2002 a steel-covered terrace had been built, while opposite were two seated stands and a covered area used as a store for tip-up seats.

The club moved around a lot in their early days. They initially played at Lea Bridge Road, Church Road and the Recreation Ground. They moved to Blackhorse lane in 1894, the Essex County Cricket Ground in 1895, Hainhault Road in 1897 and the Hare & Hounds Ground in 1901 before moving to Osborne Road four years later. The club turned professional after this and played in the Southern League alongside the likes of Fulham, Tottenham Hotspur and West Ham United. During this period the great footballer Charles Buchan, who later appeared for England, Sunderland and Arsenal, played for Leyton. They played at the Army Sports Ground before the First World War. Immediately after the war the club returned to amateur status and secured admission to the London League soon afterwards. They were champions of the London League for three successive seasons. In 1926/27, Leyton won the FA Amateur Cup for the first time by beating Barking Town 3-1 in the final at The Den. The following season Leyton, now members of the Athenian League, again won the Amateur Cup, beating North-East miners side Cockfield 3-2 at Middlesbrough's Ayresome Park. The following year they reached the final for the third successive time, this time losing to Ilford 3-1 at Highbury. Leyton also become the first amateur club to reach the final of the London Challenge Cup in 1929 and in the following year carried off the Athenian League championship for the first time. In the 1930s, Leyton reached the Amateur Cup final on two further occasions, losing both times to Dulwich Hamlet: 2-1 in 1934 and 3-1 in 1937.

Leyton were playing at the Osborne Road Ground (now called Brisbane Road) during this spell. They had secured the lease on the ground in 1930 from the council, and it was a stunning blow, at the end of 1936/37, when they were informed that the license would not be renewed and Clapton Orient would take over the ground from Leyton. Their neighbours, Walthamstow Avenue, came to the rescue, and allowed them to share their ground for a while, but afterwards Leyton led a nomadic existence until they settled down at the Lea Bridge Road Ground. Even then their troubles were not over. In 1950/51 it was decided that the Hare & Hounds pitch was not up to Athenian standards and Leyton had to play all their league games on away grounds, finishing the season at the bottom of the table. Fortunately, their landlords had contracted to drain, raise and improve the pitch and the committee set about restoring the club's fortunes.

After playing through the extra preliminary and qualifying rounds, Leyton appeared at Wembley in the Amateur Cup final of 1952 in front of 100,000 spectators. After beating Barnet in the semi-final at Tottenham they lost to local rivals Walthamstow Avenue 2-1 in the final. Leyton also won the Athenian League championship twice. Celebrating their centenary during 1968/69, Leyton were honoured with a congratulatory telegram from The Queen and were presented with an illuminated address by the Football Association. The club's financial problems began in the late 1960s and became even worse during the early 1970s. While Leyton enjoyed reasonably good playing facilities at the Hare & Hounds, costs were rising so rapidly that they nearly folded. The merger of Leyton and Wingate to become Leyton Wingate FC saved the club. A new club called Leyton, formed in 1999, occupied the Hare & Hounds ground again. They initially played in the Essex Senior League but joined the Isthmian League Third Division recently. They bought many of the seats from the old Wembley Stadium and plan to make a number of improvements to the ground.

LEYTON ORIENT
Ground: Leyton Stadium, Brisbane Road, Leyton, London E10.

Leyton Orient have been perennial strugglers and have had to fight hard to gain supporters from neighbours Arsenal, Tottenham and West Ham. They were in the top flight for only one season, 1962/63. Otherwise they have mainly struggled in the lower reaches. The club was formed in 1888 as the football section of Glyn Cricket Club (founded in 1881). One of its members suggested the name Orient as he worked for the Orient Steam Navigation Company and this was adopted. Orient's first ground was a field just off Glyn Road, but they moved to a ground at Pond Land Bridge in the early 1890s. They lost this venue when it became an electricity sub-station. They moved to an adjacent field owned by Whittles Firework Company, which after it was enclosed became known as the Whittles Athletic Ground in 1896 as the club joined the London League. Facilities were very basic and two carriages were purchased and used as dressing rooms.

The club changed its name to Clapton Orient in 1898. The ground was renamed as the Millfields Road Ground in 1902 and the club turned professional in November 1903. Considerable work was needed to improve the arena at Millfields Road after Orient's entry into the Football League in 1905. As a consequence, there were improvements to the dressing rooms and new terracing installed. A grandstand was built – but not completed until 1906 – and consisted of a narrow seated enclosure alongside Millfields Road. Opposite to where the main grandstand was later built, a large section of banking was erected to increase the ground's capacity. This was called the 'Spion Kop'. The pitch was well drained and one of the best in London. It was enclosed by neat wooden fencing. The terracing was wooden blocks that held clinker that came from the nearby electric power station. Two hundred new tip-up seats were installed in the grandstand in August 1914 and, in 1923, the board made a decision to purchase a new grandstand that held almost 3,000 spectators, valued at £30,000. Unfortunately, they struggled to pay off this large debt as attendances began to dwindle. This grandstand was situated opposite the 'Spion Kop' on the north side, where concrete terracing was also laid. To make the ground look more attractive, flowerbeds were planted around the pitch. The old stand that the new grandstand replaced was sold to Wimbledon FC and was still in use in the 1990s at Plough Lane.

A greyhound-racing syndicate bought the lease of the ground and dog racing began over Easter 1927. Unfortunately, problems soon arose between the two companies and the football club was to come off worse. There were problems concerning the dog track encroaching on corners of the football pitch. The O's were also unable to use the stadium for training purposes or use the boardroom on match days. Things came to a head in 1930 when the football club decided to leave Millfields Road. The Clapton Greyhound Stadium at Millfields Road eventually closed in December 1973 and was pulled down and replaced by houses. The ground had experienced its record crowd on 16 March 1929 when 37,615 attended a match with Tottenham Hotspur.

The club had difficulties finding a new venue to play at, but eventually found a site close to Lea Bridge Station that was overlooked by a railway track, just half a mile from Millfields. This ground was a bleak, soulless enclosure and used by the local speedway club; it was not really suitable as a football venue. It was oval in shape with wooden

Leyton Orient, July 1979. The main stand held 3,960 on eighteen rows of tip-up seats. Opposite was a covered terrace the length of the pitch. Both ends were open terracing

fencing around and in need of refurbishment. Its stands were closer to the goal line than the halfway line, which gave the stadium a lop-sided appearance. Lea Bridge's capacity was just over 20,000, with room for 4,000 under cover. It was not long before Orient ran into problems at their new ground and, after playing Torquay United on 8 November 1930, the opposition's directors complained that the wooden fence was too close to the touchline. Football League officials soon inspected the ground and ordered Orient to make immediate alterations to the dimensions of the pitch. The O's had to play their games at other venues – including two home League matches being played at Wembley Stadium and a FA Cup tie at Highbury. More problems arose when Millwall visited Lea Bridge for a League fixture on 13 March 1937. It could have been a disaster as a massive crowd arrived and many spectators broke into the ground without paying. The ground was clearly not good enough to cope with such a large crowd. The club decided to leave Lea Bridge and when they were offered the lease on the Brisbane Road enclosure, they took it, forcing its existing incumbents Leyton FC to seek pastures new. The Lea Bridge ground disappeared completely a few years later and factories now stand upon the site.

Orient played their first League match at Brisbane Road on 28 August 1937 against Cardiff City. Leyton FC had used the ground from September 1905 to 1914 and from 1929 to 1937 and it was also the sports ground of the Bryant & May Co. Ltd during the 1920s. When Orient moved to Brisbane Road the ground was commonly known as Osborne Road. The stadium was in need of improvement and repair but the first improvements did not arrive until 1949, when the large grassy hill, which was at the side of Orient's small stand and laid slightly back, was levelled and crush barriers were added to the west stand and behind each goal. A running track was added around the pitch in 1951. Terracing at the Coronation Gardens end was improved and extended for the big FA Cup clash against Arsenal in 1952, and the terracing behind the goal had further extensions, in 1959 and in 1960. The whole of the west stand terracing was improved in 1962, when smaller steps were made. The small stand held only 475 spectators and was affectionately known as 'The Orange Box'. It had stood for over fifty years when it was dismantled in 1956. The present one, bought from the derelict Mitcham Stadium (next to Tooting & Mitcham United's ground at Sandy Lane), was erected the same year, although the final wing was not added until 1962. This wing created an additional 900 seats for spectators, bringing the seating total to about 3,500.

The floodlights were first installed in 1960 and the first official match under them was the game against Brighton on 31 August. A concrete wall replaced the former wooden one in 1952. Many turnstiles have been replaced over the years and the enclosing of the back of the Main Stand was completed in 1963. The west stand area was converted into an all-seating enclosure in 1978. Work was due to start on a new stand on the Coronation Gardens end of the ground in 1996 but was halted whilst archaeologists excavated a Bronze Age settlement (3,500BC) found when the original terraces were removed. The new stand was eventually completed in 1999 and had 1,336 seats for spectators.

Orient negotiated a 125-year lease on the ground with Waltham Council in 2000 at a cost of £350,000. This enabled them to make long-term improvements. During the summer of 2003, Orient had plans approved for the redevelopment of Brisbane Road at a cost of £10m. The proposal is for 103 flats to be built on the four corners of the ground and the north terrace and west stand will be replaced with all-seater stands.

The overall record crowd for Brisbane Road was for an FA Cup tie against West Ham United on 25 January 1964, when 34,345 crammed inside, but this was almost broken on 2 May 1972, when promotion-bound Birmingham City beat Orient 1-0 before an official attendance of 33,383. This is unlikely to ever be beaten due to new safety regulations.

ALEX'S FIRST TIME: Fulham had just been relegated for the second season in succession from the First to the Third Division. On 13 August 1969 they paid a visit to Brisbane Road to play Orient in a Football League Cup first-round tie. The game ended in a goal-less draw before 8,636 spectators with Ray Goodard, a former Fulham apprentice goalkeeper, having an outstanding match for the O's.

LEYTONSTONE
Ground: Granleigh Road, Leytonstone, London E11.

The Leytonstone club was founded in 1886 and until 1894 were known as The Cedars, after the trees at the corner of Davies Lane, Leytonstone. It was after six very successful seasons that they changed their name to Leytonstone FC, and became affiliated to the

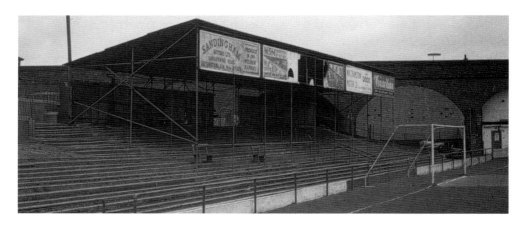

Leytonstone, March 1972. The larger of the two covered ends at this three-and-a-half-sided ground had twenty-five concrete steps. To the right, above a sixteen-step terrace, was the main stand which held 370 on six rows of seats. Opposite the main stand along half the pitch was a terrace and tiny stand with a capacity of six.

London Football Association. Leytonstone played at Granleigh Road from 1894, which was situated next to Leytonstone High Road station. It became a compact three-sided ground, located underneath a high-level railway station and surrounded by gardens belonging to local houses.

After a season in the Spartan League, Leytonstone were invited in 1908 to join the Isthmian League, bringing that competition up to ten clubs. Leytonstone did not succeed in winning the Isthmian League championship until 1937/38, although they were runners-up in 1909, 1911, 1913 and 1933. They retained the title the following season. After losing to Bishop Auckland in the semi-final of the 1939 Amateur Cup, (going down 2-1 in a replay at Darlington), Leytonstone won the Amateur Cup for the first time in 1946/47 when they narrowly defeated Wimbledon 2-1 in the final at Highbury before 47,000 fans. Wimbledon took the lead through Stannard but Noble and Smith scored for Leytonstone before half-time and these proved to be the winning goals. They retained the trophy the following season, this time beating Barnet 1-0, thanks to a goal from Groves, at Stamford Bridge before another excellent crowd of 59,605. In 1949/50 they reached the second round of the FA Cup by beating professionals Watford 2-1. The record crowd at Granleigh Road came in 1951 for a FA Cup second-round tie against Newport County, when somehow 9,740 squeezed into the ground. It seems incredible that such a crowd could fit into such a cramped venue, but the terracing which stretched behind both goals and in front of the grandstand was deceptively spacious. They won the Amateur Cup final again, this time at Wembley in 1968, by beating Chesham United 1-0 before a crowd of 52,000 after losing in semi-finals in 1958, 1961 and 1963. On top of this, they were also Isthmian League champions five times between 1946 and 1952 and again in 1965/66. The club went into decline during the 1970s and one of the few highlights was reaching the FA Cup first round again in 1973, where they lost at Hendon 3-0.

The club was badly hit by financial problems and, after amalgamating with another declining club, Ilford, they became known as Leytonstone & Ilford in 1979. Ilford's Lynn Road Ground was sold to alleviate the financial worries. The new club gained promotion at the first attempt back to the Premier Division when they became champions in 1979/80. They did very well for a time and were Isthmian Premier champions in 1982/83 and runners-up the following season. Leytonstone/Ilford were on the move again when they absorbed the debt-ridden Walthamstow Avenue in 1988, taking over their Green Pond Road Ground (see Walthamstow Avenue & Dagenham & Redbridge). Sadly, the Granleigh Road ground was sold for redevelopment. They won the Isthmian League again in 1988/89 but were denied promotion to the Conference due to ground problems. The solution was to move to Dagenham's Victoria Park Ground and to be renamed Redbridge Forest. So, in the course of ten years, three clubs had disappeared and three historic football grounds had become housing estates in east London when Walthamstow Avenue's Green Pond Road Ground was also sold for housing development.

ALEX'S FIRST TIME: I visited the unique Granleigh Road on 12 November 1985 for an Isthmian League Division One match between Leytonstone and Bromley. A paltry crowd of only 120 saw the home team win 3-0. If I remember correctly, the only part of the ground open to spectators was in front of the main stand that sat on top of about fifteen steps of terracing. There was terracing behind each goal but nothing opposite the main stand, which backed onto a railway viaduct.

LEYTON WINGATE
Ground: The Hare & Hounds Ground, Lea Bridge Road, Leyton, London E10.

This is the second part of the long and complicated history of Leyton FC. Leyton Wingate FC was formed from an amalgamation of Leyton FC and Wingate FC in 1975. The merger meant that they would use Leyton's Hare & Hounds Ground and the fresh financial impetus came from Wingate FC (see sections of Leyton and Wingate & Finchley). The first season was undistinguished but a great deal was achieved within the environs of The Hare & Hounds Ground. Wingate obtained the freehold of The Hare & Hounds Ground and were able to make improvements to its facilities. With the purchase of the ground completed in 1976 it was decided to rename it the Wingate-Leyton Stadium. The erection of new dressing rooms was the first step. However, disaster struck when the clubhouse was destroyed by fire in August 1976. With the minimal insurance money plus a great deal of effort the club managed to create a new clubhouse with greatly improved facilities.

Leyton Wingate won the Athenian League title in 1976/77 and were semi-finalists in the London Senior Cup. Ground improvements continued and after the removal of several thousand tons of wartime rubble, a modest car park was created within the ground. They won the Athenian League again in 1981/82, this time being unbeaten in the competition with 28 wins and 8 draws, and the club was elected to the Second Division of the Isthmian League. Leyton Wingate became Second Division (North) champions in 1984/85. The following season they reached the FA Cup first round proper before losing to Swansea City 2-0 at Vetch Field and soon afterwards new floodlights were installed. New terraces and a wall were built at the Seymour Road end and a new covered stand was erected in 1987.

In later years the club became increasingly frustrated with being unable to improve The Hare & Hounds Ground to their liking when planning permission was not given for other improvements due to lack of access to the site. In 1991, they made the decision to amalgamate with Finchley and move to their Summers Lane ground (see Wingate & Finchley). Leyton continued to play at the Wingate-Leyton (Hare & Hounds) Stadium after the departure of the Wingate club. When near-neighbours Leyton FC and Walthamstow Pennant decided to merge during the 1994/95 season, it was yet another move in the very complicated history of the Leyton club. Walthamstow Pennant were denied a place in the Isthmian League when a proposed groundshare at Leyton-Wingate was rejected as The Hare & Hounds Ground no longer met the league's new ground standards. Leyton FC lacked the funds to bring it up to scratch but Walthamstow Pennant's ground met these regulations so the two clubs merged and played at Pennant's Wadham Lodge arena (see Waltham Forest).

ALEX'S FIRST TIME: This was for an Isthmian League Division One fixture between Leyton Wingate and Wembley on 31 January 1987. All the facilities, including three stands, were on one side of the ground. On the other three sides there was barely room to walk around the pitch.

LONDON CALEDONIANS
Ground: Huddlestone Road, Tufnell Park, London N7.

London Caledonians were founded in Fleet Street at a meeting in Anderton's Hotel called by Hugh Scott MacPherson in 1886. All players had to be Scottish by birth or parentage. They had a hard struggle in their early days as they failed to attract local support, although they had some fine players. They usually won games at their first ground – playing fields that were part of Elm Farm, Walthamstow. They moved to the Essex County Cricket Ground, Leyton in 1889 but support was very poor. They beat past-FA Cup winners Blackburn Olympic and also beat Crouch End at Leyton to take the Middlesex Senior Cup for the first time.

They decided to try their luck in South London and moved to a ground next to the Greyhound public house at Dulwich Village in 1891. They brought Aston Villa to play at Dulwich: the bait of a £15 guarantee was considered most substantial in those days, but alas, the gate was only £14 9s 6d. After only one season they migrated back to North London to play at Tufnell Park, where they shared the ground with the Casuals for a while. There was a colony of Scots living in the area and this helped to improve crowds. Many of the club's players were Scots and one of these was John Lambie, who joined

London Caledonians, July 1974. Probably situated behind the goal and near the corner flag, the stand provided seating on ten rows of planks.

the club from Queens Park, where he had become a Scottish international. The ground was often waterlogged in those days, which caused havoc with their fixture list.

After a dispute between the club and the ground owners, they decided to seek pastures new in 1894. They moved to a piece of wasteland on the opposite side of the railway from the Tufnell Park ground. This was quickly converted into a football arena and was called Caledonian Park. With rumours that the ground was about to be built upon, the club returned to Tufnell Park in 1898. They had one brief interlude as the tenants of Barking at Vicarage Field during 1900/01, which was not a success, before returning to Tufnell Park the following season. The Calies remained amateurs throughout their history and became original members of the Isthmian League in 1905, along with Clapton, Casuals, Civil Service, Ealing and Ilford. They also shared their ground with the newly formed Tufnell Park Football Club from 1905. They were the new competition's first champions and also won the title in 1907/08 and three seasons on the trot between 1912 and 1914. They reached the first round of the English (FA) Cup in 1912/13 after beating two professional clubs, Chatham and Shrewsbury Town. They lost at Wolves 3-1 but were never outclassed. As a reward they were excused the qualifying rounds the following season and visited Huddersfield Town in the first round but lost this time 3-0.

Most of the players joined up at the start of the First World War, many enlisting with the London Scottish Regiment, so the club closed down for the duration. They had to build a new team in 1919, as only five players who played before the war were now available. They won the 1923 FA Amateur Cup final when they beat Evesham Town 2-1 (after extra time) at the Crystal Palace grounds before 14,132 spectators. They had beaten Slough 10-2 in round one, then R.A.M.C. (Aldershot), Summerstown and Ilford before beating St Albans 2-0 in the semi-final at Kenilworth Road, Luton. Jimmy McCubbin hit the winning goal with a twenty-five-yard drive, five minutes into extra time. They reached the first round of the FA Cup three times during the 1920s and were also runners-up of the Isthmian League four times. The club went into decline during the 1930s and after losing the Tufnell Park ground in 1938, the Calies initially shared Barking's Vicarage Field and also played at the Park Royal Stadium (QPR's former ground) during 1938/39, but left the Isthmian League when they were unable to find their own ground after the Second World War and did not appear again. The club was still registered with the FA in 1960.

Metropolitan Police, April 1976. The stand provided 672 seats on six rows of benches. By 1989 a steel-covered terrace had been built behind one goal.

METROPOLITAN POLICE

Ground: The Metropolitan Police Sports Ground, Imber Court, East Molesey, Surrey.

The Metropolitan Police Football Club was formed in 1919, playing friendly matches until joining the Spartan League in 1928 where they played, except for the war years, until 1960. The timber-and-steel main stand that was constructed in 1923 was doubled in size in 1934 for the additional cost of £265. During the Spartan League years, the Met Police were league champions eight times, runners-up once and League Cup winners once. They joined the Metropolitan League in 1960 and often played against Football League clubs' 'A' teams. They won the League Cup in 1969. The football ground did not really start to develop until the 1960s, when a wooden fence replaced the canvas sheet that enclosed the ground, enabling them to take a gate. This was subsequently replaced in 1973 by a tall concrete wall that completely closed off the playing area. The Blues stepped up into the Southern League in 1971, playing in the South Division under team manager Vic Rouse, the former Wales and Crystal Palace goalkeeper. Three floodlight pylons were erected in 1971, but due to the proximity of a cricket square a fourth could not be put in place. The fourth pylon was only finally added in 1993.

The Met Police moved to the Isthmian League in 1977, becoming one of the founder members of the restructured Division Two. A successful first season in 1977/78 resulted in the club finishing runners-up to Epsom & Ewell and being promoted to Division One. The club finished third in Division One in 1981/82, missing promotion by just two points. Five turnstiles were constructed in 1984 and placed at opposite ends of the ground, while substantial terracing was built around three sides at this time. The terrace at the Mounted Branch End was covered by a concrete cantilever roof in 1988.

The club finished third from the bottom and were relegated to Division Two (South) in 1984/85 despite experiencing their best FA Cup run that season, reaching the first round proper where they lost at Imber Court to Dartford. The Met again reached the first round proper of the FA Cup, losing 2-0 to Crawley Town, in 1993/94. After the Bradford fire disaster in 1985, the main stand's days were numbered due to its wooden construction and the club had no choice but to replace it. The new structure was slightly smaller and holds 284 people. This was completed in fourteen weeks during the close season of 1994 and cost £123,000 to construct. The new stand was opened as part of the club's seventy-fifth anniversary celebration with a representative game against the Army.

The club finished in the bottom two of the newly formed Division One (South) in 2002/03 but were saved from relegation when Combined Counties League side Withdean 2000 failed to gain entry into the Isthmian League due their ground situation. In a hastily arranged play-off between the second from bottom sides in Division One (North) and Division One (South), the Met beat Wembley in the two-legged play-off 6-2 on aggregate to preserve their status in Division One (South).

ALEX'S FIRST TIME: Imber Court always seems to be in immaculate condition and the pitch is one of the best in non-League soccer. Their games are rarely postponed and when everything else is called off you can usually rely on finding a game on there. I visited the venue for the first time on 14 August 1984 for a pre-season friendly against Fulham. The Met put up a good fight and lost narrowly 4-3, despite Fulham including four present and future internationals in their side. These were Paul Parker, Gerry Peyton, Gordon Davies and Jeff Hopkins.

MILLWALL
Ground: The Den, Senegal Fields, Zampa Road, Bermondsey, London SE16.

Millwall's grounds have been intimidating places to visit for away fans over the years. The club's supporters are well-known for their chants of 'no-one likes us but we don't care' and even in the 1890s their crowds gained a reputation for rowdy and sometimes violent behaviour. Millwall started life playing on the Isle of Dogs, which is north of the river Thames, but the club moved south of the river in 1910 to New Cross. The club was called Millwall Rovers when it was formed in 1885, and their first ground was a piece of waste ground at Glengall Road. The ground had no facilities or an enclosure fence. Glengall Road is now called Tiller Road and a modern housing estate is built over the area. The club moved to a field further south on the island and located behind the Lord Nelson public house in East Ferry Road in 1886. This ground had no facilities and the club stayed four years before another move – the Lord Nelson ground was due to be built over so the club moved again to their first proper enclosed ground. The new enclosure was opposite Millwall Dock Station and was again in East Ferry Road. It covered twenty-seven acres. Club members set about making changes and spent £400 on the ground.

They drained the ground and levelled the pitch and it was ready for use by to the start of 1890/91. On the west (East Ferry Road) side, a 500-seater stand was built along with some dressing rooms. A running track and some banking was laid around the ground. It was officially opened with a cycle meeting on 28 June 1890 and the first football match took place on 6 September between Millwall Athletic and London Caledonians. The visit of Woolwich Arsenal attracted a crowd of over 14,000 on 19 November 1892, with the gate money totalling £342. Millwall became one of the first teams in the South to become professional in 1893, becoming founder members of the Southern League in 1894, and winning the title in the inaugural season without losing a match. The club did not accept an invitation to join the Football League due to travelling expenses, a decision they would regret a few years later. They received notice to quit the East Ferry Road ground in 1901 when the Millwall Docks Company, who owned the land, wanted to build a timber yard on the site.

Millwall Athletic had to find a new ground quickly and, due to their poor financial state, had little money with which to do it. A field was found, about midway between the earlier Lord Nelson site and their previous ground. This ground became known as the North Greenwich ground. When they took over the site it was little more than a field for grazing cattle. Only a seven-year lease was granted to Millwall, so they decided not to spend much money on facilities at the ground. A 'Save Millwall Fund' helped raise enough money to convert it into something like a football venue. Terraces were created, a 500-capacity stand was built, the pitch levelled and a narrow band of open seating that stretched almost the full pitch length was built opposite the stand. A moveable terrace that had been used for Queen Victoria's Jubilee in Poplar Park was placed behind the railway end. The dressing rooms were nothing better than old sheds and at the beginning there was no water supply to the ground. The North Greenwich ground was opened in September 1902 with a friendly match against Aston Villa, and Portsmouth visited three days later for a Southern League fixture before a healthy attendance.

The average gate had risen to around 6,000 by 1909/10 when rumours began to circulate that Millwall were planning to move to a new ground across the river Thames, where they felt they could attract better crowds. Many fans were not happy about the move but the club decided to depart to New Cross anyway. Work on the new venue at Cold Blow Lane, New Cross was not completed on time but on 29 October 1910, Brighton became the first visitors to The Den, attracting an attendance of close to 25,000. The North Greenwich ground was beside the present Docklands Light Railway but most traces of it have long since disappeared except for an embankment, complete with some timber railway sleepers, which remained in place until the early 1990s. This was the standing area at the railway end. The new ground was developed from farmland and surrounded by railway lines. It was built at an estimated cost of £10,000 and was designed by the famous football ground architect Archibald Leitch. The capacity was estimated at 36,000 and was later increased to 40,000 with 3,500 seats. The Duke of York

Millwall, March 1981. The main stand held about 3,200. Around the rest of the ground was terracing with cover at the top on all three sides.

(later King George VI) visited the Den on 8 May 1924 and again on 1 May 1930 to watch charity matches. The record attendance of 48,672 was set on 20 February 1937, for a FA Cup fifth-round tie with Derby County. The first main grandstand at The Den was destroyed by fire after the London Senior Cup final on 26 April 1943. A bomb also badly damaged terracing opposite the stand and the Lions were forced to play home games at The Valley, Upton Park and Selhurst Park during the Second World War. Due to post-war building restrictions, Millwall found it difficult to start work on rebuilding the stand.

Millwall bought the freehold on the ground in December 1951 for £30,000. The club's first floodlights arrived in 1953 and were officially switched on for a friendly game against Manchester United on 5 October. New lights were installed in the summer of 1967. The intimidating atmosphere at The Den helped Millwall establish a record of 59 successive home League games without defeat from 1964-67. The Den also became the first ground to stage a League match on a Sunday, on 20 January 1974 against Fulham. After the closure and removal of the freight railway lines that ran close to The Den, Millwall FC were able to improve access to all areas of the ground. The main stand had seats for 3,500 spectators and there was terracing covered by a roof on the other three sides of the venue. Unusually, players entered the pitch from behind the goal at the Cold Blow Lane end. By the time of its closure, a section of the north terrace was separated to form a family enclosure and three executive boxes were added. The adjoining New Cross Greyhound and Speedway Stadium, which could be clearly seen inside The Den, was demolished in 1975 after lying unused for six years.

The club made the momentous decision to sell off The Den for redevelopment and build a new modern stadium in the local vicinity. The cost of a 20,000-seated stadium was put at £15 million. With £5.2 million from a housing company that wanted to develop the old site, plus £2.6 million each being offered by the Football Trust and Lewisham Council, that still left nearly £5 million to raise. Millwall staged the last match at the Den on 8 May 1993 against Bristol Rovers; Millwall fans not happy about the move invaded the pitch and generally helped themselves to souvenirs from the ground. The Den disappeared under a new estate of flats and houses. The New Den was opened in August 1993 with a friendly against Sporting Lisbon. The new stadium was designed by the Miller Partnership (architects) and Thorburn (engineers and project managers). The site was formerly playing fields called Senegal Fields, and was once occupied by Senegal Road. Like the old ground, the new one had railway embankments on two sides and was approached by passing under a railway arch. Simon Inglis, in his book *The Football Grounds of Great Britain*, described the new ground thus: 'The design consists of four stands which, from inside the stadium, appear almost identical. Each has a lower tier only half the depth of the upper. The cleanly defined roof structures consist of blue steel columns at the rear, bearing cross-braced cantilevered trusses under which the roof deck is suspended. The exposed trusses above the roof sheeting are in self-weathering, rust-coloured steel, which reduces the need for maintenance. Along the front of each roof, the nosings are clad in angled, silvery-white profiled steel, with floodlights neatly integrated within the cladding on both side roofs. The screen ends are in translucent sheeting with angled bars, thereby capping each open corner of the stadium in a streamlined style.' The north and south stands are identical, with 4,382 seats, and are served by a single ground floor concourse. The main or west stand holds 5,354 and houses the club offices, lounges and two levels of concourses. In its upper north corner is a stadium control room. A council-run sports centre is situated behind the north stand, offering a hall, gym, crèche, bar and changing rooms plus three floodlit five-a-side pitches.

ALEX'S FIRST TIME: As well as seeing the first ever League match on a Sunday at The Den in January 1974, my first visit was made on 6 August 1966 for a pre-season friendly between Millwall and Fulham. Fulham won 4-2 with goals from Allan Clarke, Johnny Haynes, Graham Leggat and Bobby Robson before a crowd of 4,100. My first visit to the New Den came on 8 April 1994 when Millwall beat Sunderland 2-1 before 10,244. I was very impressed by the new ground but could understand why so many Millwall supporters had not wanted to leave the old Den due to its unique atmosphere.

MOLESEY
Ground: Walton Road, West Molesey, Surrey.

The club was formed as Molesey & St Paul's United in 1889 and was connected to the local church. During the 1920s Molesey were respected as one of Surrey's strongest junior sides. After the Second World War a large influx of people to the area enhanced Molesey's status to intermediate level. The Walton Road ground was purchased in 1953 and was already equipped with a small stand. That year, the club changed its name from Molesey St Paul's to Molesey. The club joined the Surrey Senior League that season and progressed to the Spartan League in 1959. The ground had a covered area opposite the stand by 1960. It was soon all to change when the shape of the ground completely altered following promotion to the Spartan League. The covered stand was moved to the new pitch site. The turnstile entrance stayed more or less in the same place with

Molesey, November 1973. Before executive boxes were invented Molesey seemed to have them with a function room behind the three rows of benches. Opposite was a low tin shelter.

the splendid galleried stand and clubhouse complex straddling the halfway line. The clubhouse has a large viewing area fronted by an elevated seated section. This can be accessed from a metal staircase from ground level. There is an impressive fascia to the stand with the club's name paraded on it in large letters.

Molesey's list of honours through the years include the 1958 Surrey Senior League title, runners-up position in the Spartan League and cup in 1960, Spartan League Cup winners in 1962, and Surrey Senior Shield runners-up in 1975. The record crowd at Walton Road came in 1966 when Sutton United were the visitors for a Surrey Senior Cup semi-final when 1,255 paid to watch. Floodlights followed in 1971. After a period of Athenian membership, Molesey joined the Isthmian League (Division Two) in 1977/78. A financial crisis was averted in 1988 and a new board of directors began great improvements to the ground. The club was soon promoted to the First Division of the Isthmian League. A new perimeter fence went up and the seating in the stand was converted from bench to modern tip-ups. More terracing was built around the ground and a new tea bar was installed. With promotion to the Premier Division in 1993 a new covered area was erected behind the far goal and a new turnstile complex replaced the old one at Walton Road.

ALEX'S FIRST TIME: This was for an FA Cup fourth-qualifying-round tie between Corinthian Casuals and Merthyr Tydfil on 29 October 1983 that the Casuals surprisingly won 1-0 thanks to a goal from current West Ham manager Alan Pardew. A visiting supporter, angry at the defeat, threw a brick through the clubhouse window. Pardew, who at the time worked as a glazier, fixed the window. I saw Molesey play at Walton Road on 1 August 1990 when Fulham were the visitors. Fulham won 2-1 before a crowd of 300.

NETHERNE VILLAGE

Ground: Netherne Sports Club, Woodplace Lane, Hooley, Coulsdon, Surrey.

The club was formed in 1968 as Reedham Park FC and they played in the now-defunct Croydon Saturday League with varying degrees of success. They played at Higher Drive Recreation Ground in Purley in their early days with the majority of the players coming from the Old Lodge Lane area of Purley. The original name of Reedham Park was derived from the former Reedham Orphanage in Old Lodge Lane, Purley. After Higher Drive they played at Sparrows Den in Addington, the Southern Railways' Sports Club in Wallington and then finally moved to the present ground at Netherne. The club joined the Surrey Eastern Intermediate League in 1975. A series of promotions from the Third Division, starting in 1983, ended in Netherne taking the Premier Division championship in 1989. The club was promoted into the Surrey Premier League and won the Sportsmanship Trophy in 1990 and 1992, the Partington Cup in 1992, the Premier League Cup in 1993 and the Premier Division championship in 1994.

After twenty-six years, four leagues and nine divisions, the club finally made it into senior football when they joined the Combined Counties League in 1994. They finished in third position in the inaugural season and reached the Surrey Senior Cup first round proper. They lost their Combined Counties status in 2002 when they moved to the Surrey Senior League.

Netherne Sports, March 1995. Nigel Tovey enjoys a sit down in what was to become a covered shelter.

The change of name to Netherne FC was made in 1992 to identify the club more closely with the area in which they played. The name of Netherne is associated with the former nearby hospital and the clubhouse was erected by the hospital staff as their social club in 1952. At one time they had a running track surrounding the pitch.

ALEX'S FIRST TIME: My first visit to Netherne was on 18 January 1997 to see a match between Netherne and Farnham Town in the Combined Counties League that the visitors won 2-0 on a very cold and foggy day. It was a long walk up from Coulsdon South Station. The clubhouse looks like an old RAF mess hut and there is little on the ground itself as far as spectator facilities are concerned.

NORTH GREENFORD UNITED
Ground: Horsenden Hill, Berkeley Field, Berkeley Avenue, Greenford, Middlesex.

North Greenford United were playing in the Middlesex League until 1984 when they joined the London Spartan League Senior Division. Their Berkeley Field Ground had no seats or lights at this time but there was a members' bar and function room. They finished fourth at the end of their first season in the Spartan League. North Greenford

North Greenford United, August 2004. Since Bob's first visit in 1986, Berkeley Fields has been transformed with floodlights and a stand with sixty seats.

won the Harry Sunderland Trophy in 1986, beating Brent 2-0 in the final at Hanwell Town. They were elected to the Premier Division of the Spartan League in 1988. The club struggled in the Premier Division and their best season was their first, when they finished fourteenth. They left the Spartan League in 1994 and joined the Middlesex County League Premier Division, finishing sixth in 1994/95. North Greenford United moved up into senior football again when they joined the Combined Counties League in 2002/03 and finished tenth out of twenty-four clubs in their first season. They entered the FA Vase for the first time in 2003/04 but were knocked out in the second qualifying round against Mildenhall 4-1 at Berkeley Field. The club built a small stand that was half seats and half standing area in 2002 and also erected floodlights. The club finished fourteenth out of twenty-four clubs at the end of 2003/04.

BOB'S FIRST TIME: Alex and I played for the same football team for years called Putney Manresa. We toured Holland in May 1986 and played three games in Amsterdam. On our return from Sheerness Docks, Alex sloped off to bed to have a sleep while I decided to go and watch North Greenford United play Wandsworth in a London Spartan Senior Division encounter. This match took place on May Day 1986 and Wandsworth won the game 4-2 before just seventeen spectators. Berkeley Playing Fields was a very basic ground at this time with a social club and dressing room behind one of the goals. The pitch had a rail around it.

NORTHWOOD
Ground: Chestnut Avenue, Northwood, Middlesex.

The exact date of the formation of Northwood Football Club is unknown but there was a Northwood club in existence by 1902. Northwood joined the Harrow & Wembley League in 1931 and immediately found success by winning the Premier Division title in six consecutive years, from 1932 to 1937. After the Second World War, they were champions again from 1947 to 1949 and they also won the Middlesex Junior Cup in those three successive years. The club played at several different venues until their move to Chestnut Avenue in the early 1950s. Northwood had little success after this until they were elected into the Middlesex Senior League in 1969 and became runners-up in 1971. Northwood won the Middlesex League Cup on five occasions during the 1970s and the title in 1978 when they were elected to the Hellenic League. With help from the London Borough of Hillingdon, the club developed their present ground and were quickly promoted to the top flight as First Division champions. They also won the Hellenic League Cup.

Floodlights were erected and senior status was granted to Northwood in 1981. Northwood moved to the London Spartan League in 1984 and they completed a league and cup double in 1992. After considerable ground improvements, the club was elected into the Isthmian League Division Three in 1992. They won the 1993 Associate Members Trophy and were promoted to Division Two in 1997. Northwood were outstanding during 1999/2000 and won the Vandanel Trophy, lost the final of the

Northwood, July 2004. The original stand on the left is now dwarfed by the steel structure with about 200 seats. There is cover behind one goal and opposite.

Middlesex Senior Cup, and gained promotion to the First Division of the Ryman League as runners-up. In the newly formed Division One (North), Northwood flourished and won the title by one point from second-placed Hornchurch and entered the Isthmian League Premier Division for the first time in 2002/03. The transformation of the club in such a short period was remarkable.

ALEX'S FIRST TIME: My first visit to Chestnut Avenue was on 15 November 2003 for an Isthmian League Premier Division match between Northwood and Sutton United that the visitors won 2-1. This is a neat ground that has obviously only been developed in recent seasons. The clubhouse is outside the ground with the dressing rooms as part of the building. There is a small stand with cover opposite and behind the goal. Like Croydon Athletic's ground, it is situated next to a cemetery.

NUNHEAD
Ground: Brown's Field, Ivydale Road, Nunhead, London SE15.

The club was originally known as Wingfield House when they were formed in 1888. They were founded by a group of gentlemen from the stock exchange who wished to set up a home for working boys in Stamford Street, Blackfriars. They set up a sports section that included the football team. The home was moved to Wingfield House, South Lambeth Road in 1894. After playing in local leagues, the club decided to join the Southern Suburban League in 1898. They also moved to play at Hyde Farm, Balham at this time, having previously had no set ground. In 1900 they moved again to Poplar Walk, Loughborough Junction and made another move in 1902, this time to Wavertree Road, Streatham Hill. Wingfield House changed their name to Nunhead in August 1904 when they merged with a club called Honor Oak FC. They moved to Honor Oak's Ivy Ground and they entered the FA Amateur Cup for the first time.

Nunhead, May 1974. Seven concrete terraces with the entrance to the dressing rooms to their left are the only evidence of a major non-League football venue.

It was announced in April 1907 that Nunhead would be moving to Brown's Ground, and this became their home until 1938. The ground was later called the Nunhead Sports Ground. The venue had been well known even before Nunhead's occupancy as the Prince of Wales, King Edward VII, was a regular user of the grounds for shooting, and W.G. Grace was reputed to have regularly played cricket there. The ground had previously been the home of Southern United, a semi-professional club that played for a short time in the South Eastern League, as well as Deptford Invicta for a short period.

Nunhead joined the Isthmian League for 1908/09 and finished seventh in its first season. They became one of the strongest clubs in that league between 1908-1934, after which they went into decline. They won the Isthmian League championship in 1928/29 and 1929/30. The ground was an enclosure within a larger sports ground. The northern side of the venue had a quarter-length grandstand that was erected by the club in 1908. A railway embankment ran alongside the eastern boundary and a covered standing area was later built behind the goal at the opposite Ivydale Road end. Changing rooms were located opposite the stand and in front of these the only concrete terracing at Brown's Ground was eventually built, just six steps deep and around twenty metres long. A number of improvements were made to the ground in 1919, including the construction of a new pavilion and stand and the provision of a second pitch. This second pitch was used by Nunhead reserves, and the main pitch would now be shared with West Norwood. More seating was put in place in June 1920 and during the summer of 1927; repairs to the stand roof and entrances were carried out. Improvements to the dressing rooms were made in 1930 at the same time as the Supporters' Association rebuilt the pitch drainage. A confirmed record-crowd figure for Brown's Ground has not been found but the record was probably set on 23 October 1920 when Nunhead met Dulwich Hamlet in an Isthmian League fixture when an estimated crowd of about 10,000 attended.

The stand was destroyed by fire in January 1936 and many club records were among the items lost. The cost of rebuilding the stand was £700. Nunhead continued playing at Brown's Ground after the Second World War broke out and completed their South-Eastern Combination fixtures there in 1939/40. Due to their inability to pay the rent, Nunhead lost the ground in 1940 and they were forced to share Dulwich Hamlet's Champion Hill ground until Nunhead's demise in 1941. Soon afterwards, the War Department requisitioned Brown's Ground and it was subsequently used for baseball games. A local school used it as a sports field after the war and it was later transformed into a rugby playing area. The enclosure fences, stand and embankments had disappeared by 1987, but the dilapidated dressing rooms and terracing were still clearly to be seen. Even these have now disappeared.

PINNER
Ground: Cuckoo Hill, The Circuits, Pinner, Middlesex.

Pinner FC disappeared in the early 1960s due to poor facilities and lack of money. They were formed in 1892 and at this time Pinner was no more than a village surrounded by countryside. The local recreation ground (off West End Road) was used for home matches and players used the nearby Bell public house for a dressing room. They played their first game on 1 October 1892, against a team called Butterflies. The club entered the Harrow & District in 1894, but with only six competing teams the ten matches were supplemented with seventeen friendlies. Pinner moved to the Willesden & District League in 1898/99 when real success came at last, with the team winning the championship. During their first season they suffered only one defeat and also won the prestigious Middlesex Junior Cup.

The club was admitted to the London League in 1910 and finished as runners-up of the Second Division. They struggled in the higher division, however, and after just one more season, they moved down to the more suitable Middlesex League. After the First World War the club moved back to the Harrow & District League Second Division. Pinner had folded at the start of the war and had to start from the bottom once again. They played for many seasons on the large open Pinner Recreation Ground which still exists on the west side of West End Lane, adjacent to the junction with Highview. Pinner FC moved to the enclosed ground at the end of Cuckoo Hill Road (just south-west of the Recreation Ground) in 1927, when they made a big step up to the Spartan League. This ground had existed at least from the early 1900s. At that time there was a one small structure, probably a pavilion, which was located just inside the ground entrance. There was a tea hut and a small covered and seated stand at the ground. On each side of the stand there were short runs of terracing several steps high and behind it there was sufficient room for a practice pitch.

Pinner managed to continue during the Second World War and played in the West Middlesex Combination and Middlesex Senior League, but returned to the Spartan League for 1945/46 and were successful enough to enter the Premier Division the

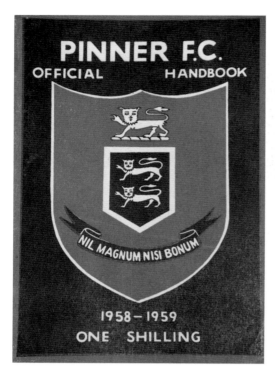

Pinner, 1959. Cuckoo Hill Road, home of Pinner, boasted a grandstand with covered terraces on both sides. Motto: 'Nothing is great – unless it is good'.

following season. Such clubs as Cambridge Town, Chesham United and Aylesbury United were in opposition, and the team struggled in such company and were relegated in 1949. They had been struggling for some time, and the loss of their enclosed ground at Cuckoo Hill in 1951 necessitated a move. This was caused by the poor financial state of the club, and their change to a council-owned pitch brought about a considerable saving of £240 per annum. The Cuckoo Hill ground remained for many years, and it was in only in the 1980s that the site was built upon with high-quality houses.

The move was to 'The Croft', situated off Cannonbury Avenue. Unfortunately, the football club was unable to charge entrance money from the dwindling number of spectators that attended home games, as it was not enclosed. The only facility was a single-storey pavilion, which served the two football pitches. Pinner entered the Southern Amateur League Division Three in 1951. Between 1952 and 1956, they were champions once, runners-up once and bottom twice. They went from the Third to the First Division and back again. Pinner never recovered from this and spent the rest of their competitive days in the Third Division. The club was eventually thrown out of the Southern Amateur League in 1961 by their fellow clubs, due to their very poor facilities. They soldiered on during 1961/62 with all matches being either friendlies or cup games, and all played away from home. The relatively small sum of £80 for the annual ground rent was difficult enough to find, so the £300 spent on installing lighting and a hot-water system in the changing rooms had all but crippled the club, after the council had refused to do this work despite owning the ground. The heart had gone out of the club, which folded during the summer of 1962.

Queens Park Rangers, January 1982. Not many at the School End for this Alliance Premier League fixture that ended goal-less on the plastic pitch.

QUEENS PARK RANGERS
Ground: Loftus Road, Shepherd's Bush, London W12.

Queens Park Rangers have played on fourteen different venues since they were formed in 1886 from the merger of two West London teams, St Jude's and Christchurch Rangers. Their first ground was at Welford's Fields, now covered by housing off Chamberlayne Road, around Bolton Gardens. They hired the London Scottish Ground (somewhere in Brondesbury) in 1888, but the pitch became so waterlogged that they left in 1890, first for Home Farm (location unknown), then to Kensal Rise Green, where Burrows Road is now situated. Rangers moved to their first enclosed pitch, which was known as the Gun Club Ground and was situated on Wormwood Scrubs, in 1891. This was located next to the present West London Athletics Stadium. This was followed by four years at the Kilburn Cricket Ground on Harvist Road. Gates rose to 3,000 at Harvist Road, so in 1896 the club secured a ten-year lease at the National Athletics Ground, later called Kensal Rise Athletic Ground, where most local cup finals were played at this time. This was north of Kensal Rise Station, between College and Chamberlayne Roads.

Rangers turned professional in December 1898 and joined the Southern League. The National Athletics Ground had been in existence since 1890 and QPR attempted to buy the ground, which had a pavilion on one side, but failed, although they still planned to erect an uncovered stand opposite. They left in April 1901 but were back the following year. Kensal Rise was again used briefly by Queens Park Rangers during the First World War when the Army took over their ground in Park Royal, but by 1917 it had been turned into allotments for the war effort and by 1921 was housed over.

Their next home was a recreation ground on St Quintin's Avenue (part of which still survives as open space). There were no facilities at this ground so the players had to change in the Latimer Arms on Latimer Road and run down the street to the pitch. After a 12,000 crowd attended a Christmas fixture *v.* Spurs, the local residents applied for an eviction order due to the problems these crowds were causing. QPR returned to the Kensal Rise Athletic Ground again, where their old landlord gave them a two-year lease at £240 a year – more than twice the previous rent. When the rent was raised again the club decided to accept an offer to play at the Royal Agricultural Society showground at Park Royal in 1904. This was a 100-acre site between the Grand Union Canal and the Great Western Railway. It was an oval arena with stands on either side and was said to be able to hold 40,000 spectators. The ground could be reached by railway but was a long way away from where most Rangers supporters lived. The society's debts forced it to sell the showgrounds in 1907 and the Guinness brewery on Cumberland Avenue now covers the site. The Great Western Railway had created a new Park Royal Stadium that lay between Coronation Road and the original Park Royal Station (which was west of the present station of that name). Park Royal was almost an exact copy of Archibald Leitch's Ayresome Park (built four years earlier). On the south, or railway side, was an impressive 4,000-seat, barrel-roofed stand with an arched gable and paddock and the remaining three sides were open terraces. Park Royal was used for the first time on 2 November 1907 when QPR played Millwall in a Southern League match watched by an attendance of 16,000. The first ever rugby league Test Match between Great Britain and Australia was held there in December 1908, but was watched by a paltry crowd of 2,014. Rangers won the Southern League in 1908 and 1912, and had it not been for the war they probably would still be using the ground today.

The Army requisitioned Park Royal in February 1915, forcing Rangers to complete their home fixtures at Stamford Bridge and at their previous ground at Kensal Rise. When they moved to Loftus Road in 1917, QPR brought most of the stand and fittings with them from Park Royal. The Park Royal Ground was used by the newly formed Park Royal FC between the wars and was replaced by new housing and industrial development in the late 1940s. There was also the Park Royal Greyhound Stadium close by, which was built in the early 1930s for greyhounds and also used by short-lived Acton and Willesden Rugby League club in 1935. This has also now disappeared under more industrial development.

Loftus Road had previously belonged to Shepherd's Bush FC, who went out of business around 1916. They were an amateur side that played in the Southern League at the turn of the century and had played at Loftus Road since 1904. Before then the rectangular site had been a dumping ground, hemmed in by houses on two sides and a school. The north side backed onto the fields of Old Oak Farm. The ground was very basic, with only the framework from the stand from Park Royal supplying their spectators with any cover. This lost its pitched roof and gable when re-erected. The three other sides were unterraced banks, with the Popular Side being backed by a rough track (later South Africa Road), on the other side of which, only twenty yards away, was the shed-like rear of one of White City's largest exhibition halls that remained in use until the late 1930s. Just up the road from this ground was the 60,000 capacity

Queens Park Rangers, December 1984. White City Stadium in the throes of demolition.

White City Stadium. This was built for the 1908 Olympic Games and was also the centrepiece of the Franco-British Exhibition of the same year. QPR had actually played in the stadium twice in 1912, when a coal strike prevented trains from reaching Park Royal.

White City remained unused until 1927 when the Greyhound Racing Association gained a lease from the Church Commissioners and they purchased the stadium in 1930. The first speedway meeting was held there in May 1928 and the Amateur Athletic Association annual championships started there in 1932. London Highfield rugby league side played their home matches at the stadium in 1933/34 and boxing events were also held there. QPR decided to see if they could attract better crowds at White City and the first game there, against Bournemouth on 5 September 1931, drew a crowd of 18,000, but ended in a 3-0 defeat. During that first season QPR also recorded their highest ever home attendance in January 1932, when 41,097 saw an FA Cup tie with Leeds United. Despite having experimental floodlights at White City, the FA would not allow the club to use them. QPR returned to Loftus Road after the second campaign at White City had not proved a success, due to falling attendances.

Improvements took place at Loftus Road when the Supporters' Club raised £1,500 to build a cover at the Loftus Road End in 1938, providing shelter for 6,000. Hammersmith Borough Council bought up the now-redundant exhibition halls behind the Popular Side in 1936 and built a large estate of flats. South Africa Road was also laid out. Rangers bought the ground's freehold and also thirty-nine houses adjoining Ellerslie Road and Loftus Road in 1948 for £26,250 and the terraces were concreted. Floodlights on four corner masts were switched on for a match with Arsenal in October 1953 but the ground still remained cramped and basic. Rangers decided to try their luck at White City again in 1962/63, but their small crowds were lost in the stadium. The lack of atmosphere also had a negative effect on the players and again they returned to their former home. White City staged its final major football match, a World Cup group game between Uruguay and France, watched by a crowd of 45,662. Speedway continued on and off until August 1983 and the last greyhound meeting was held at White City on 22 September 1984. The ground was demolished in 1986 and the British Broadcasting Corporation's new headquarters now covers the site.

The club, at last, decided to commit to Loftus Road on a long-term basis and the ground was completely transformed. This transformation took place in four stages over twelve years at a cost around £2 million. However, they tried to cram too much into too small an area and this has made it a very uncomfortable ground today. Under chairman Jim Gregory, the club and ground were modernised and they went on to the most successful period in their history. The first stand to be developed was the South Africa Road Stand in 1968, and cost only £162,000 to build. Thirty-two executive boxes were built along the back of the paddock. The roof does not extend over this paddock, however, and only covers the upper tier. The Ellerslie Road stand replaced the original stand in 1972. It has a single tier of blue seats and is a very basic stand with little leg room. This is backed by neighbouring houses and was very cheap to build. The School End stand, where visiting supporters currently sit, was converted from open terraces in 1981 and upgraded in 1993. It has two tiers and spectators have to stand up in the upper tier to see the goal line, as the stand is crammed into the smallest of spaces. The Loftus Road End is similar to the School End and was built in 1980 in place of a bank of terracing and has a pitched roof at its rear. The Lower Loft remained terracing until 1994 and in the lower north corner a control room has been squeezed in. There are a large number of seats at Loftus Road with only a restricted view. The record crowd for the ground was set on 27 April 1974 for the visit of Leeds United when 35,353 attended. Rangers dug up their notorious pitch and became the first football club in the world to play on an artificial surface in 1981 (an Omniturf pitch costing £350,000). Fulham moved in to share the ground in 2002 but returned to Craven Cottage, thankfully, in August 2004.

ALEX'S FIRST TIME: I saw Rangers play Peterborough United at the White City on 18 May 1963. There was a crowd of just over 5,000 in the ground and there was no atmosphere there at all. Spectators were some distance from the pitch and the conditions were the opposite to what they were at Loftus Road. I was able to compare the difference when I attended a QPR *v.* Millwall match in March 1966. This was Rodney Marsh's debut for Rangers after his transfer from neighbours Fulham. The home side won 6-1 and John Collins scored one of the greatest goals I have seen when he knocked himself out with a bullet header. I was close to the action and the atmosphere was electric that day.

Rainham Town, July 1972. The stand held about 250 on six wooden sections. Opposite was a covered terrace, with railway sleepers behind one goal.

RAINHAM TOWN
Ground: Deri Park, Wennington Road, Rainham, Essex.

Rainham Town FC was formed in 1945 and became founder members of the Delphian League in 1951/52. They had entered the FA Cup for the first time in 1947/48, losing in the extra preliminary round 2-1 at Clapton. They were runners-up of the league in 1956/57 and moved on to join the Metropolitan League in 1961. The club's best seasons in the FA Cup came in 1957/58 and 1958/59 when they reached the third qualifying round before losing to Chelmsford City 6-0 away and Woodford Town 2-0 away respectively. After three seasons in the Metropolitan League, Rainham decided to join the Athenian League Division Two. They won promotion to the First Division as runners-up in 1973/74. After thirteen seasons in the Athenian League, the club decided to try their luck in the Isthmian League Division Two in 1977/78.

Deri Park was built in 1945 just after the end of the Second World War. It had a concrete stand with a corrugated-iron roof with bench seating and a standing area opposite. A concrete wall surrounded the pitch with a post and rail in front. The ground was reached down a track between houses that made the site inaccessible when the club would have liked to sell the ground for redevelopment in later years. The club entered the FA Vase for the first time in 1974/75 and had their best run in the competition in 1977/78 when they reached the fifth round, where they lost at Almondsbury Greenway. The club lost their Deri Park ground in 1991 and Rainham Town collapsed three years later. Their last season came in 1993/94 when they finished bottom of the table, with only 14 points from 42 matches, and rather than be relegated decided to disband. The ground soon succumbed to vandalism, became overgrown and has been replaced by modern houses.

BOB'S FIRST TIME: This was for an Isthmian League clash between Rainham Town and Horsham on 18 October 1983 which the Zebras won 2-0 before fifty fans. The ground, at this time, had a small wood stand with six rows of benches in front of the dressing rooms, and social club. Opposite was a low covered terrace and behind one of the goals was a six-deep terrace made from railway sleepers.

Rayners Lane, March 1975. This charming tin-backed, PVC-roofed construction had disappeared by 1984. There are now two identical covered areas made of breeze block with an asbestos roof. The trees are now so dense that you can no longer see the houses behind.

RAYNERS LANE
Ground: Tithe Farm Social Club, 151 Rayners Lane, South Harrow, Middlesex.

There have not been many highs in Rayners Lane's history and they struggle on today in the lower echelons of the Hellenic League. The club was formed in 1933 and played in the Harrow & Wembley District League. The Tithe Farm Social Club was formed and the football club absorbed into it, where it has remained ever since. 'The Lane' enjoyed considerable success in the late 1930s and early 1940s and continued this pattern when they were promoted to the Parthenon League for 1945/46. They were winners of the League Challenge Cup in 1948/49 and 1952/53, runners-up in 1954/55, won the championship in 1950/51 and were runners-up in 1952/53. They joined the Spartan League in 1957 and played there until they failed to gain re-election in 1970. They then returned to the Parthenon League (now renamed the Middlesex League). This was a successful period and resulted in promotion again to the Spartan League, but after two seasons the Spartan and the London Metropolitan Leagues amalgamated, which forced 'The Lane' back to the Middlesex League. During this period they had their best run in the FA Vase, where they lost 2-1 at Kingsbury Town in the second round.

Looking for a new challenge, they joined the Hellenic League in 1978 and after two seasons won promotion to the Premier Division. The club won the Hellenic League title in 1982/83 with only four defeats in thirty games. They had their record crowd at Rayners Lane in 1983 when 550 attended a Middlesex Senior Cup match with Wealdstone. The club built a small stand that holds thirty-two spectators in 1984, three years after railing the pitch off, but the ground remains fairly basic. They had their best run in the FA Cup during 1992/93 when they reached the second qualifying round, where they lost 5-1 at St Albans City. Rayners Lane were relegated to the Hellenic League First Division in 1994, as they did not have floodlights. They resigned from that league in 1996 to rejoin the Middlesex County League and regroup. This return to the club's roots was a real benefit, with the side becoming Premier Division champions, reaching the semi-final of the Alec Smith Cup and winning the Charity Shield in the first season. Rayners Lane joined the Chiltonian League in 1998/99 and found themselves back in the Hellenic League when the two leagues amalgamated in 2000.

BOB'S FIRST TIME: This was for a match between Rayners Lane and FC Germania in a pre-season friendly on 14 August 1984. The visitors were from Canada and the match ended 1-1 before sixty spectators. A new small stand was in the process of being built, replacing the previous plastic cover.

RAYNES PARK VALE
Ground: Prince George Playing Field, Raynes Park, Grand Drive, Raynes Park, London SW20.

Raynes Park Vale FC was founded in 1995 from a merger of two clubs, Raynes Park FC and Malden Vale FC. Malden Vale Football Club was founded in 1967 and spent its first decade of existence playing in the North Surrey Youth League, Sunday Sportsman League, Thameside League and the Surrey Combination League, where a total of thirty-seven honours were obtained in junior and intermediate football. The club gained senior status in 1977 and was elected into the Surrey Senior League. The following season the Surrey Senior League changed its name to the Home Counties League, but the Vale decided to join the London Spartan League, being admitted straight into the Premier Division.

During the 1980s the club carried out improvements on the Grand Drive Ground. A new barrier around the pitch was put in place during 1986. Floodlights were installed the following year and a small new stand holding thirty seats with a covered standing area was built in 1989. The club finished runners-up to BAE Weybridge in 1988/89 in the Combined Counties League and were promoted to the Isthmian League Division Two (South) after many improvements to the ground. These included new dressing rooms, some concrete terracing and turnstiles. The club spent five seasons in the Isthmian League and had their ups and downs. The club lost most of their players when the management team left to join Hendon during the summer of 1994 and the following season saw Malden Vale finishing bottom of the league.

Raynes Park Football Club was founded in 1954, taking over from the Southern Railway football section. From these humble beginnings the club ran five senior teams on Saturday, the first team and reserves playing in the Surrey Premier League, the third team in the Surrey South-Eastern Counties League, with the fourth and fifth teams in the Kingston & District League. The merger was planned over a two-year period and finally, on Saturday 18 August 1995, the club played its first ever game as Raynes Park Vale in the Combined Counties League. They finished fourth in the league in 1997/98, their best season so far.

Raynes Park Vale, November 2003. The stand holds about 100 on wooden planks, while officials get chairs. There is also a small bit of cover in one corner.

ALEX'S FIRST TIME: I visited Grand Drive for an Isthmian League Division Two (South) match between Malden Vale and Abingdon Town on 24 October 1989 that ended in a 0-0 draw. I remember that the pitch was very boggy and the floodlights were not very bright. The ground was basic and the crowd only 100 strong.

ROMFORD
Ground: Brooklands, Brooklands Road, Romford, Essex.

Romford tried unsuccessfully to enter the Football League during the 1960s but within the next decade had disappeared and lost their Brooklands ground. Various clubs existed in Romford before the First World War, including the original Romford FC who played on a pitch at Great Mawneys. A club called Romford Victoria played on a pitch at Brooklands when it was part of a much larger sports set-up with hockey, cricket and tennis. There was another club in the town called Great Eastern (Romford), which faded after the formation of Romford. Romford FC was formed in 1929 and took over Brooklands. Admission to the London League was obtained, and their first match in that competition was against Bostall Heath. At the end of 1930/31, Cheshunt lost their ground and their place in the Athenian League and Romford were elected to take their place. Romford won the Athenian League championship in 1935/36 and also reached the semi-final of the Amateur Cup, but were beaten in the closing minutes of a thrilling match by the Casuals 3-2 at Champion Hill. They were champions again the following season and also reached the Amateur Cup semi-finals, but lost to Erith & Belvedere 4-2 in a replay at Selhurst Park.

Romford, March 1973. The main stand held about 2,000 on fifteen rows of wooden seats. To the left is the bridge over the speedway entrance. Fifteen steps of terracing completed the oval-shaped ground. Opposite the main stand was 'Clockside' – the north stand which gave shelter to those standing.

Romford Football Club Ltd was floated in 1936 and the shareholders bought the Brooklands Stadium, which until that time had been rented from Romford Sports Club. The limited company had £10,000 capital divided into 80,000 half-crown shares. They enclosed one pitch, which was turned forty-five degrees, and then built a small seated stand with the opposite side opening out onto a cricket pitch. Some terracing was also put in place. Just prior to the Second World War, the ground was fully enclosed and banking was formed all around, with a covered area opposite the grandstand, while after the war a further area of cover went up. At the end of 1938/39, Walthamstow Avenue and Romford, the two clubs at the top of the Athenian table, accepted invitations to become members of the Isthmian League. Romford finally reached the final of the FA Amateur Cup in 1949, but they lost to Bromley 1-0 at Wembley. The Brooklands ground was large enough to accommodate 18,237 in 1951 when Southall visited for an FA Amateur Cup tie. Despite finishing close to the bottom of the Isthmian League in 1958/59, Romford resigned to join the Southern League as a professional club. They were runners-up of the First Division at the end of their first season and were promoted.

Archibald Leitch & Partners were employed to design and build a new stand that could hold 2,500 spectators at a cost of £40,000 and new floodlights costing £16,000 were also erected. The stand was used for the first time in September 1964 and underneath it was a directors' lounge and dance hall with bars. The average crowd were now 3,000, and 10,500 attended a FA Cup match with Luton Town in 1965. The ground was one of the best in non-League soccer, with its mounds of terracing with crush barriers and impressive stand replete with a clock gable. Romford won the Southern League title in 1966/67, but were unsuccessful in their attempt to join the Football League.

Romford had their best season in the FA Cup during 1971/72 when, after starting in the preliminary round, they reached the second round proper where they lost to Gillingham 1-0 at Brooklands. During the 1970s, Romford developed massive debts and the club was forced to sell Brooklands in 1975. The money raised did not allow the club to proceed with the proposed new site at Oldchurch Park and despite firstly attempting to re-erect the stand at the new venue and then offering it for sale to Dagenham FC, the whole thing fell through and Havering Council withdrew the offer of the site. The last game was played at Brooklands but did not feature Romford as Hornchurch used the ground to play Chesham on 30 April 1977, as their own ground was not available. Romford's Supporters Club reformed Romford in 1992 and they shared Hornchurch's ground. They eventually absorbed the Collier Row club and used their Sungate Ground for a while before taking over Ford United's ground after Ford's move to Barkingside (see Collier Row).

BOB'S FIRST TIME: This was for a Southern League Premier Division match between Romford and Bedford Town on 11 March 1972. Romford won the game 2-0 before an attendance of 905. Brooklands doubled as a speedway venue and the main stand was similar to Cheltenham Town's main stand with fifteen rows of seats holding 2,500 spectators with 'overhead heating' according to Romford's Football League application brochure. The rest of the ground had fifteen rows of concrete terracing, with cover opposite the main stand for 1,000 people and four tall corner floodlights.

RUISLIP/RUISLIP PARK
Ground: Middlesex Stadium, Breakspear Road, Ruislip, Middlesex.

Ruislip are one of the shortest-lived clubs in the London area, lasting barely five years before going bankrupt. As part of a housing development, a new ground with banking on two sides, a seated stand (which lost its roof in the gales of 1989) and a large brick-built clubhouse with views of the pitch was built at Breakspear Road in 1985. Behind one goal close to the main entrance into the ground, a covered standing area was created where 300 spectators could stand with protection from the elements. Ruislip Town were formed in 1980 and were struggling in the Middlesex League when they dropped the Town from their name and entered the Southern League. They abandoned their former ground, which was in a field next door, and moved into the new ground. When Ruislip played Queens Park Rangers in March 1986 for an official floodlight opening, a crowd of 1,459 attended. Normally, however, crowds were paltry with usually only about twenty spectators bothering to attend matches. The ground was miles from anywhere and the club was soon beset with financial problems.

With the club finishing at the bottom of the Southern League's Southern Section in 1988/89, a merger took place with another local club called Bromley Park Rangers, enabling a new board to take over. They joined the Hellenic League Premier Division but lasted for only one year before disbanding. Another local club, Hillingdon Borough, was

Ruislip/Ruislip Park, July 2004. The stand holds 165 spectators. Hillingdon Borough now play here.

reformed in 1990 and became founder members of the Spartan South Midlands League. They were using the ground at Breakspear Road by 1997 and had plans for a new 250-seater stand so that they could move up into the Isthmian League.

ALEX'S FIRST TIME: It was amazing that a club with such a basic ground was allowed to join the Southern League but Ruislip managed it in 1985. On 25 March 1986, I attended a match in the Southern Section between Ruislip and Hastings Town, with the visitors winning an entertaining match 3-2 before one of their better crowds of ninety-two. I remember that the pitch smelt like a farmyard and it was the first match under floodlights at the ground. Most of the crowd huddled under the covered area behind the goal.

RUISLIP MANOR
Ground: Grosvenor Vale, off West End Road, Ruislip, Middlesex.

Ruislip Manor FC was founded in 1938 and spent its first season in the Uxbridge League, finishing in joint-first position. They were runners-up in the League Cup and became founder members of the Middlesex League during the Second World War. They

Ruislip Manor, May 1974. This unusual cover with wood sides and PVC roof was built in front of the tea bar behind one goal. On both sides of the ground were seated stands.

finished as runners-up to Cheshunt in their first season in the London League Division One in 1946/47, but could not be promoted as they did not have the required senior status. The club originally played on a ground at nearby Sidmouth Drive, but in 1947 moved to Grosvenor Vale and quickly enclosed the playing area from the rest of the park. This helped them obtain senior status in 1950 and they became Premier Division runners-up behind West Thurrock in 1951/52. Ruislip Manor transferred to the Spartan League in 1956, finishing third in both 1961/62 and 1962/63. In the early 1960s the Supporters' Club built the dressing rooms, which were a group of large wooden sheds, and a small stand that had an overhang and leaning posts. Opposite the main stand, there was a basic-looking structure made of corrugated iron and wood. They had a record crowd at Grosvenor Avenue for an FA Amateur Cup tie with Tooting & Mitcham United in 1962, when over 2,000 attended.

Manor were elected to the Athenian League in 1965 and after struggling for the best part of seven years, won the Second Division championship in 1972/73, losing only two games. The previous season, Manor reached the first round proper of the Amateur Cup for the only time, bowing out to Bishop's Stortford after a replay. When the Athenian League was disbanded in 1984, Ruislip Manor joined Division Two (South) of the Isthmian League. The club reached the fourth qualifying round of the FA Cup in 1990/91 for the first time, losing 5-2 at Halesowen Town after memorable home victories over Hendon and Wealdstone in the previous rounds. Promotion was finally achieved when Manor finished runners-up in 1992/93, having led the table for most of the season. In the higher league, Manor struggled to make any impact and it came as no surprise when they were relegated in 1996 and went to play in the Spartan League. Off the field the committee and supporters made improvements to the main stand and other facilities to help try to regain their Isthmian League status, and the club should have achieved this in 1998 but threw promotion away when they lost their last home game to Waltham Abbey. Since then Ruislip Manor have mainly finished in mid-table.

The spacious clubhouse at Grosvenor Avenue has three bars and a dance floor and is situated in the car park. It also has an overhanging roof attached that gives cover to some seating. A concrete outer wall encloses the far end of the ground, with the pitch enclosed by a smart new wooden fence. In the far corner of the ground is one of the most unusual buildings to be seen at a London football ground. This is a Second World War gun turret that is owned by the Ministry of Defence and guards the nearby Northolt Aerodrome. In the past it has also been used as dressing room, tea bar and as an area for officials.

BOB'S FIRST TIME: Lewes were the visitors on 11 May 1974 for an Athenian League Division One fixture, which the visitors lost 2-0. Bob remembers an altercation between the tea-bar staff and spectators who kept on obscuring their view of the action. Unfortunately, there was a veranda in front of the tea bar where spectators tended to stand. There was a lengthy cover with three rows of seats underneath down one side of the pitch. On the other side were the social and changing facilities with covered seating in front.

SLADE GREEN
Ground: The Small Glen, Moat Lane, Slade Green, Erith, Kent.

Slade Green was formed after the amalgamation of three clubs – The Wasps, St Augustine's and Southern Railway Sports. This decision was made on 6 June 1946 in a meeting at the Railway Hotel in Slade Green. The club was initially called Slade Green Athletic but were renamed Slade Green in 1986. They created a ground on a local piece of land that they named 'The Glen' (their present home). Southern Railway Sports had previously used this ground and it is close to the railway depot at Slade Green.

Green joined the Kent Amateur League in 1952 and won the Second Division title at the end of their first season in the competition. The following year they won the First Division championship, remaining unbeaten and scoring 144 goals in the process. Having gained promotion to the Senior Division, Slade Green were granted senior status and in 1960 and they overcome Mottingham 3-1 to win the Kent Amateur League Cup. They also beat Brentstonians 6-2 to gain the West Kent Challenge Cup. Slade Green were Senior Division champions in 1960/61, and shortly after this they were elected to the Greater London League. They won the West Kent Cup again in 1966, beating Bexley United, and they finished as Greater London League runners-up in 1968/69. They moved to the Kent League at the start of 1970/71.

Slade Green progressed through to the Kent League Cup final in 1983 and won the trophy, following a 2-1 win over Faversham Town. The ground was renamed The Small Glen in 1987 in recognition of the late Charlie and Glen Small who had been involved with the club since its inception. Around this time they refurbished the clubhouse at Slade Green and new dressing rooms, a referees' room, committee room, canteen and

Slade Green, April 1984. The stand was built on to the front of the dressing room; to the left are three rows of chairs. To the right are three concrete terraces.

public toilets were incorporated into the clubhouse/stand so that the ground was up to Kent League standards. A new fence was also erected around the ground. The club's greatest day came in April 1992 when a 3-1 victory over Tunbridge Wells saw them take the Kent Senior Trophy. The record attendance at Moat Lane came on 25 July 1992 when Millwall attracted 2,000 spectators for a pre-season friendly. Their best seasons in the Kent League were 1981/82 and 1995/96 when they finished sixth, and their best run in the FA Cup was 1992/93 when they reached the second qualifying round where they lost 3-2 at Wembley. Their most successful seasons in the FA Vase came when they reached the third round in 1990/91 and 1995/96. Slade Green beat Three Bridges, Whistable Town and Faversham Town before losing 5-0 at Littlehampton Town in 1990/91. They lost 2-0 to Diss Town in 1995/96, after beating Leatherhead 5-1, Saltdean United 5-1 and Newmarket Town 2-0, all at Moat Lane.

ALEX'S FIRST TIME: This was for their last game of 2003/04 when Sporting Bengal United were the visitors on 17 April 2004. Slade Green had lost their previous nine games and Sporting Bengal had won only one Kent League match all season. Slade Green eventually won 4-1 before a small crowd of thirty-four. The ground's facilities are all in one place within the main stand. There are no seats in the covered stand and the clubhouse is a little gloomy as there is no natural light.

SOUTHALL
Ground: Western Road, Southall, Middlesex.

Another sad loss was the demise of Western Road, a ground capable of holding 20,000 spectators. This was a sea of concrete terraces and crash barriers until sold for redevelopment. Southall were formed in 1871 and first entered the FA Cup three years later when they drew 0-0 at home to Leyton. They joined the West London League in 1892 and were in the Southern League Second Division from 1896 until they moved on to the London League in 1905. The club was reorganised in 1906 and went down to the West Middlesex League before moving into the Great Western League the following season. It is not clear when they started playing at Western Road, but it was probably around the turn of the century. Southall entered the FA Amateur Cup in 1897/98 and beat Fulham in the second qualifying round. The first FA Cup match against Football League opposition took place in 1904/05 when Southall faced Second Division Leicester Fosse (now Leicester City) in the sixth qualifying round but lost 4-0 at Western Road. Southall suffered their biggest defeat in the FA Cup when they lost 11-1 to Second Division Glossop in 1912/13. Southall reached the final of the FA Amateur Cup for the only time in their history in 1924/25 where they lost 2-1 to Clapton at The Den, before a 25,000 crowd. They took the lead after ten minutes through Hawkins but Gibbins soon equalised for Clapton. Gibbins scored the East London side's winner after seventy-one minutes. They also reached the semi-finals in 1927 where they lost to Leyton 2-1 at Craven Cottage.

Southall won the Athenian League title for the only time in 1926/27 when they won 18 of their 26 games and finished 5 points clear of second-placed Kingstonian. This included eight-goal home victories over Summerstown and Windsor & Eton. By the mid-1930s Southall were in a very bad way financially and on the playing side. The club merged with Park Royal, who had a wealthy owner, and much money was ploughed into improving their Western Road Ground. A vast concrete terrace was created on the existing grass banks. A wooden grandstand was built on the far side with changing rooms. The grandstand was eventually gutted by fire, and a new stand with dressing rooms underneath was built on the opposite side. The ground was tested to the full when Watford visited the ground for an FA Cup third-round tie in January 1936, when a crowd of 19,094 saw the Hornets win 4-1. Southall had beaten Swindon Town at home 3-1 in the first round and then had an easy 8-0 victory over Newport IOW after the club had started their cup run from the extra preliminary round. Spectators had to wait until 1955/56 for the next first-round appearance in the FA Cup against Hastings United, where they lost 6-1.

Southall did not create a useful team again until the 1952/53 campaign when they reached the semi-final of the Amateur Cup, but were narrowly defeated by the ultimate winners, Pegasus, 2-1 in a replay at Fulham. After this, one by one nearly all their players moved to other clubs, yet despite these defections Southall managed to finish second from the top in the Athenian League table in 1954/55, a point behind champions Tooting & Mitcham. The club went into decline after this. They left the Athenian for the Isthmian League in 1973/74 and the following season finished as runners-up of the

Southall, April 1981. Both seated areas are shown: to the left is a tiny building in front of the clubhouse with room for about twenty people, in the middle the main stand seating 300 on five rows of planks. Opposite was a small covered terrace. Everywhere else there was concrete terracing, providing a huge theoretical capacity.

Second Division. They changed their name to Southall & Ealing Borough in 1975 but reverted to their original name five years later. After years of mediocrity, Southall suddenly fought their way to the final of the FA Vase in 1985/86. It took them eleven games to reach their Wembley final where they lost 3-0 to Halesowen Town before a crowd of over 11,000. Southall were relegated to the Third Division of the Isthmian League in 1993 and after seven further seasons of struggle lost their Isthmian League status in 2000 after finishing bottom of the table. Southall had left their Western Road ground in 1992 after a floodlight pylon collapsed. The team moved to Harefield in 1992 and to Tring Town in 1996. The Western Road Ground was demolished in March 1996. The club outlined plans in 1996 to move to a new stadium at Glade Lane, Southall but nothing came of this.

With the demise of Southall FC (1871) from the Ryman League Division Three in 2000, a split took place within the club. Two clubs were formed out of the original club; both were given senior status by the Middlesex County Football Association. Southall Town FC was founded in March 2000 and after negotiation with the Hellenic League, the club was accepted into Division One (East). A ground-share agreement was negotiated with

Yeading FC. Southall Town's first season in the Hellenic League went well and the club was promoted from Division One (East) into the Premier Division. Southall FC, the other club, currently use the ground of Chesham United and play in the Combined Counties League.

ALEX'S FIRST TIME: What a ground! A sea of terracing with a small stand perched on top of one side. This ground could easily have held close to 20,000, even in the 1980s. Unfortunately, Southall did well to attract 200 spectators to their games and the cost of the ground's upkeep must have been prohibitive. I saw Southall play Kingsbury Town in a Middlesex Charity Cup game at Western Road on 13 December 1983 that the home team won 4-1.

STAINES TOWN
Ground: Wheatsheaf Park, Wheatsheaf Lane, Staines, Middlesex.

Wheatsheaf Park has had a major refurbishment in recent years with the club on the up and up. Staines FC was formed in 1892 and the club was known as Staines Albany at the turn of the century. They merged with another local club called St Peter's Institute and joined the Great Western Combination in 1905. Staines played at The Lammas, also known as Ashby Recreation Ground in Wraysbury Road. The club folded in 1914 but a new club called Staines Lagonda emerged after the First World War and joined the Hounslow & District League, moving to the Great Western Suburban League in 1920. They played at the Mill Mead ground and found success in the FA Amateur Cup when they fought their way through to the last sixteen in the early 1920s. Mill Mead was also known as Hammond's Farm or Wicks' Farm. While at Mill Mead, players changed at the White Lion pub in the High Street, walking to the ground through the town.

The club joined the Spartan League in 1924, and changed its name to Staines Town the following year. Due to financial problems they lost their Mill Mead ground and their Spartan League status in 1935. The land was used for construction of the reservoir around 1940 and the stand was used as a store for the engineers' equipment. Eventually, a temporary home was found in Shepperton Road, Laleham where they stayed until the new ground at the Wheatsheaf was built and opened in 1951. The first structure, called the Green Hut, housed changing rooms, a boardroom and a tea hut. During the 1960s a stand was built close to the halfway line and a covered enclosure went up behind the right-hand goal. Short spells in the Parthenon and Hellenic League preceded the return to the Spartan League in 1956. They won the Athenian League Division Two title in 1972/73 and moved on to the Isthmian League the following season. A precast concrete cover was erected opposite the grandstand in 1975, while in 1981 the cover behind the goal was lost when the area of land it occupied was sold for housing, causing the pitch to be moved forward. A crowd of 2,750 spectators packed Wheatsheaf Lane to see Staines defeat Banco di Roma in the Barassi Cup final during 1975/76, after 70,000 had seen the first leg in Rome's Olympic Stadium.

Staines Town, November 1973. The same designer seems to have built Addlestone's stand. Six rows of benches were provided for spectators. Opposite was a long low covered area.

By the early 1990s, the stricter ground-grading requirements forced Staines to leave Wheatsheaf Park. Staines moved to ground share with Chertsey Town in 1995 but after three years returned to the Wheatsheaf, having carried out the necessary improvements to maintain their Isthmian League status. With its desirable location close to the river Thames, it attracted the attention of a development company who offered to part-finance the construction of a new ground as part of a larger project to build a health and sports club. Planning permission for a £6.5 million scheme was granted in 2000 and the Football Foundation also awarded a grant for this development. Due to the scale of the reconstruction work, Staines Town were forced to spend twenty-two months away from Wheatsheaf Park, during which they played their home matches at Walton & Hersham, Chertsey Town and Egham Town.

The football stadium was completed and the first game on the revitalised ground was against Carshalton Athletic on 22 February 2003. The ground had been almost completely rebuilt. There is a massive brick building built close to where the old clubhouse used to be. This houses the privately owned Thames Club, whose facilities include a swimming pool, a gymnasium, a spa and sauna room, a restaurant and banqueting facilities. There is a well-elevated grandstand attached to this building with a high roof. It presently holds 288 spectators but can be extended to hold 500 if the demand ever arises. There is a viewing gallery running along the top of the seating tier with bar area behind, and this is used by Staines as their clubhouse. A small strip of terracing has been squeezed in at the bus-stop end and there is a long and low prefabricated shelter opposite the grandstand with steps stretching along its length. There are four corner pylons for the 400-lux floodlighting system.

ALEX'S FIRST TIME: I saw an Isthmian League Division One encounter between Staines Town and Bromley on 13 April 1985. There was a crowd of about 200. The ground was pleasant but basic and only a short walk to a very picturesque section of the river Thames.

SUTTON UNITED
Ground: Borough Sports Ground, Gander Green Lane, Sutton, Surrey.

Two clubs, Sutton St Barnabus and Sutton Guild Rovers, merged in 1898 to form the current club. After one season of using both grounds, all matches were played at Manor Lane. The ground was roped off but spectators had a free view and an enclosed site was needed. Funds became available to fence the ground off a couple of years later. Manor Lane remained Sutton's home until grounds at Rose Hill, the Fairfield Ground at Collingham Road and London Road were used, prior to United gaining the use of a pitch called 'The Find' in Grove Road. They moved to their present ground in August 1919. It was called the Adult School Sports Ground in Gander Green Lane ground in those days. The venue had already been in existence for seven years and had a small wooden stand. The club secured admission to the Athenian League in 1921 and won the championship in 1927/28 with 43 points from 27 games.

The Sports Ground was renamed the Borough Sports Ground after the local council purchased it from the local school in 1934. It had a cinder running track with a post, and rail-and-picket fencing around the playing area. The two stands were at the side of the ground and rough banking stretched around the oval-shaped site. There was a fence, which divided the ground from the Recreation Ground next door. The club had to wait eighteen years before they won the Athenian League title again in 1945/46 and that season Sutton also did well in FA Cup, beating Guildford, Wimbledon, Walton & Hersham, Tooting & Mitcham and Gillingham (by nine goals to three) to reach the first round proper. Amateur international centre forward Charles Vaughan scored 68 goals in this season and later signed as a professional for Charlton Athletic.

During the 1940s the Collingwood Road end was extended, banked and terraced with railway sleepers and a car park was created between the ground and the railway. A new grandstand was opened in 1953 at a cost of £3,000. It held 1,100 seated spectators and is still used today. Sutton United won the Athenian League championship in 1957/58 and in their first appearance in the London Senior Cup final gained a excellent victory over Finchley. The club accommodation under the stand was not completed until 1961 and this included dressing rooms, clubrooms and bars. Floodlights soon followed. The club visited Wembley twice for Amateur Cup finals in 1963 and 1969, but lost both games. They had a great FA Cup run in 1969/70 which culminated in a 14,000 crowd squeezing into Gander Green Lane for a fourth-round visit of Leeds United, who won 6-0. To make sure the match took place at Sutton's home, the council strengthened the terracing and renewed banking, fences and gates. Bench seating was borrowed from The Oval cricket ground and arranged around the track. The club took over the

Sutton United, April 1976. Both built in the 1930s, the left hand stand held 125, the other 132. Opposite was the current main stand, built in 1959. There was a running track round the pitch at this time.

running of the ground in 1975 and Sutton reached the final of the FA Trophy in 1980/81 but they lost again at Wembley, this time to Bishops Stortford. The athletics club, who had shared the ground, moved out, and the club replaced the two original wooden stands with the present structure in time for the entry into the Conference League in 1986. The track was no longer required and it was squared off at the Gander Green Lane end, terracing being built instead. Sutton reached the third round of the FA Cup in 1987/88 where they met Middlesbrough at Gander Green Lane. They had beaten Aldershot and Peterborough United to reach this stage. A tight match saw Sutton grab a replay with Mark Golley's late header but they lost the game at Ayresome Park to an extra-time goal. They were paired with Coventry City in the FA Cup in January 1989 and pulled off a shock victory by beating them 2-1 with goals from Tony Rains and Matty Hanlan. The run ended at another First Division side, Norwich City, with an 8-0 defeat in front of over 23,000 at Carrow Road.

Sutton were relegated back to the Isthmian League in 1989/90 after a run of eight straight defeats as United finished in the third relegation spot. They won the Isthmian League title again in 1998/99 in their centenary year to return briefly to the Conference.

ALEX'S FIRST TIME: I have visited Gander Green Lane on many occasions. They have had a succession of very entertaining sides over the years and the atmosphere is always warm and friendly. I visited for the first time on 19 April 1986 for an Isthmian Premier Division match with Hitchin Town that the U's won 4-1. This was before the strangely shaped wooden stands disappeared on the Rec. side of the ground.

Thames Association, 1928. (Aerofilms, ref. 24264)

THAMES ASSOCIATION
Ground: West Ham Stadium, Prince Regent Lane, Custom House, London E13.

Thames Association was a football club created to occupy the newly constructed West Ham Stadium. A sports ground had previously existed on the site before the building of the arena and was known as the Custom House Sports Ground. Narrow soil embankments surrounded a rectangular playing field with a small enclosure centrally located on the south side. The ground was surrounded by allotments. The West Ham Stadium was completed in 1928 and the most popular use of the stadium proved to be greyhound and speedway racing. The record attendance for the stadium was the 64,000 that watched a speedway international meeting between England and Australia. The first dog meeting on 4 August 1928 attracted more than 56,000 spectators – a record for the sport. The claimed capacity was 120,000 and the venue was the largest ground ever used regularly by a Football League team in England. The playing arena was an enormous oval shape and the stadium was similar in appearance to Wembley Stadium. It was surrounded with two banks of different levels of concrete terracing. There were two seating enclosures, but these held only about 5,000. These were located on each side of the ground and extended partly around each end.

Thames were always going to struggle to attract new support with established clubs like West Ham United, Clapton Orient, Leytonstone and Ilford on their doorstep. Their first game in the Southern League was at Aldershot on 23 August 1928 that was drawn 2-2. The first home match at the West Ham Stadium was for the visit of Brighton Reserves when a crowd of 3,000 attended. This small crowd would have looked lost in this vast arena and to make matters worse the visitors won 2-0. Despite finishing fourteenth in the Southern League, the club applied unsuccessfully for entry into the Football League.

The club was already £3,000 in debt by the start of 1929/30, but finished third in the table and again applied to join the Football League. Amazingly, they were successful despite their poor crowds. They joined the Third Division (South) and before the season began had improved the pitch by returfing it and also installing a new drainage system.

The first Football League match at the West Ham Stadium attracted a new record 7,000 crowd that saw Thames win 4-1. However, the attendances quickly declined and when Luton Town visited on 6 December 1930, only 469 spectators paid to watch the match. In contrast, the speedway club was attracting crowds of about 25,000. Thames' final season started brightly when a new record crowd of over 8,000 attended a 0-0 draw with Exeter City on 29 August 1931. After a run of defeats the club found themselves at the bottom of the League – where they stayed. The season had been a disaster throughout and they finished bottom with only 7 wins in 42 games. On 3 June 1932, a press release stated that the club had decided to withdraw its re-election application. Secretary Mr H.R. Milbank stated: 'Lack of funds prohibits us from continuing in the League. Indeed we are disbanding altogether and will not compete in any competition.'

The West Ham Stadium survived until 1972, when the site was sold for redevelopment. The final speedway meeting took place on 23 May 1972 and the last greyhound meeting took place three days later. The stadium was demolished and replaced with housing, and no traces remain today.

THAMESMEAD TOWN
Ground: Bayliss Avenue, Thamesmead, London SE28.

Thamesmead was created in the late 1960s as a new town on the Thames close to Abbeywood. Thamesmead Town was formed in 1970. Their first ground was The Meridian Sports Ground in Charlton. They joined the London Spartan League in 1980 and won the 'Third' Division title in 1979/80 and by the end of the 1980s were playing in its Premier Division. They moved to their present ground at Bayliss Avenue in 1988 and opened the ground with a match against FA Cup holders Wimbledon before a record crowd of 400. They nearly beat this during 1994/95 when 363 saw a Kent League encounter with Dartford. Thamesmead Town joined the Kent League Division One in 1991 and, in 1993/94, they finished fourth and reached the semi-final of the League Cup but lost to Ramsgate. This division was renamed the Premier Division in 1998. They were Kent League runners-up on goal difference in 1999/2000, winning 23 of their 34 games, and could have won the title if they had not had 3 points deducted. During 2002/03, they missed the runners-up spot on goal difference. They have entered the FA Cup since 1994. Their best season in that competition came in 1998/99 when they lost to Harrow Borough in the second qualifying round, and also 2003/04 where they lost to Thame United at the same stage. They have faired better in the FA Vase and in 1995/96 reached the fifth round by beating Chipstead, Ashford Town (Middlesex), Arlesey Town, Brentwood and Chichester City before losing 2-1 at home to Canvey Island. They also reached the fourth round in 2000/01 before losing to Rushall Olympic in a replay.

Thamesmead Town, August 1988. By 2004 a stand with 144 seats had replaced this bit of cover.

BOB'S FIRST TIME: This was for Thamesmead Town *v.* Bromley Athletic in the London Spartan League Premier Division on 23 August 1988. Newly promoted Thamesmead Town won 1-0 before fifty fans. Bayliss Avenue was a fairly new ground and had dressing rooms and a social club behind one goal and a bit of cover on the halfway line with one chair in it.

THAMES POLYTECHNIC
Ground: Kidbrooke Lane, Well Hall, Eltham, London SE9.

Thames Polytechnic are today playing at Intermediate level but they have a long history. The club was formed in 1888 and initially played under the name Woolwich Polytechnic Young Men's Christian Institution. From 1888-1895 they played at Charlton Park. By 1900 a new recreation ground had been acquired at Church Manorway, Plumstead, with four football and three cricket pitches. Here the polytechnic's soccer club spent their early years until the ground was required for new railway sidings during the First World War. Fortunately, twenty acres at Kidbrooke Lane, Well Hall, Eltham, became available shortly afterwards – thus began the polytechnic's long association with Eltham.

Woolwich Polytechnic obtained senior status and entered the London League Division Two in 1900/01. The club transferred its allegiance to the Amateur Football Alliance in 1911 and, after failing to gain admission to the Southern Amateur League, played in the Southern Olympian League, which included many well-known clubs, among them Cambridge Town and Highgate. The club also reached the semi-final of the AFA Senior Cup in 1912/13 before being beaten at Ipswich Town 3-2 before a record crowd. Two famous players appeared for the club at this time: Charlie Buchan who subsequently played for Sunderland, Arsenal and England, and Gordon Hoare, the English amateur international and Woolwich Arsenal player who was a member of the club's London League side from 1901-03. Woolwich Polytechnic finished at the top of the Eastern Division of the London League in 1945/46 and won the Dewar Shield, beating Edgware Town, the winners of the Western Division, by three goals to one. Another landmark of the early 1950s was the completion of a grandstand on the club's ground at Well Hall. The poly were forced to leave the London League in 1956 after a row over which league their reserve side should play in. The club was accepted into the senior section of the Kent Amateur League (Western Section) but returned to the London League in 1963/64. This competition eventually became the London Spartan League in 1974/75.

The next milestone was in 1971 when the name of the Woolwich Polytechnic was changed to Thames Polytechnic. New training facilities became available at the polytechnic's Dartford Campus ground in 1979/80 and, although welcomed, it took the players away from Well Hall, and the general atmosphere suffered. Training continued at Dartford until 1982 when the much-delayed construction of the Rochester Way relief road began. In compensation for the loss of land the polytechnic were granted sufficient cash to allow a floodlit all-weather area to be constructed at Well Hall. One of the best seasons in recent years saw the poly finish third in the London Spartan League in 1984/85 but they moved to the Kent League the following season. The club was still playing at Well Hall by 1998 but in the Kent County League. The eighty-seater stand was still in place but its roof was in need of repair. One of their most famous players of recent years is John Regis, who in 1982/83, at the age of sixteen, received the Player of the Year award. However, he was also interested in athletics and pursued his sprinting career. John became a world-class sprinter who specialised in the 200 metres, and went on to win a silver medal at the World Championships in Rome as well as other major medals.

Thames Polytechnic, April 1986. The cover consisted of five concrete steps. The dressing rooms and social facilities are in the half-timbered building.

BOB'S FIRST TIME: There was a large turnout of groundhoppers for a match between Thames Polytechnic and 4 Area Metropolitan Police in a Kent League Division One match. Thames lost 4-2 before a crowd of sixty. The football ground consisted of a railed-off pitch on one side of a large sports field. There was a cover with five concrete steps on the halfway line and close to the corner flag was a large two-storey social club with dressing rooms.

THURROCK/PURFLEET
Ground: The Thurrock Hotel, Ship Lane, Purfleet, Essex.

This is a club that has come to prominence over the last few years from a humble beginning. Purfleet Football Club was founded as recently as April 1985, when two junior clubs, Rainham WM and Fondu, merged. The first competitive game was played on 24 August 1985 against Canvey Island Reserves in Division One of the Essex Senior League and resulted in a 3-0 win. The club's ground forms part of the Thurrock Hotel and Oasis Leisure Complex and at first consisted of two pitches and dressing rooms in the hotel. The whole site was originally Aveley Technical College until permission was granted to create a leisure centre on the redundant space. Midway through the first season the playing area was turned round and work started on the dressing-room areas to become a self-contained unit away from the main hotel complex. At the end of the season, Purfleet had finished third in the league and were granted senior status by the Essex County FA. They were also winners in the League Cup, defeating Burnham Ramblers 2-0 in the final. Within a year, an impressive 300-seat stand was built along

Thurrock, March 1996. On Bob's original visit in 1986, players changed in the hotel behind and there was no spectator shelter. The stand holds 220 and there is cover behind both goals.

with new changing facilities and floodlights. The floodlights went up in January 1988 and the first game under them was an Essex Thameside Trophy match against Pennant that the visitors won 2-1. Behind the far (eastern) goal the dressing rooms and tea bar were built, all housed in a pleasant brick-built building fronted by a small flowerbed.

An application was made to join the Isthmian League and after finishing as Essex Senior League champions they were duly elected. Purfleet finished runners-up to Harlow Town in Division Two (North) in their first season and were promoted to Division One but they were soon relegated into Division Two (North).

Purfleet had their best ever run in the FA Vase in 1990/91, reaching the last thirty-two. They finished winners of Division Two and won the Loctite Trophy the following season. Covered terracing was installed for some 800 people in 1993/94 to achieve the 'A' grading required for promotion, and the club finished runners-up to Bishop Stortford to gain promotion to the Premier Division. An attendance record of 1,578 was set in 1996 when West Ham visited for a pre-season friendly. This was beaten in July 1998, when West Ham were again the visitors, when the crowd was 2,572. The club changed its name to Thurrock during the summer of 2003 and continues to do well in the Premier Division.

BOB'S FIRST TIME: Bob visited what was then called the Essex Sports & Leisure Centre shortly after the ground had opened, so facilities were rather basic. Purfleet played out a 2-2 draw with Brentwood in their first match in the Essex Senior League Division One on 26 August 1986. The ground consisted of a wooden fence that enclosed the ground, a brick dugout and dressing rooms in the hotel. The ground has changed out of all recognition in recent years.

TOOTING & MITCHAM UNITED
Ground: Imperial Fields, Bishopsford Road, Morden, Surrey.

One of the best non-League grounds in the country disappeared when Tooting & Mitcham sold their former Sandy Lane ground for redevelopment and moved to their new one at Imperial Fields in 2002. The Tooting part of the club that was to become Tooting & Mitcham United in 1932 was originally founded in 1887 as Tooting Graveney and played their first matches on Figges Marsh. They won the South-Western Cup in 1898 and 1900. After an amalgamation with local rivals St Johns, from the neighbouring village of Balham, admission was gained to the Surrey Suburban League. Mitcham Vestry gave the club notice to quit their ground and they moved to the Lonesome Ground in Streatham that proved most unsatisfactory as it was underwater for most of the winter. The club was playing at the North Surrey Poultry Farm at Gorringe Park by 1907/08 and they won the Suburban League before moving again to a field beside the railway on what is now the Ridgeway. They successfully applied to join the Athenian League in 1914 but this league closed down after only one game.

The club was re-formed under the title of Tooting Town in 1919. The club's headquarters were at the Forester's Arms and a tenancy of two pitches on Tyrell Poultry

Tooting & Mitcham United, September 1976. Replacing an old wooden grandstand, this stand was started in about 1958 and never completed as the final third envisaged on the right was never built. Apart from the enclosure in front there was no covered terracing. The other three sides of the ground had extensive concrete terracing.

Farm was taken at £60 per annum. After winning the Southern Suburban League, they secured admission to the London League. Some of the committee members decided to purchase their own ground and the venue at Sandy Lane, Mitcham, was secured with a local dairyman, Mr Brown, advancing the extra £450 needed to complete the purchase. Sandy Lane was quickly enclosed and a local firm of contractors designed and erected the wooden stand that cost £600 and seated 360. Tooting experienced some difficult financial times, owing mainly to the proximity of the Mitcham Wanderers club who played at Streatham Lane.

Mitcham had been formed in 1912 by a group of lads from Lower Mitcham who used to frequent Ern's Coffee Shop at Cranmer Green. The first eleven competed in the Wimbledon League and their teams came very much into the limelight in junior ranks in the years following the First World War, when they won many local cups, including the London Junior Cup and the Surrey Junior Cup. Mitcham Wanderers moved to Streatham Lane in 1922 and senior status was attained. They joined the London League (First Division) and were quickly promoted to the Premier Division in the following season. They were champions in 1928/29 and runners-up the following season. With both clubs in the London League a merger seemed logical and this took place in 1932, with the new club playing at Sandy Lane. The existing stand was lengthened by adding four more bays to increase the seating capacity to 600. The club moved upwards into the Athenian League in 1937. Terracing was built at the Sandy Lane end in 1946, along with a new fence and turnstile block. The terraces were extended right around the ground in time for an Amateur Cup tie with Leytonstone that attracted over 10,000 fans. New dressing rooms were built at a cost of £3,500 and were opened by Sir Stanley Rous in December 1950. Prior to this the players had to use two former army huts, after the original dressing rooms were destroyed in the Second World War.

Tooting & Mitcham won the Athenian League championship twice in 1949/50 and 1954/55 and were invited to join the Isthmian League in 1956. They went on to win the championship in 1957/58 and 1959/60. The club considered buying one of the massive stands at the soon-to-be-demolished Mitcham Stadium in 1957, which was next door to Sandy Lane. The stand was eventually moved to The Eyrie at Bedford Town. The club had a great run in the FA Cup during 1958/59. Over 10,000 saw Bournemouth and Northampton Town beaten at Sandy Lane in the first and second rounds. In the third round, Nottingham Forest attracted 14,300 to Sandy Lane on a frozen January day and Tooting came close to pulling off a major shock before a late penalty meant a replay at the City Ground Nottingham, and an eventual 3-0 defeat. A crowd of over 17,000 saw the championship decider against Dulwich in May 1960. During the 1960s there were more ground improvements, including a new clubhouse in March 1962 and new floodlights. Arsenal visited to open them (the lighting was upgraded in 1985). There was another large crowd at Sandy Lane for an FA Cup tie against Crystal Palace in 1974, and the following season saw the club reach the fourth round of the cup, this including a tie with Swindon that was watched by 7,500 spectators.

Tooting went into decline after this and finished in the bottom two of the Isthmian League in 1983/84 and were only saved from the drop as Staines Town did not have the required ground grading. There was no reprieve in 1988/89 when the club was relegated for the first time in its history. Fourth place was attained in 1993/94 and promotion missed by just two points, but relegation to Division Two became a reality at the end of the 1996/97 season when a miserable run of results saw only 8 points gained from the final 20 league games, and they finished bottom of Division One with only 32 points. The club's best season for many years came in 2000/01 when they reached the quarter-finals of the FA Vase before defeat came at the hands of eventual winners Taunton Town. Even more importantly, the Ryman League Second Division championship was won, despite a huge fixture backlog.

Sandy Lane became very dilapidated and neglected in its latter years but work started on the new ground at Bishopsford Road in 1999 after many delays, and was completed for the start of 2002/03. The club secured a ninety-nine-year lease on the ground, which is owned by former Palace chairman Ron Noades. The new site had previously been used by Crystal Palace as a training ground. The club decided to call the new ground 'Imperial Fields' and the large site features a large floodlit all-weather pitch, changing rooms and club buildings. The large 600-seat main stand is fitted out with black-and-white seats that spell out TMFC. The stand is elevated so all seats have an excellent view of the playing area. There are identical terraces at the Bishopsford Road and Wandle ends of the stadium, each with a capacity of 1,200, and room for 300 beneath small open-backed covers.

ALEX'S FIRST TIME: I visited Sandy Lane for the first time on 26 November 1977 for an FA Cup first-round tie between Tooting & Mitcham and Northampton Town. The Cobblers won 2-1 before a crowd of 3,513. The ground was in good condition in those days and well looked after. The terracing was impressive enough but the stand was almost full and helped create a great atmosphere. I was sad to see this ground disappear, but I attended the first ever match at the new Imperial Fields on 30 July 2002 when the club met a Chelsea XI in a pre-season friendly before an attendance of 1,500. It is refreshing to see a new ground that is interesting to look at and well designed.

TOTTENHAM HOTSPUR
Ground: White Hart Lane, Tottenham High Road, Tottenham, London N17.

The club was formed by a group of cricketers back in 1882 who initially called the club Hotspur FC. Their first ground was on Tottenham Marshes and they stored their homemade goalposts at Northumberland Park railway station. The players had to cross the Great Eastern railway line to reach their pitch. They changed their name to Tottenham Hotspur in 1885 and in September 1888 they moved to their first enclosed ground, at nearby Northumberland Park. This new venue was behind the Northumberland Arms on Trulock Road, close to the present ground. A stand was finally built in 1894 but it blew down in a gale soon afterwards. The following year, the club turned professional. Northumberland Park saw its record crowd when over 14,000 spectators watched a match with Woolwich Arsenal in April 1899. The roof of a tea bar collapsed under the weight of spectators, causing several minor injuries. The ground at Northumberland Park was an open Recreation Ground for many years but is now covered by a school.

Spurs needed a better ground to deal with their large crowds. They found Beckwith's Nursery, behind the White Hart Inn on Tottenham High Road. Charrington's, the brewers, owned the nursery and they initially wanted to build houses on the site. However, the landlord of the nearby White Hart public house wanted a football club so that he could improve his trade by serving Spurs fans on match days. The Tottenham directors then approached Charrington's and agreed a tenancy. To start with, the new ground had very limited facilities and Spurs brought over the wooden stand they had used at the Northumberland Park ground that provided cover for 2,500 spectators. The new ground was instantly successful and crowds were close to the 10,000 mark. Spurs ended their first season at White Hart Lane as Southern League champions. They also became the last non-Football League side to win the FA Cup when they beat Sheffield United in a replayed final at Burnden Park, Bolton in 1901. As a consequence, the club expanded the terracing to hold 32,000. Five hundred seats were placed in their basic main stand.

Tottenham used the issue of 5,000 shares to help them purchase the ground's freehold in 1905. Their next move was to purchase the land behind the Paxton Road End (then known as the Edmonton End). When they were elected to the Football League Second Division in 1908, the ground had grown in size and now held approximately 40,000. Within a year they were promoted to the First Division and in September 1909 they opened their first major stand for the visit of Manchester United. This was designed by Archibald Leitch, and was a larger version of the stands he had built at Fulham and Chelsea. The new west stand had 5,300 seats, a paddock for 6,000, and a mock-Tudor gable on its roof. A year later, the model of a cockerel, perched on a ball, was placed on the roof. The cockerel and ball had cost £35 and had been crafted by W.J. Scott, a former Spurs amateur who worked for a coppersmiths on Euston Road. There was a new rival for the supremacy in North London when Arsenal moved from Plumstead to a new ground at Highbury. To make matters worse they 'stole' Spurs' place in the First Division in 1919. After winning the FA Cup again in 1921, Spurs set up offices at the Red House, a former restaurant, at 748 Tottenham High Road. They covered the Paxton Road End in 1921, and the Park Lane End in 1923 with an almost identical roof, designed by Leitch. He also played a major role when the east side of the ground was at last developed in 1934. This had been a plain uncovered terrace area but the new development would transform this side of the ground. It cost a massive £60,000 to build the new east stand but it was a matter of keeping up with what had been going on at Highbury, where Arsenal had invested huge amounts of money in modernising their stadium. The scheme was not as grand as it seemed at first glance, as in reality it was a classic Leitch double-decker stand placed above the existing east terrace. To make way for this a row of houses behind it had to be demolished and a roof gable housed the press box ('The Crow's Nest'). There were 5,100 seats on the upper tier, standing for 11,000 on the mid-tier (which became known as The Shelf), and uncovered terracing on the lower level for a further 8,000, Tottenham's east stand was one of Leitch's last major works before he died in 1939.

During the Second World War, Arsenal moved to play at White Hart Lane when Highbury was bombed. During heavy bombing in London, the east stand was used as a mortuary for a time. The pitch at Spurs was poor and in an attempt to improve it, 3,500 tons of sub-soil were dug up from the pitch and dumped on Hackney Marshes, and a new surface laid in its place during 1953. Floodlights were installed on four corner poles soon afterwards and extra lamps were mounted on the two stand gables in 1957. The cockerel was moved from the west to the east stand gable in 1958. The 1960s and early 1970s was a period of great success for the club. Not only did they do well in domestic competitions, but they also won the European Cup Winners' Cup and UEFA Cup. Yet for all the club's wealth, its redevelopment policy remained conservative and very little was done to improve the ground despite the money made from these successes. There were some improvements to the floodlights and the rear sections of each end terrace were converted to seating. Corner sections were added to the west stand in 1968 and at the Paxton Road end in 1972, adding 2,100 seats. It became clear by 1975 that the club needed to replace the ageing wooden west stand. The costs of the new stand rose from £3.5m to £6m in the process of being built and, when completed, only held 6,900 seats due to so many executive boxes being included in the development. The demolition of Leitch's much-loved but ageing west stand began in November 1980 and Sir Stanley Rous opened the new west stand on 6 February 1982 before a game against Wolves. It had a double layer of glazed executive tiers. White Hart Lane's capacity was now 48,200, including 17,600 seats, while average gates topped 35,000.

Due to the Bradford fire of 1985, Spurs were facing stringent demands for safety work to be done to the older stands. Despite spending nearly £500,000 on the ground, the club was told to cut the capacity on the Shelf (part of the east stand) due to its limited number of exits. In January 1987 the decision was taken to renovate the existing stand at a cost of £4.8m. This included a new roof (not completed until 2000) to improve cover for spectators and a new TV gantry and floodlights were put in place. A restaurant and bar was added, the concourses refurbished and the upper tier was given new seats. Thirty-six executive boxes were added. These turned out to be the most retrogressive,

Tottenham Hotspur, August 1986. Archibald Leitch's east stand with press box and cockerel above.

badly managed and overpriced stand refurbishments ever carried out in British football as costs rose to £8.6m. To make matters worse, the fans were very unhappy with the new development. After a great deal of lobbying, a small terrace holding 3,000 spectators remained in place in the new development, but this was replaced with seating in 1994 when White Hart Lane became an all-seater stadium. At this time the Park Lane Stand was demolished to make way for a new structure. The construction of this new 8,517 seat south stand cost £9 million and was completed by mid-1995. This brought all four stand roof lines to the same level, with the ground's overall capacity now only 33,157. The next development was the replacement of the north stand upper tier, which cost another £6m.

ALEX'S FIRST TIME: It was a very hot day when I saw Tottenham Hotspur play Manchester United on 10 September 1966 in a crowd of 56,295. I remember very little about the match as I felt so ill because of the heat. This was a shame as some of the best players of the era were playing, including George Best, Bobby Charlton, Denis Law and Jimmy Greaves. The ground was packed and I saw very little of the action.

TUFNELL PARK

Ground: Recreation Ground, Huddlestone Road, Tufnell Park, London N7.

Tufnell Park was founded in 1905 and the club started their competitive career in the London League in 1907. Tufnell Park reached the second round of the FA Amateur Cup in 1910/11 (losing 4-1 at Bromley), but one year later they reached the semi-finals before losing to Eston United at Stockton. They had another successful run two years later, when they again reached the semi-finals but they lost to Northern Nomads, in a game played at Herne Hill. The club established themselves as a famous amateur club after making tours to Spain, Denmark, Sweden, Czechoslovakia, Germany, Belgium, Holland and France before the war. The club closed down during the First World War but re-emerged again in 1918/19 when they played in the United Senior League, eventually finishing as runners-up.

The club joined the Isthmian League in 1919 and the first two seasons were very encouraging, with two third-place finishes. However, they often struggled in the league and had to seek re-election in 1928 and 1930, although they managed to finish third again in 1937/38. Tufnell Park reached the final of the FA Amateur Cup in 1919/20 after beating Stanley United in the semi-final in a match played at Bishop Auckland. Unfortunately, they lost the final to Dulwich Hamlet 1-0 (after extra time) at The Den, watched by a crowd of 25,000. Their best run in the FA Cup came in 1921/22 when they narrowly beat Ilford 1-0 in the fifth qualifying round, before facing Grimsby Town in the next round. The amateurs forced a notable 1-1 draw at Cleethorpes but lost the replay by 4 goals to 1.

Tufnell Park, April 1983. The Barrass Stadium was one of many venues used after the Second World War. The main stand had twenty rows of seats, while on the opposite side a covered terrace ran the length of the pitch.

For many years they had shared their ground with London Caledonians and both now needed to find a new ground. Tufnell Park had moved in with the Calies in 1905. The main entrance to the ground was (and still is) in the south-east corner, off Tufnell Park Road. The ground was known as the Recreation Ground, Junction Road and was also used for cricket. When the ground was first used it was partially enclosed by houses on two sides with little in the way of facilities. Later the ground was fenced in to form a proper enclosure and by 1914 a grandstand was built on the south side of the ground with other adjacent structures, and some terracing along the Campdale Road side of the ground. North London Polytechnic, the landlords, reclaimed Tufnell Park's ground in 1939.

Tufnell Park continued to play during the hostilities, sharing the ground of Golders Green FC (later named Hendon FC). The team played for one season (1940/41) in the Herts & Middlesex Senior Amateur League, but all fixtures after this were either friendly matches or cup competitions. They twice played at Wembley Stadium, where they contested the final of the Middlesex Red Cross Cup in 1944 and 1945. When peace resumed the club had to search around for a new ground, and settled on groundshare with Cheshunt at their Albury Ride venue. For a post-war history of the club, see the section on Haringey Borough.

The ground was oval in shape and the grandstand was capable of seating around 500 spectators. It had a simple pitched roof that was supported by five wooden stanchions. After Tufnell Park and London Caledonians were forced to leave this venue, it remained in use as a sports ground. The grandstand remained intact until the 1970s before being taken down. A school building had been tacked on to one end of the grandstand by the time it was demolished and half of the former football pitch had been tarmacked. It was still maintained as a sports ground by the University of North London in the 1990s.

TWICKENHAM
Ground: The Beveree, Station Road, Hampton, Middlesex.

There was a club called Twickenham that played in local leagues before the Second World War, but this does not seem to be connected with the later club of that name. They played in the South-West Middlesex League and the club's main honour of note was the winning of the Middlesex Junior Cup in 1923. A new club was formed in 1943 and joined the Middlesex League. They played under the guise of the Brentford FC reserve team during 1943/44 and became joint champions (with Edgware Town) in 1944/45. They moved up a level and joined the Corinthian League in 1945, but the team had a poor season and finished second from bottom in the table.

Twickenham became Brentford's nursery club in 1945/46 and played some matches at Griffin Park. They entered the FA Cup during 1946/47 but lost at Acton Town 2-1 in the extra preliminary round. Twickenham joined the newly formed Home Counties League in 1949, but the league's name quickly changed to the Metropolitan & District League and Twickenham finished in sixth place out of nine clubs. Twickenham were out of their depth at this level and in 1953 decided to move down to the Parthenon League (formerly the Middlesex Senior League) and won the Premier Division championship in 1958/59.

The club played at an open sports ground in Hanworth Road from their formation, but solved their ground problems in 1952 when they controversially managed to obtain a seven-year lease on The Beveree in Station Road, Hampton. Hampton FC were also keen to obtain the lease but Twickenham gained it by virtue of the mayor's casting vote. Luckily for them, he was a prominent member of Twickenham FC! For some years there was bad feelings between the two clubs until Hampton won back the lease at The Beveree in 1959. During Twickenham's occupation, there were few facilities at The Beveree. When the club lost their Beveree ground, a new one was found at Ivy Bridge, Twickenham Road, in Isleworth. This was probably little more than a field and most likely not enclosed. Some years were spent here, but by the mid-1960s the club had moved on again, this time to Redlees Park, which was also just off Twickenham Road with the entrance off Worton Road. This ground possessed a pavilion but little else. The club moved to Heston Park in 1969, and this was again a non-enclosed ground; the club folded around 1974.

UXBRIDGE
Ground: Honeycroft, Horton Road, West Drayton, Middlesex.

The original Uxbridge club was formed as long ago as 1870. In those days, the club wore a white strip, before changing to the current red strip in 1880. The club was successful during its first ten years and two of their players, the Heron brothers, gained full international caps for England. They also entered the FA Cup for the first time in 1873/74 and beat Gitanes 3-0 at home in the first round. The club became members of the Southern League and reached the FA Amateur Cup final in 1897/98, where they lost to Middlesbrough 2-0 at the old Crystal Palace ground. Uxbridge nearly folded with a deficit of £130 at the turn of the century but recovered and joined the Great Western Combination League in 1906/07.

They played at The Common, Colne Farm, Hillingdon House Farm and Cowley Road before the First World War. The club became known as Uxbridge Town in 1919 and may have reformed after the war when they joined the Athenian League. Uxbridge finished bottom at the end of their first season and were not re-elected but rejoined the league from 1924. Uxbridge moved to the RAF stadium at Uxbridge in 1923, but suffered a severe blow when they lost the lease on the stadium in 1937 and, consequently, their place in the Athenian League. The club may have re-formed again at this time, as they were called just plain Uxbridge when they re-emerged in 1939 to join the Great Western Combination League, and continued to play during the Second World War before joining the London League in 1944/45.

The club became a limited company in 1948 and a large house called Honeycroft, at Cleveland Road in Cowley, was bought and converted into a ground. This is now part of Brunel University. The club has played regularly in the FA Cup since 1945/46 and they have reached the third qualifying round five times. They joined the Corinthian League in 1948, finished as runners-up in their first season and were champions in 1959/60. Uxbridge rejoined the Athenian League in 1963/64 but were relegated in 1967.

Uxbridge, December 1975. The original Honeycroft had a stand built in 1958 holding about 400 on seven rows of wood seats. Opposite was terracing the middle part covered. Behind one goal was terracing.

Uxbridge were in debt by the 1960s and the ground was mortgaged. An investment company served them with a notice to quit their ground. The club purchased its current ground in 1978; this is also called the Honeycroft and they spent over £170,000 improving it. A new stand emerged in 1979 and they played Arsenal to mark the opening of the new floodlights in 1981. This attracted a record crowd of 1,000. Uxbridge finished third in the Athenian League in 1981/82 and were elected to the Isthmian League. They had their best season in the FA Vase in 1983/84 when they reached the fourth round before losing to Irthlingborough Diamonds. More success came in 1984/85 when they were runners-up of the Second Division (South) and reached the final of the AC Delco Cup in its inaugural year, losing 3-1 to Sutton United. New covered accommodation was built in 1984 and the following year terraces were created behind the goals. The grandstand was enlarged in 1987. The club beat Brentford in the Middlesex Charity Cup final in 1993, when the Bees included names such as Joe Allon, Simon Ratcliffe and Terry Evans. The 1993/94 season closed with the London Challenge Cup final at Honeycroft against Welling United. In an eventful game the Reds won 3-0. Recently their best finishes in the league have been fifth, in 1997/98 and 2002/03. They entered Division One (North) when the league was reorganised in 2002.

ALEX'S FIRST TIME: I have seen a match at their old RAF stadium that still exists today. This was a game between the FA Colts and the Combined Services FA, and was played on 5 March 1985. The Colts included Paul Ince, Neil Ruddock and David Howells in their line-up. The grandstand was large and the pitch was surrounded by an athletics track. I visited the Honeycroft at West Drayton on 29 January 1994 for a match between Uxbridge and Croydon. The ground was neat and well looked-after.

VIKING GREENFORD
Ground: Avenue Park, Western Avenue, Greenford, Middlesex.

The club started life as a youth team formed in 1945 and the first match was played at Ravenor Park, Greenford against 342 Squadron ATC. The young Viking team became founder members of the Ealing Youth League in 1948 and they progressed quickly through the many divisions of the old Dauntless League, before joining the Nemean (AFA) in 1956. The club made an historic tour of the Soviet Union in 1965 and played one of the top Ukrainian teams, losing 10-1 to Desna Chernigov before 10,000 all-seated spectators at the Yuri Gagarin Stadium. Viking undertook another extraordinary tour to Czechoslovakia three years later where they drew 2-2 with Sokol. However, that night, forces of the combined Warsaw Pact invaded the country and the town was surrounded by troops. Viking moved into the Middlesex League in 1970/71, finishing in the runners-up spot in the first season.

The club moved from Churchfields to Avenue Park, Greenford in 1967. Over the years they developed this once-derelict site into a fine ground with excellent facilities, including a covered stand behind one of the goals. Floodlights were erected in 1992. The club switched to the Hellenic League in 1980, finishing in third position in 1982 and then runners-up in 1985/86, securing promotion to the Premier Division. The club gained senior status in 1987 after a great deal of effort to improve the ground's facilities. Unfortunately, the clubhouse was completely destroyed by a fire later that year and they were also relegated at the end of that season. On Friday 7 July 1989 the local MP, Harry Greenway, officially opened the new clubhouse and changing facilities. The cost was partially covered by insurance but they had to raise the rest of the money themselves. Travelling was, however, becoming a problem, the nearest opponents being Wallingford Town, and the club was accepted into the Combined Counties League.

Viking Sports, August 1986. A hole cut in a caravan was the only cover. By 2004 cover had been erected behind the goal.

Viking celebrated their Golden Jubilee in 1995 by finishing as runners-up in the Co-Co League to Ashford Town. Since then the club has had little success until 1999/2000 when they reached the League Cup final but lost to Walton Casuals 4-2. Severe financial constraints had a detrimental effect on any ground or clubhouse improvements. The club erected a £10,000 security fence to try and curb the problem of vandalism at the ground. The club changed their name from Viking Sports to Viking Greenford in 1999; however, they decided to disband in 2003 after further insurmountable problems.

BOB'S FIRST TIME: This was for a match between Viking Sports and Sharpness in the Hellenic League Premier Division on 30 August 1986. Viking lost 2-0 before sixty spectators. At this time, the stand consisted of a caravan parked diagonally next to a corner flag with an opening cut into it with eight chairs inside. A cover behind the goal replaced this and had two concrete steps underneath. There were also four corner floodlights by 2003.

WALTHAM FOREST
Ground: Wadham Lodge, Brookscroft Road, Walthamstow, London E17.

When near-neighbours Leyton FC and Walthamstow Pennant decided to merge during the 1994/95 season, it was yet another move in a very complicated history of the Leyton club. (For a history of Leyton FC, see sections on Leyton and Leyton Wingate.) Pennant Football Club was formed as a junior side in 1964 and initially joined the South-West Essex League, where they spent eight years. They progressed quickly, winning the league's junior, intermediate and senior cups in successive seasons in the late 1960s. This was followed by the Premier Division title in 1972/73. Pennant joined the Metropolitan London League in 1974 and in their first season won the league title and the London Junior Cup. Senior status was attained in 1983 and Pennant joined the London Spartan League. In their first season finished fourth in the Senior Division, enough to secure a place in the Premier Division. The club changed its name to Walthamstow Pennant in 1988 to keep alive a famous footballing name after neighbours Avenue were swallowed up by Redbridge Forest. Floodlights were installed at the club's Wadham Lodge ground for the first time during 1988/89, the official switch-on coming in a match with Leyton Orient that attracted a ground record of 860.

Walthamstow Pennant's best season came in 1990/91 when a tight race for the league title was eventually won by one point from Barkingside. A single-goal victory over Haringey Borough secured the double in the League Cup. A treble was denied, however, when Haringey reversed the score in the final of the London Senior Cup. A best ever season in the FA Vase completed the season's achievements as Pennant reached the last sixteen before losing at Littlehampton Town. Leyton FC were denied a place in the Isthmian League when a proposed groundshare at the Hare & Hounds Ground was rejected as it did not meet the league's new requirements and the club lacked the funds to bring things up to standard. This contrasted with Walthamstow Pennant's situation, whose ground met them, and the Isthmian League gave its blessing

Waltham Forest, July 2004. Wadham Lodge has steadily developed from being an enclosed field. There is now a 300-seat stand and cover at both ends.

to the merger of the two clubs. Prior to this Leyton had continued to play at the Wingate-Leyton (Hare & Hounds) Stadium after the departure of the Wingate club to amalgamate with Finchley. A new stand was built, covered terracing erected and a 'B' grading was achieved to launch the newly named Leyton Pennant for 1995/96. Fourth place that season was followed by a period of struggle and a failure to win any of the last nineteen league games in 1999/2000, which led to relegation to Ryman Division Two. The club changed their name to Waltham Forest during the summer of 2003. As well as the stand, the ground now also has cover behind one of the goals and concrete terracing on the other two sides.

BOB'S FIRST TIME: This was for a match between Pennant and Penhill Standard in the London Spartan League. The match was played on 31 March 1984 and Pennant lost 3-2. Bob was the only spectator in the ground. There were also two watching over a wall and eleven watching from the clubhouse. At this time the ground consisted only of a large two-storey social and changing facility that served several pitches.

WALTHAMSTOW AVENUE
Ground: Green Pond Road, Walthamstow, London E17.

Walthamstow Avenue was originally formed in 1900 by schoolmaster Parkin Davidson, as a team for boys of Pretoria Avenue School. They stayed together when they left

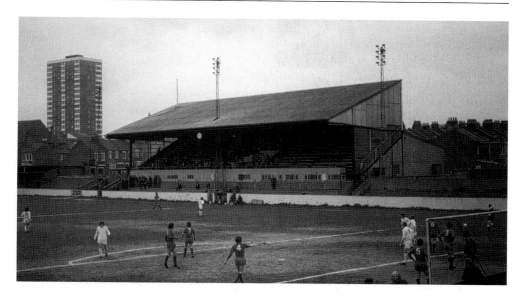

Walthamstow Avenue, March 1972. The magnificent main stand held 1,170, thirteen deep. Opposite and behind one goal were covered terraces, and a twenty-five-deep open terrace was behind the other goal.

school and played as Pretoria Avenue Old Boys and then Avenue United before becoming Walthamstow Avenue in 1903. They played on a pitch within the Barclay Estate at Whipps Cross and then at Lloyd Park for a number of years before the First World War. There was a rule that all the players should reside in Walthamstow and in an avenue. After playing in the Walthamstow & District League, the Stoke Newington & District League, the Stamford Hill League and the South Essex League, they joined the Spartan League. With the limited number of grounds available, Avenue accepted a ground-share deal with Walthamstow Grange until 1920 when they were given a rough field with a stream running through it, which had formerly been allotments, in Green Pond Road. Appeals were launched in an effort to buy the land and they bought the freehold for £25.

A six-foot fence soon enclosed the ground and pipes were laid by the council to divert the stream. The ground was opened on 21 December 1921 after a wooden stand, with a clubhouse at the back, and new terracing had been built. There were also dressing rooms with baths and 3,000 saw the first league game against Slough. Avenue played in the Spartan League from 1921 and then transferred to the Athenian League in 1929. They proceeded to win the league title five times before the Second World War. Green Pond Road was banked up with sleeper terracing and the club attracted 12,500 for a FA Cup second round replay with Stockport County in 1938/39. A fire swept through the ground soon afterwards, destroying the clubhouse and stand, but the club members immediately got to work and a new grandstand that could hold over 1,000 spectators was opened by Stanley Rous on 26 August 1939. It was 40 feet high, 135 feet long and had a members' and VIP enclosure. There was a new clubroom, two large dressing rooms, a referee's room, secretary's office, boardroom and Supporters' Club facilities, in all costing £6,000.

Walthamstow Avenue celebrated their first season in the Isthmian League by winning the championship in 1945/46 with the record of 100 goals and 42 points. The title was won again in 1945/46, 1952/53 and 1953/54. The Avenue reached the final of the FA Amateur Cup during 1951/52 for the first time where they defeated Leyton 2-1 and attracted a 100,000 crowd to Wembley Stadium. The following season, they reached the fourth round of the FA Cup with wins over Wimbledon (3-0), Watford (2-1) and Stockport County (2-1) before holding Manchester United 1-1 at Old Trafford. They bowed out in the replay 2-5 at Highbury. The FA Amateur Cup was won again in 1960/61 with the 2-1 defeat of West Auckland Town after they had beaten Hitchin Town 1-0 at White City in the semi-final. There was little major success after this but they did reach the FA Cup second round in 1967/68, where they lost at home to Bournemouth.

The club accumulated huge debts of over £1 million during the next two decades and crowds were as low as 150 by the time it folded. Avenue were relegated for the first time in 1987 and disbanded in May 1988. The club's assets and debts were taken over by Leytonstone/Ilford. The last game was played at the Green Pond Road ground against Borehamwood in May 1988 when Leytonstone/Ilford finished as champions of the Isthmian League. To stay at Green Pond Road and play in the Conference League would have meant spending £70,000 to bring the stand up to safety certificate standards. The club had no long-term intention of staying there and so changed their name to Redbridge Forest and moved to share Dagenham's ground. A new club called Walthamstow Avenue was formed in 2000 and they joined the London Intermediate League.

ALEX'S FIRST TIME: I visited Green Pond Road only once, on 28 February 1989, for an Essex Senior Cup semi-final between Leytonstone/Ilford and Grays Athletic that ended in a 0-0 draw. The match went to extra time and there was a better than average crowd in attendance of 400. The only way into the ground was through the marvellous old stand, which remained until the end. Most of the crowd stood on the terraces despite all the seating that was available. This ground was a great loss to the London non-League scene when it was demolished soon afterwards.

WALTON & HERSHAM
Ground: Sports Ground, Stompond Lane, Walton-on-Thames, Surrey.

Walton & Hersham were formed in 1946 with the amalgamation of Walton FC and Hersham FC. Walton (The Swans) were founded in 1896, and were runners-up in the Surrey Senior League four seasons running before winning it in 1916/17 (from Hersham on goal average). They were admitted to the London League in 1937 and won the League Cup during their first season. Hersham (The Robins) were a much younger club and were founded in 1926. They won the Surrey Senior League championship in 1935/36. Two seasons later they were runners-up in both the League and the Charity Shield and reached the final qualifying round of the FA Cup before losing to Folkestone. They entered the London League in 1939.

Walton & Hersham, October 1973. Built in 1963 with a capacity of about 600 the only change has been the replacement of wood benches with plastic bucket seats. Opposite, a covered terrace stretches the length of the pitch

The club was offered their present Stompond Lane Ground in 1908 but turned it down. However, the ground was eventually bought in 1933 for £7,000. The first wooden grandstand stood on the site of the current one and changing rooms were added next to it. The council owners created a cinder running track and this was used by the local athletics club. They continue to share the ground with the football club. After the war the Supporters' Club built a tea hut and covered the area opposite the stand. Hersham's ground was taken over for agriculture on the outbreak of war and afterwards new houses were built on the site. As they now had no suitable ground of their own they approached Walton to discuss an amalgamation, this taking place in 1946, and they used the Stompond Lane ground for home matches. They joined the newly formed Corinthian League and, following a poor first season, they won a hat-trick of championships. They were elected to the Athenian League in 1950 and finished as runners-up. They reached the FA Amateur Cup semi-final in 1951/52 and 1952/53 before losing to Walthamstow Avenue and Harwich & Parkeston respectively. A record crowd of 10,000 attended Stompond Lane in 1952 when Crook Town visited for an FA Amateur Cup match. The Swans reached the FA Cup first round for the first time in 1957/58 but Southampton won easily 6-1 before a 6,000 crowd at Stompond Lane. To accommodate this crowd, the grass banking either side of the stand was made safe and chairs placed behind the goals. Concrete terracing already existed behind the Hersham Road goal.

Floodlights were introduced during the 1960s and the old wooden stand was taken down and replaced with the present 600-seat structure, with dressing rooms underneath. The old dressing rooms were turned into a clubroom. The club had the most successful period in their history after the appointment of Alan Batsford as manager in 1967. They won the Athenian League championship in 1968/69 for the first time and reached the first round of the FA Cup during the next two seasons. Walton & Hersham were elected to the Isthmian League in 1971 and the club had a marvellous season in 1972/73. They overcame Exeter City 2-1 in the FA Cup first round before losing disappointingly to Margate in the next round. Kingstonian were beaten 2-0 in the Surrey Senior Cup final and the runners-up spot was achieved in the league. They also reached a Wembley cup final when 41,000 spectators saw them beat Slough Town with a last-minute goal from Roger Connell in the FA Amateur Cup final. The following season, Brian Clough's Brighton side visited Stompond Lane in the FA Cup first round. After a goal-less draw, Swans pulled off a sensational 4-0 victory in the replay at The Goldstone Ground. When Batsford left for Wimbledon the following season, this fine team broke up. Relegation soon followed in 1975, but they again reached the FA Cup first round, where they lost narrowly to Crystal Palace at Selhurst Park.

The Swans nearly went out of business in the early 1980s and were saved by a takeover from a local consortium. After twenty years out of the top flight, Walton at last gained promotion in 1993/94. Swansea City won 2-0 at the Lane in the FA Cup in 1994/95 but the club was relegated again in 1996. A splendid late-season run, along with a superb away record, enabled promotion to be gained on the last day of the campaign with a win at Wokingham Town the following season, but they were relegated again in 1999/2000.

ALEX'S FIRST TIME: The pitch at Stompond Lane is some way from the stands due to the athletics track. This ground is a pretty tree-lined enclosure with most facilities painted with large amounts of green paint (the club's colours). I saw an encounter with Staines Town on 12 November 1988, along with 230 other spectators, which ended 2-2 in the Isthmian League First Division.

WALTON CASUALS
Ground: Franklin Road Sports Centre, Waterside Drive, Walton-on-Thames, Surrey.

Walton Casuals have only risen to prominence in recent years. A Sunday team formed by a group of ex-servicemen became Walton Casuals in July 1948 and they played on a pitch at Elm Grove Recreation Ground. They joined the Surrey Intermediate (Central) First Division and were promoted to the Premier Division at the end of 1952/53. The Stags moved to the Western Section in 1965 before joining the newly formed Surrey Senior League in 1968. The Casuals moved to their current ground at Franklyn Road, and two years later they became founder members of the Suburban League. They spent nine years on the move after this. Having played at neighbours Walton & Hersham for a season, they then spent eight years at Addlestone's Liberty Lane Ground before returning in 1980 to the club's present home at Franklyn Road. The reserves had remained at Franklyn Road, where they played in the Surrey Combination League, but the ground facilities were not good enough for the Suburban League. Walton took the Suburban League (Southern) championship in 1982/83, after a twenty-three-match unbeaten run, and The Stags just failed to retain the title the following season, finishing runners-up to Sutton United reserves. They reached the Surrey Premier Cup final in 1987 and rejoined the Surrey Senior League in June 1992. The club were winners of the Surrey Premier League Challenge Cup in 1993/94, defeating Holmesdale in a replay.

Walton Casuals, July 2004. At the time of Bob's visit in March 1995 a canvas awning in front of the clubhouse was the only cover. An amazing transformation has seen the erection of this cover, a 112-seater stand opposite and cover behind both goals.

Walton Casuals were promoted to the Combined Counties League in 1994/95, after the installation of floodlights, enabling The Stags to taste senior football for the first time. 2000 saw their first honour as a senior side, when they lifted the CCL Challenge Cup, beating Viking Greenford 4-2. Huge improvements have been made at the ground in recent years with new stands and covered areas.

BOB'S FIRST TIME: This was for a Surrey Premier Challenge Cup quarter-final replay against Chessington & Hook United. The first match had ended in a 2-2 draw and the replay was on 25 March 1995 before fifty-five spectators. The Casuals won 3-2, with two goals in extra time. A canvas awning on the front of the social and dressing room building was the only cover.

WATFORD
Ground: Vicarage Road, Watford, Herts.

Like most clubs in the London area, Watford started in modest circumstances. The present Watford FC was formed as Watford Rovers in 1881 and they played in Cassiobury Park until 1883, before spending six years at the Rose & Crown Meadow (now covered by Market Street), followed by one season at Colney Butts Meadow, off Wiggenhall Road. The club changed its name to West Herts in 1893 and were based at the West Herts Sports Ground. The name changed again to Watford after absorbing another top local side Watford St Mary's (who played at 'The Bog' on Wiggenhall Road) in 1898.

The West Herts Sports Ground came into being in 1890 and to be able to use the ground, the club had to change their name to West Herts. The football pitch was marked out in the north-west corner of the site. There was pavilion that had a clock tower, which stood close to the west touchline. On either side were low stands, while there were only ropes on the opposite touchline (nearest Cassio Road). Cover and banking had been erected behind one of the goals by 1906. The club spent £160 on a new stand in 1907 and, at this time, the ground was in a quaint rural setting.

Watford became a limited company in 1909 and became tenants at the West Herts Sports Club, paying £50 a year rent. The dowager, Lady Essex, was so appalled by Watford continuing to play after war broke out in 1914 that she persuaded the West Herts Sports Club to evict them. It was only after the intercession of the local Benskins Brewery that West Herts relented and Watford were able to resume at Cassio Road after the war. After entering the new Football League Third Division in 1920, Watford soon outgrew the ground. One stand at the Park End had been dismantled during the war so brewery drays and hay wagons had to be used instead. Watford fans resented members of the West Herts club grabbing the best seats. The ground had too many vulnerable entry points, while the players' bath water had to be carried up to the pavilion in buckets. A new ground became a priority, especially after a record 13,000 crowd (of which over 1,000 gate-crashed) somehow packed in for a derby against Luton Town in March 1921. Cassio Road is still used today for hockey, tennis, cricket and squash and staged its final Watford game, against Gillingham, attended by 5,000 spectators, in April 1922.

Vicarage Road recreation ground remained Watford's first choice for a new ground and, as a former gravel pit, it already had sloping banks on three sides. Benskins bought the site in 1921 for £2,300 and loaned Watford £12,000 for ground improvements. The new east stand cost £7,000 to build and was a conventional structure, 45 yards long, with a pitched roof and 3,500 seats. The Vicarage Road End was built up by hard core and covered in clinker, while on the west side, a stand from Cassio Road was re-erected and named the Union Stand. At the Rookery End was a small, low wooden cover, also brought over from Cassio Road. Vicarage Road was opened on 30 August 1922, in front of only 8,000 spectators. Watford's finances were boosted by the start of greyhound racing at Vicarage Road in October 1928. The ground required few changes as there was already a wide track around the pitch. During the 1930s, concrete terracing was laid by the players. Rudimentary floodlights were erected in 1953 along the side-stand roofs, and these were replaced by corner pylons in 1960.

The first improvements for some time took place when the Supporters' Club funded a new roof over the Rookery End terracing in 1959. Watford gained long-term security at the ground in 1968 when they were given a 150-year lease by Benskins. Soon afterwards, Watford had their highest ever crowd (34,099 v. Manchester United) in February 1969. In the summer of 1969 they spent £45,000 on an extension to the existing east stand that added 1,700 seats. The Greyhound Racing Association spent £200,000 on new equipment, kennels and outbuildings in 1975 when it returned after a six-year break. Watford installed a £40,000 electronic scoreboard at the Vicarage Road End in 1978 and nearly every barrier and rail was replaced the following year. The banking in the corner between the Rookery and Shrodells Stand was terraced for the first time (these were cinder with wooden blocks before this) and all access points were redesigned. The GRA's lease ran out in 1979 and the dog track was removed. The east stand paddock had 2,200 seats added, and next to this the open terracing was replaced by 280 bucket seats in 1982.

Perhaps the club's greatest achievement was reaching the FA Cup final in 1984 after Graham Taylor's management and Elton John's finance had managed to bring them up

Watford, April 1985. Built in the 1930s the west stand was replaced by the Sir Stanley Rous Stand in 1986.

from the Fourth to the First Division in the late 1970s and early 1980s. Watford decided to build a precast concrete west stand costing £2.2 million, which was opened officially on 18 October 1986 by Elton John and named after the club president, Sir Stanley Rous. The Rous Stand brought Vicarage Road's seating total to 6,906. In April 1991, Watford agreed a ground-share deal with non-League neighbours Wealdstone (see Wealdstone). Watford redeveloped the two remaining terraces at Vicarage Road into seated stands. The north stand, at the Vicarage Road end, was opened in October 1993. The stand holds 5,796 seats and is covered by a 'goalpost' supported roof with angled floodlight gantries extending from this steelwork. The south stand (Rookery End), at the opposite end of the ground, is larger than the north stand with seats for 7,000 and was opened in March 1995.

ALEX'S FIRST TIME: I saw Fulham win a Second Division relegation struggle at Vicarage Road on 16 October 1971. They won 2-1 thanks to a last-minute own-goal from Keith Eddy. I stood on the cinder terraces called the Bend and was amazed League grounds still had such terraces at this time. The former east stand seemed to be leaning/resting against the wall of the factory behind it and the ground was in great need of modernization at that time.

WEALDSTONE
Ground: Lower Mead, Station Road, Harrow, Middlesex.

Wealdstone were one of the leading non-League sides during the 1980s but went into decline and eventually lost their Lower Mead ground, which led to a nomadic

Wealdstone, October 1972. The stand holding 300 came from Summerstown FC in 1928. Both ends were covered and there was open terracing on the opposite side.

existence. Wealdstone was founded in 1899 and they competed in the Willesden & District League, but after a lean time they disbanded in 1902. They reformed again six years later and won the Middlesex Junior Cup and the championship of Division Two of the London League by 1912/13. After closing down during the First World War, the club was re-formed in 1919. The club was loaned £1,650 to buy their new ground at Lower Mead in 1921 and this was ready for use at the start of 1922/23. The club applied to join the Athenian League, but were rejected so they moved to the Spartan League instead. Wealdstone remained in this league until 1928 when they were finally accepted into the Athenian League.

The late Charles Brady, who became president in 1921, was the leading light at the club. He helped to secure their ground at Lower Mead, and when Summerstown FC, who played at Garratt Lane, Earlsfield, was wound up, their grandstand was removed and rebuilt at Lower Mead. This stand remained at the ground until it was bulldozed in the early 1990s. Brady also negotiated the sale of the northern part of the Lower Mead ground to a cinema company, and they used these funds to improve facilities at the ground and clear debts. When the ground at Lower Mead was built, the area around it was rural and close to a farm. The first building at the ground was a small wooden stand, placed where the open terrace was laid after the Second World War, and dressing rooms soon followed. A terraced area was built called the Elmslie End, named after an old clubman. The Elmslie End and the Cinema End were roofed during the 1960s. Except for a lean period in the mid-1930s, Stones were usually among the leading clubs in the Athenian League.

Wealdstone featured in the BBC's early experimentation with 'outside broadcasts'. They showed two cup ties live from Lower Mead when they played Edgware Town and Colchester United in the late 1940s. The large open terrace opposite the main stand was created after the Second World War when the land behind it was sold for housing. Lower Mead saw some large crowds and their record attendance came when 13,504 attended for an FA Amateur Cup match with Leytonstone in 1949. They won the Athenian League title for the first and only time in 1951/52.

Wealdstone left the Athenian League for the Isthmian League in 1964 and turned professional. They joined the Southern League in 1971. They won the First Division (South) title in 1973/74 and then spent five years in the Premier Division. They became founder members of the Vauxhall Conference but were relegated for the first time in their history in 1981. Wealdstone won five trophies the following season and rejoined the Conference League straightaway. Their greatest season in 1984/85 saw them become the first club to complete the double of the Vauxhall Conference title and the FA Trophy in the same season. During the 1980s the club continued to improve the ground. They built a new gymnasium in 1984, made repairs to the stand the following year and put in segregation gates and new floodlights in 1986.

After being relegated back to the Southern League in the early 1990s, the club struggled financially and the club's owner decided to sell their Lower Mead ground for redevelopment. This was a great loss to London non-League football as the ground had plenty of character and atmosphere. When redeveloped it became yet another superstore. Property millionaire David Morritt sold the site for £6.5 million and was able to clear the club's debts of over £1 million. He initially wanted to move the club to Willesden Stadium, but was refused permission by Brent Council. There was a long-drawn-out battle between Mr Morritt and the club's supporters over the money received from the sale of Lower Mead. The loss of Lower Mead led to ground-shares with Watford, Yeading and Edgware Town from 1995. The club lost huge amounts of money while ground-sharing at Watford.

Wealdstone rejoined the Isthmian League in 1994/95 but had to start at the bottom, playing in Division Three. After two successive promotions, the club had moved up to the First Division. However, they struggled to make an impact at this higher level, finishing sixteenth in 1999/00, and only just avoided relegation in the following two seasons. They joined the newly formed Division One (North) in 2002/03 and finished ninth. A proposed new £4.5m development was planned in 2000 at the Prince Edward Playing Fields in Harrow. The plan was for a new stadium to be built with community leisure facilities, bars, offices and shops. This was given planning permission by the council but the club still needed to raise the funding. Work commenced on the new complex in June 2003.

ALEX'S FIRST TIME: I visited Lower Mead on 2 December 1989 for a Southern League Premier Division match between Wealdstone and Atherstone. Despite a horrible day, 541 spectators attended the match that the Stones won 3-1. This felt like a proper football ground with a small stand, two covered ends behind each goal and a large terrace opposite the stand.

WELLING UNITED
Ground: Park View Road, Welling, Kent.

Welling United have been using Park View Road as their home ground since 1977. The ground's previous users were Bexleyheath & Welling and Bexley United and football

Welling United, February 1981. Originally built in 1952/53, the covered side has been refurbished several times. Opposite is the main stand and there is open terracing behind both goals.

was probably first played at the ground around 1925. By the late 1930s there was a substantial grandstand on the ground with dressing rooms underneath, but this suffered bomb damage during the blitz. The club failed to survive the Second World War and for five years the ground was virtually derelict. The stand was demolished and the rest of the stadium became vandalised. Bexleyheath & Welling were reformed in 1951 and played in the Kent League. Two ex-Nissen huts were hastily erected for dressing rooms. A new grandstand was built and cover was erected opposite. The club changed their name to Bexley United during the 1950s. Bexley United were the only non-League side that had a youth team in the South-East Counties League during the 1960s. They went into debt when they spent substantial amounts on the ground. The existing stand was enlarged, the whole of the opposite side was covered and the slope reduced on the pitch. They were still getting excellent crowds in the 1960s, often over 3,000. The club played their last home game in April 1976 in front of 222 spectators, then went into liquidation.

Welling United came into existence in 1963, formed by Barrie and Graham Hobbins, who remain directors of the club. They began as an under-15 team playing in the Eltham & District Junior League on Sundays. They changed to playing on a Saturday in 1971 and attained senior status during the course of their rapid progress through the Greater London (later the London Spartan) League during the 1970s. Welling's first ground was Danson Park, and they later played at a private sports ground in Butterfly Lane, Eltham before taking over their present Park View Road ground from defunct Bexley United in January 1977. Welling were granted a fifteen-year lease but the ground had been vandalised and a fire had damaged the stand. The first match was on 26 August 1977 and since then, as well as repairing the damage to the stand, new boundary walls, perimeter fences, turnstiles and terracing have all been installed. Welling left the Spartan League in 1978 and spent three years in the Athenian League before succeeding at the second attempt in gaining election to the Southern League. After one season in the Southern Division they became Premier Division members when the league reorganised in 1982. They won the championship in 1985/86 – 23 points clear of runners-up Chelmsford. After promotion to the Vauxhall Conference, Welling only avoided an immediate return when Nuneaton were demoted for off-field reasons.

Welling first appeared in the FA Cup competition proper in 1986. In 1988/89 they reached the third round for the first time as they beat Bromsgrove Rovers and Bath City before meeting Blackburn Rovers at Park View Road, narrowly losing 1-0 before an attendance of 3,850 on 7 January 1989. The following season they managed their first Football League scalp when they beat Gillingham at Park View Road in a first-round replay before 4,100. Erith & Belvedere joined Welling United at Park View Road in 1998 when they sold their own ground at Belvedere. In order to preserve their own identity, money raised from the sale of their old ground was spent on building their own grandstand, offices and social facilities at Welling's ground. After clearing away the terracing and rudimentary shelter that previously occupied the cricket-ground side of the ground, work on erecting the new stand started. The stand stretches from the halfway line towards the Danson Park end, with the new clubhouse situated alongside it. The roof of the stand is supported by a large external girder and seats 568. New dressing rooms, to be used for games involving Erith & Belvedere, are housed beneath the stand.

ALEX'S FIRST TIME: A new record attendance was set for a Welling United match at Park View Road when I visited the ground on 15 November 1986. This was for a first-round FA Cup tie against Maidstone United. The crowd was 2,100 and the match ended in a 1-1 draw.

WEMBLEY
Ground: Vale Farm, Watford Road, Sudbury, Middlesex.

Wembley FC was formed in 1946 when two local junior sides, Sudbury Ratepayers Association and Sudbury Rangers, amalgamated and began playing in the Middlesex League. They finished fourth in their first season and won the championship in the second. They were then elected to the Spartan League, competing in the Western Section, and won the championship in 1950/51. Their first ground was an unfenced roped-off pitch at Vale Farm and Wembley Council had purchased this area as a sports facility in 1928. A wooden pavilion, near the entrance, housed the dressing rooms. The club had to vacate the ground when the cricket season began, and if they had not finished their fixtures, home games were played at the Glacier Sports Ground in Alperton.

The ground was enclosed in 1948, and three years later the council offered the club a twenty-one-year lease that allowed them to develop the ground. Terracing and a small enclosure were quickly erected on the rugby side of the ground for the start of 1951/52, along with grassed embankments around the pitch. That season they also became founder members of the Delphian League, but finished bottom in their first campaign. However, they were runners-up to Dagenham in 1955/56. The first section of the elevated wooden main stand was opened on New Year's Day 1955 and over £1,000 was spent replacing the small enclosure with covered accommodation that ran from one penalty area to the other. This stand was opened with a game against Grays Athletic on

Wembley FC, October 1972. The six-deep wood stand seemed to be a smaller version of that at Wealdstone. Opposite was a covered side built in 1956.

18 August 1956. They moved to the Corinthian League in 1956/57 and soon afterwards the pitch was properly enclosed and railed off, the main stand was doubled in size and more terraces were laid down in front of the pavilion. This was funded by the Supporters' Club and the club chairman. This led to improved attendances at Vale Farm that were usually around the 1,000 mark. Their record attendance is said to have been a Middlesex Senior Cup match against Hendon during 1959/60 when 2,000 came to watch the game.

The pavilion was refurbished and the bar and dressing rooms improved in 1961. Floodlights were used for the first time against Erith & Belvedere in March of that year. A new clubhouse was built adjacent to the main stand with part of the pavilion being demolished, and a larger entrance provided. Wembley joined the Athenian League in 1963/64 and were runners-up in 1967/68 and 1974/75. With financial help from Brent Council, the club was able to demolish the old dressing rooms and a new complex costing £20,000 was built behind the main stand in 1974. With these improved facilities, the club was elected to the Isthmian League the following year. New lights were installed at Vale Farm in 1981 and rails around the pitch and hard standing were also improved. Sadly, the ground lost its pretty elm trees to Dutch elm disease in 1977. Wembley had their best season in the FA Cup during 1980/81 when they reached the first round for the first time but lost 3-0 at Enfield.

The club could have easily gone to the wall in 1992 when a fire gutted the main stand while the covered terrace on the rugby side was condemned. Wembley quickly replaced these when the remaining terrace was raised and covered with a new roof, beneath which 450 seats were added. New toilets, turnstiles and a tea bar were constructed in 1993 and turnstile facilities and the boundary fence were improved two years later. Old British Rail ticket booths were used in the new turnstile block.

ALEX'S FIRST TIME: This was for a Middlesex Senior Cup second round tie between Wembley and Wealdstone on 3 February 1987 that attracted an attendance of 300, most of whom were visiting fans. Wembley pulled off a surprise by winning the match 3-1. The Wasps Rugby Club played next door in those days.

WEMBLEY STADIUM
Ground: Wembley Stadium, Stadium Way, Wembley, Middlesex.

There are several books on the history of Wembley and the brief outline below of its history can never cover the full story. Wembley Park was chosen as the site for the British Empire Exhibition in 1920. It was announced the following year that the exhibition's centrepiece would be a national sports stadium, where the FA Cup final would be played in future. The stadium was the most advanced in Britain, and the use of ferro-concrete was responsible for Wembley's swift construction in just 300 working days, from January 1922 to April 1923, at a cost of £750,000. The focal point was the entrance, the famous twin towers, 126 feet high. Both ends were open, and the two stands covered only the seated section for 25,000 spectators. The terraces were timber steps with cinder infill on the lower tier, concrete on the upper, plus 10,000 bench seats were planned in five rows around the perimeter area. The players' tunnel was initially at the western end of the stadium and was wide enough for the players to enter the pitch side by side. The FA's president, Sir Charles Clegg, signed a twenty-one-year contract with Wembley's owners and the first event to be held in the stadium was the FA Cup final of 1923. Wembley was besieged by over 200,000 people who wanted to see the match and the King. It was a miracle no one was hurt and that there was no violence despite the crush and lack of segregation.

Three days after the exhibition's opening, the second Wembley cup final took place, this time an all-ticket crowd of 91,695 watching Aston Villa *v.* Newcastle. The next six-figure crowd to watch a cup final was in 1950, when Arsenal played Liverpool. Since then many games except midweek replays have drawn 100,000 crowds (Wembley had a capacity limit of 92,000 for midweek night games). Once the exhibition closed in October 1925, after 30 million people had visited it, the organizers wound up their company and the site was put up for auction. but no one was initially interested. Fortunately, the Greyhound Racing Association wanted to hold meetings at the stadium. It cost £100,000 to install the necessary facilities, but this was soon earned as 50,000 attended the first race meeting in December 1927. The rugby league cup final was staged at Wembley for the first time in 1929 and was held there every year, apart from 1932, until the stadium's demolition. The first speedway event took place at Wembley on 16 May 1929 and was a regular event until 1956. Speedway made a comeback in the 1970s but the last meeting was held at Wembley on 5 September 1981. Wembley continued to host the World Championships every year until 1981.

The building of a 250-seater restaurant behind the Royal Box took place in 1938. This was designed by Sir Owen Williams, who was also the architect of the Empire Pool. This

Wembley Stadium, April 1978. A small crowd for the Varsity match.

steel-and-glass construction was designed to be dismantled for cup finals but never was.

After the Second World War, the stadium had a major facelift in order to stage the 1948 Olympics. Among the improvements was the building of the Olympic Way, linking the stadium with Wembley Park Station. The present players' tunnel and dressing rooms were built at the opposite end to the original ones. The Olympic torch was above the tunnel. Bench seats were temporarily installed at both ends. The entire operation ended in a loss of £200,000. The stadium company's profits began to fall steadily after this, as greyhound racing and speedway lost their popularity. Floodlights were finally installed in 1955 at a cost of £22,000. The first game was a representative match between London and Frankfurt in the European Fairs Cup in 1955, but the first time lights were used for a major match was for a game between England and Spain on 30 November 1955.

Wembley's most significant facelift came in 1963, when £500,000 was spent completely reroofing the stands and covering both ends for the first time. This gave cover for all 100,000 spectators, of which 44,000 were now seated. A 300-feet-long suspended press box and television gantries were built at this time and Wembley staged its first ever all-floodlit international when England beat Northern Ireland 8-3 on 20 November 1963. As well as the FA Cup and FA Amateur Cup finals (since 1949) being played at Wembley, it was also used for the European Cup finals of 1963, 1968 (when Manchester United won) and 1971, and the European Cup Winners' Cup final in 1965 (when West Ham won). The most important football event held at the stadium was the 1966 World Cup final when the home nation triumphed by beating West Germany 4-2.

The next big change to the ground came when the Wembley Stadium Company decided to make Wembley all-seater in the late 1980s. New seating was placed on the existing terracing behind each goal, as well as executive suites being incorporated. Four thousand new seats were placed high under the Wembley roof in 1989, in the Olympic gallery. The stadium was able to stage its first all-seated events the following year. They were forced to work within the limitations of the original stadium and this only showed how outdated it had now become. For example, despite Wembley's efforts to improve sightlines by increasing elevation, the backless seats at the front of the terracing offered a poor view in comparison with other parts of the stadium. The first all-seated FA Cup final was in 1990 when Manchester United played Crystal Palace. They fought out an exciting 3-3 draw in front of a capacity crowd, now reduced to 80,000. After years of speculation, the decision was made to redevelop Wembley and build a new stadium. The last match took place on 7 October 2000 when England played Germany in a World Cup qualifying match. The Germans won 1-0 with a goal from Hamann after fourteen minutes and the England manager, Kevin Keegan, resigned after the game. The old stadium was finally bulldozed in September 2002 after years of haggling over what should replace it. Unfortunately, the twin white towers were not saved and incorporated into the new development. The new stadium is due to open in 2006.

ALEX'S FIRST TIME: After playing eleven matches to reach their first Wembley cup final in 1975, Fulham ran out of steam in the final where they lost 2-0 to West Ham United. This was my first ever match at Wembley and the match passed so quickly. This was fortunate as it was quite a crush on the terracing at the Fulham end of the ground. The atmosphere was terrific and it is an experience that I will never forget – despite the result.

WEST HAM UNITED
Ground: The Boleyn Ground, Green Street, Upton Park, London E13.

The club was formed as Thames Ironworks FC in 1895 and were a works team created by A.F. Hills, who owned the largest shipyard on the Thames. Their first ground was at Hermit Road. It was partially enclosed but had no facilities for the fans. The pitch initially had no grass on it, but the Ironworks played their first match there, drawing 1-1 with the Royal Ordinance reserves, on 7 September 1895. After a very satisfactory inaugural season the club were elected as founder members of the First Division of the London League. Thames Ironworks decided to leave Hermit Road and move to a new ground that was located in Browning Road, just off East Ham High Street. This ground was used until April 1897 when Mr Hills paid £2,000 for the construction of a new ground at Canning Town called the Memorial Ground. Brentford were the first visitors, in a London League match played on 11 September 1897, and the Hammers finished the season as London League champions.

The Memorial Ground was an enormous arena with an oval-shaped playing area that was surrounded with an inner running track and an outer cycle track. On the west side there was a seated and covered stand and opposite there was uncovered seating. Earth embankments were formed behind each goal. Photos of the ground show that the spectators had very awkward views of matches, due to the placing of the cycle track that seemed to dominate the arena. Thames Ironworks joined the Southern League Second Division in 1898 and won its title at the end of their first season to gain promotion. The relationship between the club and its benefactor, Mr Hills, rapidly deteriorated. He was disenchanted as he believed in amateurism and, after the FA examined the club's books, it was clear that they had been paying some of their players and employing agents to sign players. They were forced to turn professional and become a limited company. By 1900, the club was in financial difficulties and Hills had overstretched himself on other deals and was unwilling to plough any more money into the club. The club and Hills parted company and the team was renamed West Ham United.

The club's lease on the Memorial Ground was due to run out in 1904, and it was obvious that this would not be renewed, as Hills owned the ground. The last game at this venue was against Swindon Town in the Southern League on 30 April 1904. The Hammers found their present ground at Upton Park, which had been a potato field behind the Elizabethan mansion of Boleyn Castle. This area had a better catchment area for supporters and crowds instantly improved. A new stand was built in time for the first visit of Millwall in September 1904, which attracted a crowd of 10,000 spectators. The ground was named after a house on Green Street that had been built in 1544 and was itself named after Anne Boleyn (Henry VIII's second wife). It was known as Boleyn Castle because it had two prominent turrets. Unbelievably, this was pulled down during the 1950s, an act of extreme vandalism by the local authority. But when United arrived at Upton Park in May 1904, the Catholic Ecclesiastical Authorities owned both the castle (which was then being used as school) and the football ground. The new main stand was built in the west side of the ground and it had a long, low roof that covered bench seats on a raised tier, with a narrow standing area in front. The players had a changing hut in the ground's north-west corner and the press and directors had a small pavilion in the south-west corner. The remaining three sides were uncovered banks with wooden barriers and a picket fence around the perimeter. A larger west stand was built in 1913 that included dressing rooms, and the embankments around the ground were increased and improved.

The Hammers were elected into the Football League Second Division in 1920 when it was expanded and crowds increased to an average of around 20,000. The club won promotion to the First Division and reached the final of the FA Cup in 1922/23, playing in the first Wembley final. A new double-decker west stand was erected in 1925 and the existing west stand roof was moved to cover the south bank. The east bank was also covered at this time. This side of the ground became known as the Chicken Run and was a very basic construction that somehow was not demolished until the late 1960s. A crowd of 43,528 managed to fit into Upton Park for a Second Division match with Charlton Athletic on 18 April 1936. The club's offices were destroyed during the Blitz and the south bank was partially destroyed by a V1 flying bomb in 1944. This was not

West Ham United, May 1983. The South Bank was virtually empty for the European Youth Championship match between Italy and Turkey.

repaired until the 1950s. New floodlights were switched on for the first time for a friendly with Spurs in April 1953 and a new main entrance on Green Street was built in 1958 – but necessitated the demolition of the last remaining turret of the Boleyn Castle. The north bank was covered in 1961 and four years later, an extra bay was added to the west stand. The Chicken Run was finally demolished in May 1968, despite protests from the fans who loved to watch games from there. A new east stand was opened in January 1969, which was a narrow structure, with a cantilevered roof. It had 3,490 seats, with a paddock for 3,300 spectators in front. There were no barriers or aisles, so fans had to endure a constant surge as the play moved from end to end. The new stand brought Upton Park's capacity up to 42,000, including 8,740 seats, and the following year this was surpassed when 42,322 witnessed a local derby with Spurs. Soon afterwards, seats were installed in the west stand paddock, and some terracing, with restricted view, was closed in the north-west corner of the north bank.

A school occupied the land between the west stand and Green Street, and the club bought this in 1991 so that they had more room with which to expand the ground. They purchased the 3.6 acre site for £1.6 million and the new land helped with gaining access to the landlocked North Bank. The completed Bobby Moore Stand was opened in February 1994 at a cost £5.5m, and holds 7,595 seats on two tiers, plus twenty executive boxes. The stand also has a wide ground floor concourse with the usual facilities for spectators. The Centenary Stand opposite was squeezed into a very small area due to lack of space. It holds 5,686 seated spectators on two tiers, cost £2.3m to build and was opened by the MP John Prescott in February 1995. The roof has a goalpost structure and has an additional canopy where disabled fans can watch the game in comfort. West Ham sought to raise their seating capacity from 26,000 to 40,500 in 1999. The local council granted planning permission and the new project was to include a new west stand with two tiers of executive boxes, plus a museum. Also included were extensions to the Bobby Moore Stand and Centenary Stand with the whole project costing £35m. The new Doc Martens Stand (West) was opened in November 2001 with 15,247 seats and was built behind the existing stand that was finally demolished in May 2001. After completion the pitch was moved towards it so that a new east stand could be built.

ALEX'S FIRST TIME: The first two times I saw Fulham play at Upton Park they lost 6-1 and 7-2 after taking the lead on both occasions. World Cup star Geoff Hurst hit four and England teammate Martin Peters scored twice in their 6-1 victory on 5 November 1966 for my first visit, before a crowd of 23,016. The home supporters were very hostile and the view from behind the goal was terrible. I was unable to see the first ten yards of the pitch. The Chicken Run stand looked as though it had been put together from a Meccano set, as it seemed to be all nuts and bolts and iron stanchions.

WEST NORWOOD

West Norwood was a well-known club in London around the turn of the century. They were formed in 1887 and were originally called Stanley FC, but a year later changed this to the 'Novices' and played their matches on Streatham Common. They changed their name again in 1889 after the local *Norwood Press* suggested a more suitable title for the club would be West Norwood. The club moved to a new home ground, at Hyde Farm, Balham (Nunhead FC used this ground from 1898-1900). This site later became a school in Hydethorpe Road. West Norwood amalgamated with Herne Hill FC in 1893 and they became the South London League Division Two champions in their inaugural season. The team also became known as the 'Bantams' at this time. They experienced a single season in the London League (1900/01), but this proved to be a too high a grade of football for them. The club had moved to a new ground at Highview Park in West Norwood in 1898 and remained amateurs, but became a properly constituted limited liability company. West Norwood remained at this venue until 1902 when they moved to the Herne Hill cycling track in Burbage Road. This was a properly enclosed ground, which was principally used for cycle racing. It was created in the 1890s with the intention to also use it for football and athletics. It was used by Crystal Palace during the First World War when they lost their own ground. It had an ornate grandstand that remains in use today – but probably not in its original form. The club found a ground in Clapham after this and joined the Suburban League. The team won little during their history but did secure the London Senior Cup in 1907 by beating West Hampstead 4-1.

During the Edwardian era, West Norwood reached the fourth qualifying round of the FA Cup in 1901 and 1903 (where they lost at Queens Park Rangers and Fulham respectively). They thrashed Northfleet United 6-1 at home at the same stage, only to be beaten 9-1 at home by Accrington Stanley in 1906/07. Their record in the FA Amateur Cup was not impressive, as they never went beyond the second round proper. After the First World War, West Norwood returned to the Isthmian League, and also went to play at Gorringe Park in Mitcham. The four seasons after the war were disastrous, as the team finished close to or at the bottom of the table. They were unsuccessful in their bid for re-election and returned to the London League for one season, before their election into the Athenian League for 1924/25. They lost their ground at Gorringe Park around 1926, and in 1926/27 had to play all of their matches on opponents' grounds. They lost their London League status in 1927 when they were unable to find a new home. The club was forced to join the Surrey Senior League but a new ground was eventually found at Ranleigh Gardens, Fair Green in Mitcham. They played their first fixture there against Dorking on 3 November 1928. West Norwood rejoined the London League in 1937/38 but slipped back to the Surrey Senior League for 1938/39, and didn't appear again after the Second World War.

WHYTELEAFE
Ground: Church Road, Whyteleafe, Surrey.

Whyteleafe Albion were successful in local football during the 1920s before joining the Spartan League in 1929. In that year, a small wooden stand seating around 200 was erected at their New Barn Lane ground. The club's stay in the Spartan League only lasted two seasons however, and they subsequently folded during the Second World War. Whyteleafe FC was formed in 1946 and in their early days had junior status, playing in the Caterham & Edenbridge, the Thornton Heath & District and the Croydon Leagues. They were champions of the Thornton Heath League in 1951/52 and won various local cups. They progressed to the Surrey County Intermediate League (Eastern Division) in 1954 and were Division One champions in 1955/56. Senior status was obtained in 1958 and Whyteleafe entered the Surrey Senior League. At this time, the club left their New Barn Lane School ground, which was inadequate for senior football, and purchased their present ground in Church Road, which had previously been farmland. They began playing on the new ground at the start of 1959/60 and the existing farm buildings were converted into a clubhouse with bar and dressing rooms. The grandstand at New Barn Lane is still intact today, and is now part of a school playing field. Football continues to be played at the ground.

Whyteleafe won the Surrey Senior League and were runners-up in the League Cup in 1968/69. The floodlit training area and stand were built in 1971 and the banking on the north side was terraced as the club left the Surrey Senior League for the London Spartan League in 1975. A new stand was erected around 1978. This stand is quite ugly with its thick concrete pillars and strange-looking roof, but it has a character all of its own. The club moved into the Athenian League in 1981 when floodlights were installed, and the dressing rooms were moved to a new location on the top bank, enabling the clubhouse to be extended.

Whyteleafe, September 1974. This cover and terrace were the only spectator facilities at the time. By 2004 there was shelter on all four sides.

Whyteleafe have twice reached the fifth round of the FA Vase: in 1980/81, when they lost to Basildon United, and again in 1985/86 when they lost 4-1 to Stevenage Borough at Church Road. The club entered Division Two (South) of the Isthmian League in 1984 and a highly successful season in 1988/89 saw the club win promotion as runners-up of Division Two (South). The club almost reached the first round of the FA Cup in 1998/99, but lost narrowly to Welling United, and also won through to the last thirty-two in the FA Trophy that season before going out to the eventual winners Kingstonian in front of a record home crowd of 945. For the first time ever the club reached the first round proper of the FA Cup in 1999/2000 when a crowd of 2,164 easily beat the previous season's record in a match that saw them hold League opponents Chester City to a 0-0 draw before going down 1-3 in a replay at Chester. An imposingly tall stand was built at the Church Road end of the ground just in time for the big match thanks to a superb effort from club members. Whyteleafe moved into the newly reorganised Division Two (South) and finished in fifth place in 2002/03, their highest ever position in the Isthmian League.

ALEX'S FIRST TIME: Church Road is a pleasant ground that is in a surprisingly rural setting considering how close it is to London. I visited the ground on 15 December 1984 for an Isthmian League Division Two (South) match when Hungerford Town were Whyteleafe's opponents. The clubhouse sold Fullers Beers on draught, which was a big plus.

Willesden, September 1977. Opened on 9 December 1965, the huge concrete stand offered covered and open seating. Opposite were six steps of terracing with about twenty park benches randomly placed.

WILLESDEN
Ground: King Edward VII Ground, Donnington Road, Willesden NW10.

There was a club called Willesden Green who had one season at a senior level when they were members of the London League in 1898/99. They were followed by Willesden Town who played in the London League Division Two from 1898-1905 and 1920-1921. This club was professional in the early years and their ground was on the north side of King Edward's Recreation Ground. They were playing at QPR's former ground, the Park Royal Stadium, by 1920 – but by this time most of the spectator facilities had been removed to Loftus Road. They seem to have folded in the early 1920s. A senior amateur team was selected from players residing within the Borough of Willesden to visit Holland to play in a tournament in April 1946. Willesden FC was founded in June 1946, and the nucleus of those players who visited Holland formed the main part of the team. The club were elected to the Middlesex Senior League and won the championship at their first attempt.

The club wanted to play at the King Edward VII Recreation Ground, but it was not available for football at this time. They eventually found a ground at the Paddington Recreation Ground. This was also used by Paddington United but was not enclosed and had few facilities. When Willesden played Queens Park Rangers on 8 May 1947 in a charity match a huge crowd of 8,000 (the club's all-time record attendance) saw the match, that was played at the King Edward's Rec. The following season, the club was told that they needed to play at a properly enclosed ground, where a gate could be taken. Willesden Borough Council was approached about the King Edward's enclosure and the club was given permission to use it. They were elected to the Spartan League

Division One (Western Section) in 1947/48 and were champions again. The club was promoted to the Premier Division and continued there until elected to the Delphian League in March 1951. Owing to ground difficulties, they had to withdraw from the Delphian League and were elected to the Parthenon League in 1953/54. Willesden resigned to join the London League in 1957/58, and two seasons later became one of the founder members of the Aetolian League. The local council informed the club that major improvements were to be made to the King Edward VII Stadium in 1957. While these works were carried out, Willesden Council provided the club with a temporary ground.

At the start of 1958/59, the ground was ready and the work had included a freshly sown pitch and a new boundary fence. A new grandstand, with 750 seats, was built in 1965 and was a cantilevered structure on the east side of the ground, but many of the seats were uncovered. A shallow-stepped terrace was also built opposite the stand and either side of the stand. The club never filled this stand and the new capacity of the ground was far greater than would ever be needed. New floodlights soon followed but the ground was, by now, essentially an athletics stadium. That meant football spectators were some way from the pitch.

Willesden returned to the Spartan League in 1963 and on to the Greater London League in 1966. After a moderate start, they were champions in 1967/68 and were promoted to the top division. Willesden moved into the Athenian League Second Division in 1971/72 and in three seasons later finished fourth (of fifteen), just five points behind champions Egham Town. A struggling team finished next to bottom in 1976/77, but despite their poor showing, they were elected to the enlarged Isthmian League. They struggled at this level and finished bottom of the new Second Division. The following season it was a similar story, when only Corinthian Casuals prevented them from receiving the wooden spoon again. Things were becoming desperate at the club and the local support had virtually disappeared. Willesden's next two seasons were ones of struggle and, with the crowds now well below the 100 mark, the writing was on the wall for Willesden. The club folded in 1982 and it was announced by the local council that the site was to be developed into the National Hockey Stadium. The Hockey World Cup was played here during the 1990s. The ground did not change that much but the grass pitch was removed and an artificial 'plastic' one replaced it. The ground still remains and is mainly used as an athletics stadium.

BOB'S FIRST TIME: When Bob visited the ground, Willesden played Bedford Town for the first ever time in a FA Cup preliminary round match on 3 September 1977. Under the management of Barry Fry, Bedford managed to lose 4-3 after leading 3-0 in what Bob describes as one of their worst performances. Kevin Blackwell, who became the Leeds United manager in May 2004, 'was not having the best of days' in the Bedford goal.

Wimbledon, July 1975. The metal railings were an attractive feature of Plough Lane. The south stand held about 300.

WIMBLEDON
Former ground: Plough Lane, Wimbledon, London SW19.

Wimbledon were still an amateur club in 1964 and did not join the League until 1977. Their rise to the First Division and great FA Cup success have been followed by a decline and eventual move to Milton Keynes in controversial circumstances. The club was formed in 1889 as Wimbledon Old Centrals by former pupils of the Old Central School in Camp Road, close to Wimbledon Common. Their first match was played on 2 November 1889, but the pitch was no more than a reasonably flat area of boggy grass. This was probably in the vicinity of Robin Hood Road, an unsurfaced road that still passes over the common today. Their next ground was probably close to Rushmere Pond, close to Wimbledon village. The players initially used a cottage as changing rooms, but after 1892, they used the Fox & Grapes public house in Camp Road. The following year they moved their headquarters to the nearby Swan pub. The club moved up a level and joined the South London League, then the Clapham & Herald League. They were on the move again in August 1901 to a ground close to Pepy's Road and Worple Road West. The nearby Cottenham Park School was used as dressing rooms. The club joined in the Southern Suburban League in 1902/03 and became a senior club two years later. They played in the South London Charity Cup final versus Nunhead in April 1905, and it was at this time that they dropped the 'Old Centrals' from their name. Soon afterwards the club entered the FA Amateur Cup and FA Cup for the first time.

Wimbledon FC moved to Grand Drive near Raynes Park Station in 1907/08, but the ground's exact location is unknown. There was a clubhouse and the ground was enclosed. They stayed there for only a year before another move to a ground to the west of Merton Hall Road, then they moved to the Malden Wanderers Cricket Club ground in Burlington Road for 1909/10, which is south of the current New Malden Station. Wimbledon FC was on its last legs due to financial problems, and folded on 3 September 1910.

Meanwhile, a new local team was emerging by the name of Wimbledon Borough FC, which had been created by local council workers. Their home ground was at Coppermill Lane on the site that is now the Wimbledon Greyhound and Speedway Stadium. Wimbledon FC re-emerged in 1912 and, after talks, the Borough team amalgamated with them to form a new Wimbledon FC. A new ground was found at nearby Plough Lane, which was a swampy former refuse tip, and the first match was played there on 9 September 1912. A stand was brought over from Clapton Orient's Millfields Road ground in 1923, re-erected on the Plough Lane side and called the south stand. It was narrow, seventy-five yards long and had about 1,500 bench seats. This stand was damaged by a bomb during the Second World War, but was rebuilt around 1952. It remained looking the same until it was finally bulldozed along with the rest of the ground.

The ground was mainly developed between 1958-63, thanks to the patronage of chairman Sydney Black. The new main stand was built on the north side of the ground in 1958. This comprised of a covered seated area with an uncovered paddock in front. The roof was extended in 1979 and seats added to the paddock. Underneath was the club's main lounge area with a supporters' tea room and directors bar. The Sportsman pub was built in the north-west corner at the same time. A cantilevered cover was erected over the west terrace end in 1959, and the following year eight floodlight pylons were installed at a cost of £4,000. These were replaced by a four-pylon system in 1965, which was bought from Sheffield United. Sydney Black purchased the ground's freehold from the council in 1959 at a cost of £8,250, and then generously donated the deeds to the club.

The Dons dominated the Isthmian League in the early 1960s, and in 1963 beat Sutton United in the final of the FA Amateur Cup at Wembley. They turned professional in 1964 and joined the Southern League, and won promotion to the top division at the end of the first season. During the mid-1970s, the Dons won the Southern League title three times in succession and also had great runs in the FA Cup. They were finally elected into the Football League in 1977 in place of Workington. The Dons went from the Fourth Division to the First in just nine seasons, and won the FA Cup in 1988, beating Liverpool in a memorable final.

Unfortunately the ground was not good enough for top-flight football and the club was limited in the extent that they could improve its facilities. Had Wimbledon stayed in the lower divisions Plough Lane may have survived, but the club made plans to relocate to a new purpose-built stadium in the locality. There was a plan to build a 20,000-capacity all-seater multi-purpose stadium on a disused sewage works in Wandle Valley, a few hundred yards from Plough Lane. Merton Council granted planning permission but it changed hands from Tory to Labour in 1990 and they changed their mind about the planning consent. The Taylor Report stipulated that all stadiums in the top two divisions should be all-seater by 1994, and it was clearly uneconomic to redevelop Plough Lane as it was such a small site. Wimbledon took what they hoped would be a temporary move and ground-shared with Crystal Palace. They replaced Charlton Athletic, who had just moved to Upton Park after sharing Selhurst Park. Plough Lane staged its final first-team match in May 1991 against their new landlords, Crystal Palace.

Plough Lane remained in use until April 1998 for Wimbledon reserve and youth team matches. However, only the main stand was licensed for spectators and the rest of the ground, although mainly intact, looked very run down by the time the ground was all demolished in the spring of 2002. A 2,000-acre site in Beddington Lane, between Mitcham and Croydon, was also considered for a relocation of the club within the Borough of Merton, but in September 1991 the council ruled out this development as well. This was followed in 1992 by an offer from the Greyhound Racing Association to redevelop the Wimbledon Greyhound Stadium into a 15,000-seater venue for dogs and football. The Dons would replace the speedway team that had moved out the previous year, but Merton Council would not sanction this either. The by-now-very-unpopular Merton Council later would not allow a supermarket to be built on the Plough Lane site, which is now completely flattened and has an unclear future.

Sam Hammam sold his interests in the Dons to Norwegian businessmen. When they announced plans to move the club to Milton Keynes in 2002 there was a major revolt by the club's fans, who not only refused to watch Wimbledon play anymore but also formed their own club called AFC Wimbledon. The new club seems to be going from strength to strength but they could not afford to buy their old ground back at Plough Lane. After an attempt by AFC Wimbledon to ground-share with Tooting & Mitcham United at their new ground at Imperial Fields was turned down by Merton Council in early 2003, the club, who were already sharing with Kingstonian, stepped in to buy their Kingsmeadow ground for £2.5m in late 2003. The K's, who have financial problems, are now their tenants. Meanwhile, the original club struggled for their existence, and some of Wimbledon's attendances before their move to Milton Keynes were below 2,000 at Selhurst Park. Wimbledon FC finally moved in October 2003 but are struggling to gain local support at the bottom of League One and went into administration in 2004.

ALEX'S FIRST TIME: I watched the Dons play regularly at Plough Lane in the late 1960s, as they were one of my local teams. Wimbledon beat Margate 4-0 in the first match that I watched at Plough Lane on 19 February 1966. There was a crowd of 2,825. Their crowds in their Southern League days were often better than after they joined the Football League. The ground changed little over the years, despite their rise up the leagues.

WINGATE & FINCHLEY
Ground: Abrahams Stadium, Summers Lane, Finchley, London N12.

Wingate FC was formed in 1946 to provide Saturday football for Jewish players in London. The club was named after Orde Wingate, a maverick British Army Officer who led the Chindit campaign in Burma during the Second World War. He was not Jewish but was 'an enthusiastic advocate of the Zionist cause'. Wingate were elected into the Middlesex Senior League and for the first two seasons rented pitches at the Indian Gymkhana Club, Osterley and Gunnersbury Park, Acton. They paid a deposit of £1,000 in 1948 to secure some land off Hall Lane, Hendon and the ground was opened in August of that year, when Kingsbury Town were the visitors for a Middlesex Senior

Wingate, April 1972. The Maccabi Sports Ground is now part of the M1 about one-and-a-half miles north of junction one.

League match. The ground was situated between the A41 (Watford Way) and the Midland railway line. The club raised £9,000 to complete the purchase of the ground, which was also used for many other sports. This included a four-lane cinder athletics track around the main football pitch, tennis courts and a second football pitch. Extensive improvements were made at Hall Lane, including the construction of a 2,000-seater grandstand in the summer of 1951. This was situated on the railway side of the ground and had an interesting design. The cantilever roof meant that the 800 seated spectators did not have any obstructions in their way. With their new facilities, the club decided to move up to the London League in 1952. Further improvements saw the completion of a concrete-post and tubular-rail barrier around the ground and the installation of a modern dressing-room block later in the 1950s. Wingate were elected to the Delphian League in 1962 and a season later moved into the Athenian League.

The ground had been under threat for some time due to plans to extend the M1, and in 1972 they received a compulsory purchase order on Hall Lane. The last match at the ground was an Athenian League game against Uxbridge on 6 May 1972. They could have moved to the recently built Copthall Stadium but instead decided to move to a fairly undeveloped ground at Brickfield Lane, Arkley. Unfortunately, the local council would not give them planning permission to bring the new ground up to Athenian League standards. Wingate were forced to divide their home fixtures between Arkley and Finchley's Summers Lane ground over the next three seasons.

There was a long dispute with the Ministry of Transport over compensation for the loss of the Maccabi Stadium. Wingate were forced to leave the Athenian League at the end of 1974/75, despite finishing third, due to the ground situation. Some members of the club decided to amalgamate the club with Leyton FC to become Leyton-Wingate (see Leyton Wingate), while other elements decided to concentrate on youth football. Wingate played in junior football until 1984 when they joined the Herts County League and soon moved on to the South Midlands League. Their ground at Brickfield Lane was in a pleasant location but had only a pavilion and a railed-off pitch, so they were unable to move up through the pyramid system as the ground was not good enough.

Finchley FC (see Finchley) were in financial trouble and facing extinction by 1990. This eventually led to the two clubs being merged to become Wingate & Finchley. Wingate entered into discussions with Barnet Council, the owners of Finchley's Summers Lane ground, and an agreement was reached whereby Wingate were given a 125-year lease of Finchley's ground. The club changed the name of the stadium to the Abrahams Stadium and the new club spent £400,000 on improvements to it. The pitch was returfed and moved closer to the grandstand. This left room for an all-weather training area on the site of the former covered terracing, which was demolished. New covered terracing has since replaced this. The art deco grandstand, built in 1931, was lovingly restored and other facilities were upgraded to a higher standard. Since moving into Summers Lane, Wingate & Finchley have won promotion to the Isthmian League.

WOODFORD TOWN
Ground: Snakes Lane, Woodford Green, Essex.

This tells the story of a club that rose to prominence during the 1950s then suffered a long, slow death as they drifted towards insolvency and their final demise in 2003. Woodford Town FC was formed at the same time as a new football ground was opened at Snakes Lane in July 1937. They were elected to the South Essex League and built a wooden 180-seater stand just before the Second World War. Woodford joined the London League in 1947 and continued with improvements to the ground. A new front entrance was created from Snakes Lane in 1947 and two years later a second seated stand, made of concrete and corrugated iron, was built on the Finchingfield Avenue side of the ground. The record attendance for Snakes Lane of 7,000 visited the ground in November 1950 for the visit of Colchester United in an FA Cup fourth qualifying round tie. Extra banking was created behind both goals, but United won easily 7-1. A fierce gale destroyed the wooden main stand in November 1952 and it cost £5,000 to build a replacement. This was officially opened in September 1954. It seated over 300 and incorporated new dressing rooms and a social club. The club had large crowds during the 1950s, but attendance became very poor during the last few years of the club's existence. Woodford Town were founder members of the Delphian League in 1951/52. Ten seasons later they transferred to the Metropolitan League before turning professional and joining the Southern League for one unsuccessful season in 1971.

The entrance to the ground was down an alleyway and the ground was surrounded by houses, which gave it an enclosed feel. The quality of the floodlights at Snakes Lane was notorious; they were mounted on conventional pylons but the lighting was not consistent across the whole pitch. Despite their inadequacies, the Southern League allowed the club back into its ranks for a second time in 1982. Woodford reached the first round of the FA Cup in November 1986 and played local rivals Orient at Snakes Lane. The club flattened the banking at the Snakes Lane end and erected a large

Woodford Town, March 1972. The main stand had four rows of benches. Opposite was a flimsy stand with PVC sheeting and behind one goal was wooden terracing.

temporary stand to help hold the 2,464 fans that filled the ground. Orient won the match narrowly, scoring the only goal.

For financial reasons, Woodford resigned from the Southern League at the end of 1986/87 and replaced their reserves in the Essex Senior League. They were shown the door at Snakes Lane in 1993 after a row with the ground's landlords, Redbridge Council, over the club failing to pay their rent. Another side called Woodford FC used the ground for a while but they soon went to the wall. A fire destroyed the clubhouse and badly damaged the stand in September 1996 and the council had to demolish the whole structure soon afterwards. Despite having no home of their own, Woodford Town continued to play in the London Spartan League. They shared the grounds of Greenwich Borough, East Ham United and Leyton before settling at Clapton's Old Spotted Dog Ground. They rejoined the Essex Senior League in 1999 and had hopes of a return to Snakes Lane, but this never happened. The departure of the management and most of the players midway through 2002/03 brought an end to the club after sixty-six years of existence. Snakes Lane still exists but has been badly vandalised. The main entrance and external wall are still intact, as were all six floodlight pylons, plus the stand on the Finchingfield Avenue side of the ground in 2003.

ALEX'S FIRST TIME: I saw Woodford Town play Clapton in the Essex Senior Cup first round on 21 September 1982. The visitors won 1-0 before a crowd of 110. The ground was already very run down by this time. The toilets were the worst that I have had to use at a football ground and the floodlights were awful. One could hardly see what was going on at the far end of the ground. However, the rest of the ground was interesting, if a little dilapidated.

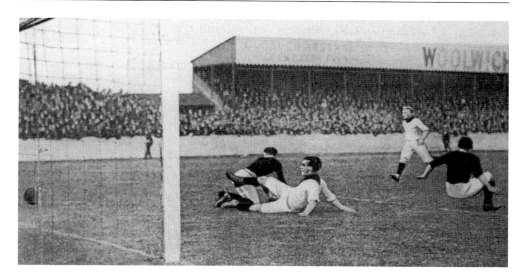

Woolwich Arsenal, September 1905. The Manor Ground at Plumstead is packed for the visit of Liverpool on 2 September 1905.

WOOLWICH ARSENAL
Ground: Manor Fields, Manor Way, Plumstead, Kent.

Before their move to North London in 1913, Arsenal played in south-east London, close to Plumstead. The club was formed as Dial Square in 1886 and were named after the Royal Arsenal workshops at Woolwich, where most of the players were employed. They soon changed their name to Royal Arsenal and played in red shirts donated by the former club of two of their players, Nottingham Forest. They played their first 'home' match on Plumstead Common in January 1887. This ground was not ideal, as army horse manoeuvres kept churning up the pitch. The club moved to a former pig farm, next to the Sportsman's pub on the edge of Plumstead Marshes, in September 1887. As this ground was usually waterlogged, they moved to a pitch next door for a match with Millwall in March 1888 and decided to stay there.

Woolwich Arsenal used the Manor Field for the next two years, but facilities were very basic and military wagons were used as stands. The players had to walk about 100 yards from their dressing rooms at a public house in Plumstead High Street to the football ground. Some spectators were able to watch for free from an embankment formed by a huge overground pipe, the southern outfall sewer. The club moved to the Invicta Ground in September 1890 and this ground had one stand on its east side with concrete terracing. Remnants of this terracing can still be seen today in the back gardens of homes in Hector Street.

Woolwich Arsenal became London's first professional club and they joined the Football League in 1893. Due to the high rent on the Invicta Ground, Woolwich Arsenal decided to form a limited company to raise the £4,000 needed to buy their former home at the Manor Field. The club members worked hard to build facilities at Manor Field: an iron stand holding 2,000 on the north side and banking were built. Gates in their first season averaged 6,000, the highest for the Second Division. The Boer War started in 1899 and this took away many of the spectators and club members, who were working overtime at the local munitions factories to produce weapons for the war. A cover was placed on the south side of the ground to prevent spectators watching matches without paying and a large bank of terracing was built and named the 'Spion Kop' after a well-known battle during the Boer War. This greatly helped in accommodating the increased crowds.

The ground was quite isolated and, even though there was a station close to it, train services were poor and slow. The ground was also very basic and, with more London clubs springing up, many supporters decided to watch their football elsewhere. The club's new owner, Sir Henry Norris, proposed in 1910 that Woolwich Arsenal and Fulham should amalgamate and play at the White City Stadium in West London. Fortunately, the Football League refused to sanction the merger, and then would not allow Woolwich Arsenal to share with Fulham at Craven Cottage. The club was struggling financially by 1912 and Norris declared that the club needed to move elsewhere in London. This situation was not helped when Woolwich Arsenal were relegated to the Second Division in 1912/13, as crowds plummeted. In February 1913, Norris announced that the club would be moving to Highbury in North London. Many fans were very unhappy about the move and Tottenham Hotspur also protested about another professional club moving into their territory. Only 3,000 spectators attended the last match at the Manor Ground on 26 April 1913, and today there is no trace of this ground (see the section on Arsenal for future developments at the club).

YEADING

Ground: Beaconsfield Road, Hayes, Middlesex.

Yeading are a club that has risen rapidly up the pyramid system from humble beginnings. Yeading Youth Club was formed in 1960 and changed their name to plain Yeading in 1965. Early days were spent in the Hayes & District Youth League and the Uxbridge District Leagues. After finishing as Premier champions in 1967, Yeading joined the South-West Middlesex League, winning the championship twice and taking the Middlesex Junior Cup for the first time in 1968/69. They were promoted to the Middlesex League and finished as champions at the end of their first season. Season 1972/73 saw the club sweep all four trophies – league and cup – in the Middlesex League. Yeading gained senior status in 1984 and joined the Spartan League.

Yeading had moved to their Beaconsfield Road ground in 1985, which was on the site of a former school. The ground is not pretty and had a gasworks on one side and derelict land on the other. Club members developed the derelict land into a football ground in just six months, after gaining a fifty-year lease. A two-storey clubhouse, which contains a committee room and large bar on the first floor, was built. This has been developed into the impressive Warren Suite that now plays host to regular sportsman's dinners, wedding receptions and other private functions. A crowd of over 3,000

Yeading, August 1989. Since this photo, the seating has been increased from 78 to 330. There is also cover behind one goal and in front of the social club.

attended a match with a strong Spurs side to celebrate the switching on of new floodlights in 1986.

The club retained their hold on the League Cup in 1986/87 and also won the league. They went unbeaten all that season and as a result were elected to the Isthmian League Division Two (South). Yeading became the first Middlesex club to win the FA Vase in 1989/90. In the final, they beat Bridlington Town 1-0 in a replay at Elland Road, after a 0-0 draw at Wembley. They also gained the Division Two (South) title that season. More success came in 1991/92 when promotion to the Premier Division was achieved. After a year of consolidation, 1993/94 saw the club reach the FA Cup first round proper for the first time. They held Gillingham to a 0-0 draw in a game played at Hayes' Church Road ground, but they lost the replay 3-1. Yeading beat Conference side Telford United in the FA Cup in 1994/95 to reach the first round again. The match was shown on BBC's *Match of the Day* as they held Colchester United to a 2-2 draw. Unfortunately, they lost the replay 7-1. That season, Yeading finished in their highest ever position of ninth in the Premier Division. Two seasons later they finished fifth but were relegated the following season with virtually the same players. One bright spot in 1997/98 was the FA Trophy victory over Yeovil Town. A goal-less draw in Somerset in front of over 2,000 people was followed by a 1-0 replay win at Beaconsfield Road. Yeading reached the third round of the FA Cup in 2004/05 where they lost to Newcastle United 2-0 at Loftus Road.

ALEX'S FIRST TIME: I visited Beaconsfield Road fairly soon after they moved into the ground on 7 February 1987. They beat Corinthian Casuals in the quarter-final of the Spartan League Cup before a crowd of 116, with Hector Walsh hitting a hat-trick in a 4-2 victory. The impressive clubhouse and main stand were already in place at this time.

BIBLIOGRAPHY

I would like to thank Bob Lilliman for helping me out with obtaining some of the books in this bibliography.

Arsenal – A Complete Record *Fred Ollier.*
Athenian Football League 1912-84 (3 volumes) *Mike Wilson.*
Book of Football – A complete history and record of the Association & Rugby Games 1905-06.
Caxton's Association Football (Vol.1) *A.H. Fabian & Geoffrey Green (eds).*
Charlton Athletic *Richard Redden.*
Cottage Chronicles (Fulham) *Dennis Turner (ed).*
Crystal Palace – A Complete Record *Mike Purkis with Rev. Nigel Sands.*
Dulwich Hamlet – 100th Anniversary Souvenir Brochure 1893-1992.
Football Club History Database – *Website by Richard Rundle.*
Football Grounds from the Air – Then & Now *Aerofilms.*
Football Grounds of Great Britain/England & Wales *Simon Inglis.*
Football League – Grounds for a Change *Dave Twydell.*
Fulham – Complete Record/ Fact & Figures *Alex White & Dennis Turner.*
Gone But Not Forgotten series *Dave Twydell (ed.).*
Greater London League Handbook 1965/66 & 1966/67.
Groundhopper Magazine.
Groundtastic Magazine.
History of the FA Amateur Cup *Bob Barton.*
History of Hampton & Richmond Borough FC *Tony Nash.*
History of Non-League Football Grounds *Kerry Miller.*
History of Queens Park Rangers *Mark Shoul.*
History of the Southern League *Leigh Edwards.*
Homes of British Speedway *Robert Bamford & John Jarvis.*
Homes of Non-League Football *Peter Miles.*
Illustrated History of Arsenal 1886-2002 *Phil Soar & Martin Tyler.*
Leyton FC History *David Chapman*
Leyton Orient – A Complete Record *Neil Kaufman & Alan Ravenhill.*
Millwall – A Complete Record *Richard Lindsay.*
Millwall – Lions of the South *James Murray.*
Non-League Club Directory 1982-present.
Non-League Football Grounds of Kent *Mike Floate.*
Non-League Football Grounds of Essex & East London *Peter Miles.*
Non-League Football Grounds of Great Britain *Tony Williams (ed.).*
Nunhead FC 1888-1949 *Mick Blackman.*
100 Years of Playing the Game, History of Finchley FC 1874-1974 *Harold Whidden.*
Pyramid Football magazine and website.
Queens Park Rangers – A Complete Record *Gordon Macey.*

Rejected FC – Histories of ex-Football League Clubs (Vol. 2) *Dave Twydell.*

Spartan League – A Retrospective Review of Personalities & Records 1907-67.

The Spartan Football League 1907-1975 (3 volumes) *Compiled by Mike Wilson.*

Spurs – A Complete Record *Bob Goodwin.*

Sutton United Handbook 1898-1948.

Sutton United FC 1898-1973.

The Bridge – A History of Stamford Bridge *Colin Benson.*

Tooting on the Move *Jeff Brooks.*

To the Palace for the Cup *Ian Bevan, Stuart Hibberd & Michael Gilbert.*

United We Stand – Sutton United 1898-1998 *Dave Farebrother (ed).*

Various club websites including Merstham, Brook House, Ruislip Manor and Edgware.

Watford FC *Oliver Phillips.*

West Ham United – A Complete Record & Illustrated History *John Northcutt & Roy Shoesmith.*

Who Killed Cock Robin? – The History of Croydon Common *Alan Futter*

Other local titles published by Tempus

CHARLTON ATHLETIC FC
Images of Charlton Athletic FC   David Ramzan   0 7524 1504 2   £10.99

CRYSTAL PALACE FC
The Men Who Made Crystal Palace FC   Rev. Nigel Sands   0 7224 3291 5   £14.99
Crystal Palace FC Classic Matches   Rev. Nigel Sands   0 7524 2733 4   £12.99
Crystal Palace FC 100 Greats   Rev. Nigel Sands   0 7524 2176 X   £10.99

FULHAM FC
The Men Who Made Fulham FC   Alex White   0 7224 2423 8   £19.99

LEYTON ORIENT FC
Images of Leyton Orient FC   Neilson N. Kaufman 0 7524 2094 1   £11.99
The Men Who Made Leyton Orient FC   Neilson N. Kaufman 0 7524 2412 2   £25.00

MILLWALL FC
Images of Millwall FC 1885-1939   Chris Bethall & David Sullivan   0 7524 1849 1   £12.99
Images of Millwall FC 1940-2001   Millwall FC Museum   0 7524 2187 5   £12.99
Millwall FC Classic Matches   Chris Bethall & David Sullivan   0 7524 2705 9   £12.00

QUEENS PARK RANGERS FC
Images of Queens Park Rangers   Tony Williamson   07524 1604 9   £10.99

TOTTENHAM HOTSPUR FC
Images of Tottenham Hotspur 1882-1952   Roy Brazier   07524 2044 5   £12.99
Images of Tottenham Hotspur Since 1953   Roy Brazier   07524 2924 8   £12.99

WEST HAM UNITED FC
Founded on Iron: Origins of West Ham United   Brian Belton   0 7524 2928 0   £9.99

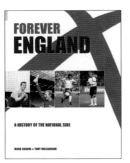

Forever England: A History of the National Side
Mark Shaoul & Tony Williamson
The definitive history of the English national side. From the days of the amateur gentlemen of the 1870s to the present day, Forever England is an insightful and fascinating account of the history of the country's national football team, and covers the careers of England's all-time greats and is an essential read for everyone who is interested in the history of the Three Lions.
0 7524 2939 6

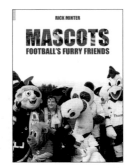

Mascots: Footballs Furry Friends
Rick Minter
Meet the Mascots in this remarkable illustrated guide. It reveals a crazy and colourful world of glamour, fun and rivalry, where football's pecking order works in reverse! The book includes a low-down on every mascot, with profiles of characters in the Premiership, Football League, Scotland and beyond.
0 7524 3179 X

If you are interested in purchasing other books published by Tempus, or in case you have difficulty finding any Tempus books in your local bookshop, you can also place orders directly through our website
www.tempus-publishing.com